Anglo-Norman parks in medieval Ireland

To Terry.
Best Wishes
Fiona

Anglo-Norman Parks in Medieval Ireland

Fiona Beglane

FOUR COURTS PRESS

Typeset in 10.5 pt on 13.5 pt AGaramondPro by
Carrigboy Typesetting Services for
FOUR COURTS PRESS LTD
7 Malpas Street, Dublin 8, Ireland
www.fourcourtspress.ie
and in North America for
FOUR COURTS PRESS
c/o ISBS, 920 NE 58th Avenue, Suite 300, Portland, OR 97213.

A catalogue record for this title is available
from the British Library.

ISBN 978–1–84682–569–9

SPECIAL ACKNOWLEDGMENT

The author and publisher are grateful for financial support towards the publication
of this book from the County Kildare Archaeological Society, Sligo Institute
of Technology, Galway County Council and Laois County Council, and to
NUI Galway for a travel bursary towards the cost of fieldwork.

Printed in England
by TJ International, Padstow, Cornwall.

To Ed
for all the coffees and dinners

Contents

List of figures

Acknowledgments

The core of this book started life as my PhD thesis, and so I owe a great debt of thanks to my supervisor, Kieran O'Conor, for our interesting and useful discussions and for his knack of keeping me focused on the primary aims of the project. I must also express my gratitude to my examiners, Elizabeth FitzPatrick and Mark Gardiner, for their insightful comments on the thesis. The original inspiration for the project, and the methodological basis, was the research of Leonard Cantor, who, between the 1960s and 1980s, carried out ground-breaking work on the parks of medieval England. There are a large number of other people who I would like to thank for their help and contributions towards both the original study and this volume, in particular Rory Sherlock and Kieran O'Conor for their comments on draft material, again keeping me on the straight and narrow, Michael Potterton at Four Courts Press and the anonymous reviewers.

The practical and fieldwork assistance provided by Gareth Boyle, Olive Carey, Mary Dillon, Owen Doherty, Cathal Farrell, Bri Greene, Martina McCarthy, Fergal Nevin and Blathnaid O'Neill was invaluable for the case studies. I must also gratefully acknowledge the archaeologists and historians who shared their unpublished data with me. They are Vincent Butler, Anne Connon, Pam Crabtree, Sean Denham, Alan Hayden, Matilda Holmes, Brian Hodkinson, Patricia Lynch, Ciara MacManus, Finbar McCormick, Rosanne Meenan, Eileen Murphy, Margaret Murphy, Emily Murray, Kathleen Ryan, David Sweetman and Claire Walsh. The websites run by Will Johnson, Ian MacInnes and Edward Gonzalez-Tennant were beacons of light in a sea of murk. The library staff at the IT Sligo, National Library of Ireland, NUI Galway and Trinity College Dublin were extremely helpful in sourcing information, books, images and articles and for this I am truly grateful, as I am to the various copyright holders who generously allowed their images to be used without charge: Alexandre Dulaunoy, Stephen Hall, Google DigitalGlobe, Karena Morton, Christoph Oldenbourg, Roger Sargent Wildlife Photography, Rory Sherlock and the Royal Society of Antiquaries of Ireland. The project benefited hugely from information and comments on drafts from, as well as discussions with, Sean Adcock, Emma Arbuthnot, Nora Bermingham, Stefan Burgh, Eve Campbell, Ruth Carden, Miriam Clyne, Christy Cunliffe, Marion Dowd, Tom Finan, Joe Fenwick, Betty Gray, Karina Hensel, Nóilín Ní Iarnáin, John Fletcher, Patrick McAfee, Noel McCarthy, Theresa McDonald, Sam Moore, Paul Murphy, Paul Naessens, Enda O'Flaherty, Chris Read, Damien Shiels, Peadar Slattery, Spencer Smith, Terence

Reeves-Smyth, Jacqueline A. Stuhmiller, Naomi Sykes, Arnaud de Volder and John Waddell, and again I thank them for their interest in the topic.

Another group of people who were essential to the project were the landowners, tenants and residents of Loughrea, Maynooth, Dunamase, Carrick, Nenagh, Carlow, Glencree and the surrounding areas. Across the board I was welcomed with enthusiasm, interest and information. In particular, I would like to thank the following for allowing more detailed survey work on their lands: John Brennan, Tony Brennan (RIP), Patrick Daly, Michael Dowling, Anne and Denis Fortune, Martha and John Geoghegan, Joan and Reggie Hodgins, Martin Keary, Paddy Lawlor, Mrs Manton, Roger Satchwell and Claire Smyth. I would also like to thank a number of people whose local knowledge added greatly to my understanding of the parks: Joe Dunne, Maura Hawkins, Brendan Hynes, Michael Linnane, Bill Mulhern, Micky Murphy (RIP) and Seamus O'Grady.

Finally, and very importantly, I would like to express my thanks to Ed and to my parents and friends for their support over the past few years. This has not been easy for any of them, as I have been grumpy, obsessed by field-boundaries and unsociable for most of that time. In particular, Ed has borne the brunt of it, but has uncomplainingly kept me well supplied with endless cups of coffee and hot dinners.

CONVENTIONS

The following dating conventions have been employed:

Early medieval	*c.*400–*c.*1100
High medieval	*c.*1100–*c.*1350
Anglo-Norman	1169–*c.*1350
Late medieval	*c.*1350–*c.*1600
Later medieval	*c.*1100–*c.*1600
Medieval	*c.*400–*c.*1600
Post-medieval	*c.*1600–*c.*1850
Modern	*c.*1850–present

CHAPTER ONE

Introduction

In October 1305 William Waspayl was sentenced to be imprisoned for three years and to pay damages to Richard de Burgh, earl of Ulster. His crime was that on a number of occasions he and his men had entered de Burgh's park at Balydonegan (Dunganstown/Oakpark) near Carlow Castle (fig. 1), where they threatened the parkers, poached deer, stole firewood and broke up and then stole the palings of the park for firewood. In addition, Waspayl had dug a pit immediately outside the park, which he claimed was to trap foxes, although de Burgh argued that it was designed to catch deer.[1] This episode provides us with a picture of one type of Anglo-Norman park: the most prestigious form, which was owned by a great magnate, stocked with deer and timber and overseen by a number of parkers. It gives us a glimpse of the social issues surrounding emparkment as well as the more practical concerns of how to enclose a park and what to keep in it.

This book adopts a multidisciplinary approach to the study of Anglo-Norman high-medieval parks in Ireland and draws upon archaeological, historical and place-name evidence in order to generate a broad understanding of the role of parks in medieval landscapes and mind-sets. Key topics explored include the form and function of medieval parks in Ireland, their occurrence and location in the Irish landscape, the status and identity of their owners and a comparison with parks elsewhere, particularly those in England.

Archaeologists have often ignored the social and practical aspects of medieval life, focusing instead on the description of architectural remains and excavated evidence. In both Ireland and Britain, the emphasis has traditionally been on the castle as the centre of medieval life. For decades after the publication of Leask's *Irish castles and castellated houses* in 1941, researchers both in Ireland and elsewhere studied castles from an architectural perspective that stressed their role as military structures, while neglecting or at best playing down their social context. Furthermore, they have commonly been considered in isolation rather than being examined within their wider landscape.[2]

---

1 *CJRI*, ii, p. 136; Gibbons and Clarke, 'Deer parks' (1990/1), 4–5; Murphy and O'Conor, 'Castles and deer parks in Anglo-Norman Ireland' (2006), 51–70. 2 Brown, *English castles* (3rd ed. 1976), passim; King, *The castle in England and Wales* (1988), passim; Leask, 'Irish castles, 1180–1310' (1936), 143–99; Leask, *Irish castles and castellated houses* (1941), passim; Sweetman, *Medieval castles of Ireland* (1999),

1 In the fourteenth century Carlow Castle, Co. Carlow, was held by Richard de Burgh, earl of Ulster.

Nationalistic sentiment contributed to this process of neglect and as a result, later-medieval studies in Ireland were the poor relation within Irish archaeology and history. During the Gaelic Revival of the late nineteenth century the early medieval period and some aspects of prehistory were seen as the 'Golden Age' of Irish civilisation, untouched by Viking or Anglo-Norman society, and hence worthy of study by patriotic Irishmen. This idea continued well into the twentieth century, and after the formation of the state in 1922 it was promoted due to the need to reinforce national identity.[3] As a result, the study of the later-medieval period was perceived as the study of the archaeology and history of English settlement in Ireland, and so was considered to be of marginal importance by many Irish scholars.[4] One particular outcome was that the later-medieval castles were largely ignored. These were seen as symbols of oppression rather than as integral elements within the Irish landscape, and, as a result,

passim. **3** Cooney, 'Building the future on the past: archaeology and the construction of national identity in Ireland' (1996), passim; O'Sullivan, 'Nationalists, archaeologists and the myth of the golden age' (1998), passim; Waddell, *Foundation myths* (2005), pp 113, 204–5. **4** Barry, *The archaeology of medieval Ireland*

associated manorial features such as medieval parks also suffered scholarly neglect.[5] Additionally, by comparison with England, the number of contemporary documentary sources is limited, both due to poor survival over the centuries, and due to the loss of many records in the Four Courts fire of 1922. In the absence of detailed research, scholars have often assumed that the Anglo-Normans directly transposed ideas on the appropriate form of the manor from the well-studied areas of the south and midlands of England to Ireland, a problem also identified by Scottish researchers.[6]

Things are improving, however, and the last three decades have seen a flowering in medieval studies, with an increasing emphasis on the role of the castle in peacetime and on the aesthetic aspects of castle design and siting. In Ireland, McNeill discussed the use of stone building materials as an expression of prestige, rather than military need, and the development of domestic space to provide increased comfort over high levels of security.[7] O'Keeffe took a more theoretical approach, considering the role of the castle in creating identity in terms of gender and ethnicity, arguing that depending on the perspective of the spectator, castles embody different meanings.[8] Furthermore, he attempted to identify landscapes designed with aesthetic principles in mind, suggesting that the surroundings of the very early fourteenth-century castles at Ballymoon and Ballyloughan, both in Co. Carlow, may be examples of this.[9] The practical aspects of the landscape have not been forgotten either. O'Conor identified the importance of the castle as the manorial centre for administration, arable and pastoral agriculture, the provision of speciality foods such as rabbits, pigeons and freshwater fish and semi-industrial activities such as milling.[10] These works show the evolution of castle studies from a purely functionalistic approach, which saw castles solely as military establishments, to a more rounded interpretation in which castles are seen as symbols of power and authority and as integral aspects of wider society and landscape.

One important outcome of this broader view of castle studies has been a growing interest in the archaeology of the landscape outside the castle gate, including the way in which views from the roof and the windows of a castle can

(1987), p. 1; McNeill, *Castles in Ireland: feudal power in a Gaelic world* (1997), p. 2; McNeill, 'Lost infancy: medieval archaeology in Ireland' (2002), 552–6; O'Conor, 'Castle studies in Ireland: the way forward' (2008), 329–39. **5** McNeill, *Castles in Ireland*, pp 2–3; O'Conor, 'Castle studies in Ireland: the way forward', 332. **6** Oram, 'Castles, concepts and contexts: castle studies in Scotland in retrospect and prospect' (2008), 355; Reeves-Smyth, 'Natural history of demesnes' (1997), p. 550. **7** McNeill, *Castles in Ireland*, pp 77, 142–7. **8** O'Keeffe, 'Concepts of "castle" and the construction of identity in medieval and post-medieval Ireland' (2001), 69–88. **9** O'Keeffe, 'Were there designed landscapes in medieval Ireland?' (2004), 52–68. **10** O'Conor, *The archaeology of medieval rural settlement in Ireland* (1998), pp 26–33; O'Conor, 'Motte castles in Ireland: permanent fortresses, residences and manorial centres' (2002), 173–82; O'Conor, 'Medieval rural settlement in Munster' (2004), pp 235–9.

provide an insight into the medieval mind-set.[11] It is possible to gain an appreciation of a modern landscape by physically standing within it or by observing it from a building such as a castle. Sometimes, this can give an insight into how the area would have looked and how it was perceived in the medieval period, but often the details of the layout of a manor are obscured by more recent developments. This is where manorial extents and inquisitions post-mortem can provide valuable information. For example, in 1287 the lands of Thomas de Clare included the manor of Baliduwil, Co. Kerry, which was described as follows:

> there are there 184 acres in demesne, whereof they extend each acre at 3*d.*;
> 5 acres of meadow at 8*d.* an acre; a pasture containing ½ acre of common
> [*currach*] and moor, good for plough horses and cows, extended at 2*s.*; a
> park containing 4 acres good for oxen and for osiers for carts, extended at
> 12*d.*; a garden and curtilage with easement of buildings there are worth 4*s.*
> a year. There are there 2 *Betagii* who hold 46 acres of land, whereof they
> extend each acre at 3*d.*; there is there also an old mill which cannot be
> extended at any price because it is laid low. The works of the said *Betagii* are
> worth 9*d.* a year; pleas and perquisites nothing because there are no tenants
> there. Total, 68*s.* 7*d.*[12]

This gives us an insight into one of the many manors owned by de Clare. Although it was only a minor manor, it included buildings and arable, pasture and meadow lands held by the lord as well as by the betaghs, or unfree Irish tenants, and gardens and the remains of a mill. There was also a park of four acres. This particular example is the smallest of the enclosures documented as a medieval 'park' and is evidently a very different type of enclosure to the hunting park at Balydonegan, mentioned above. As well as a smaller size, it had the more modest aim of corralling cattle and providing osiers, or willow rods, demonstrating the wide range of functions to which a medieval park could be put. Documentary details like this can be combined with fieldwork to recreate medieval landscapes and a number of excellent studies of individual parishes and manors have been undertaken in the last decade using such methodologies.[13]

Parks and forests have been widely studied in England,[14] whereas research in Ireland has been extremely limited in this area. In later-medieval terms, a forest

11 McNeill, 'The view from the top' (2006), 122–7; Creighton, 'Room with a view: framing castle landscapes' (2010), 37–49. **12** *CDI*, iii, no. 459. **13** For example, Lyttleton and O'Keeffe (eds), *The manor in medieval and early modern Ireland* (2005), passim; Doran and Lyttleton (eds), *Lordship in medieval Ireland* (2007), passim; FitzPatrick and Gillespie (eds), *The parish in medieval and early modern Ireland: community, territory and building* (2006), passim. **14** For example, Mileson, *Parks in medieval England* (2009), passim; Fletcher, *Gardens of earthly delight* (2011), passim; James, *A history of English*

2 Part of the earthwork ditch at Curtlestown, Glencree, Co. Wicklow. The slope of the ditch is indicated.

was a legally defined zone in which the king had control over hunting and timber resources. By contrast, a park was a relatively small area of land that was enclosed by a wall, fence or hedge, and as at Balydonegan and Baliduwil, parks were used to keep animals including deer, and to grow trees for timber, firewood and craft purposes.[15] In England, a park seems to have been an essential manorial feature, with their numbers around the year 1300 estimated at between 1,900 and 3,200.[16] Park-breaking, as described at Balydonegan, was often a political act and was common practice in England,[17] striking at the heart of a lord's ordered manorial landscape, a theme that will be further explored in Chapter 6.

The first Irish medieval park to be subject to archaeological scrutiny was at Glencree, Co. Wicklow. In the early twentieth century the physical remains of what was believed to be an arc of the boundary of the park was identified by Westropp at Curtlestown, within the bounds of the royal forest described by Le Fanu.[18] Much of this remained at the time of the county inventory and is still

forestry (1981), passim; Young, *The royal forests of medieval England* (1979), passim. **15** Rackham, *The history of the countryside* (1987), pp 125–6, 129–38. **16** Rackham, *The history of the countryside*, p. 123; Cantor and Hatherly, 'The medieval parks of England' (1979), 71–85. **17** Mileson, *Parks in medieval England*, p. 155. **18** Le Fanu, 'The royal forest of Glencree' (1893), 268–80; Westropp, 'Earthwork near

there today (fig. 2).[19] In the past three decades a number of researchers have attempted to collate documentary evidence for parks on a regional scale. The earliest of these was Weir, who discussed documentary evidence for a number of post-medieval parks in Clare but also unfortunately extrapolated this evidence backwards in time to make the assumption that these parks had been in continuous use since shortly after the arrival of the Anglo-Normans.[20] Gibbons and Clarke reviewed documentary evidence for deer parks in Carlow, with a detailed account of the historical evidence for the high-medieval park at Balydonegan and a discussion of a number of other examples that are probably of post-medieval date.[21]

The first attempt at a national census was by Reeves-Smyth, who mapped the general location of eight high-medieval deer parks, but did not identify them on the ground; unfortunately, due to a printing error on the map, the medieval parks were shown as nineteenth-century features and vice versa.[22] All of these sites were east of the Shannon apart from a single example from Loughrea, Co. Galway. O'Conor collated a list of parks in Munster and, later, with Murphy, expanded this to Ireland as a whole.[23] This work identified fourteen high-medieval parks that had a similar geographical spread to that found by Reeves-Smith, and noted that some of these may have had functions other than the keeping of deer. These works formed the basis for my own review of both archaeological and documentary evidence for deer parks, which provided a preliminary listing of sites where fallow deer remains have been found and attempted to cross-reference these with the sites identified by Murphy and O'Conor.[24] With the exception of Westropp's work in 1913, none of these studies included any fieldwork to identify the parks, to examine their placement in the landscape or to investigate the features forming the parks and their boundaries. It could be argued, therefore, that an interdisciplinary study incorporating both fieldwork and documentary evidence was long overdue.

As the example from Balydonegan demonstrates, deer were an important feature of the parks of the great magnates. Fallow deer were introduced by the Anglo-Normans, specifically to be stocked in parks, so that they are intrinsically linked to the role of parks. Much of the zooarchaeological evidence in Ireland is scattered through a range of unpublished and published reports, most of which have not been collated or interpreted as a body of material. Nevertheless, in

Curtlestown, Co. Wicklow' (1913), 185–6.   **19** Westropp, 'Earthwork near Curtlestown, Co. Wicklow', 185–6; Le Fanu, 'The royal forest of Glencree', 268–80; Grogan and Kilfeather, *Archaeological inventory of county Wicklow* (1997), p. 105.   **20** Weir, 'Deer parks of Clare' (1986), 54–5.   **21** Gibbons and Clarke, 'Deer parks', 4–5.   **22** Reeves-Smyth, 'Demesnes' (1997); pers. comm.   **23** O'Conor, 'Medieval rural settlement in Munster', passim; Murphy and O'Conor, 'Castles and deer parks in Anglo-Norman Ireland'. **24** Beglane, 'Deer and identity in medieval Ireland' (2010), passim.

addition to my own paper on fallow deer, two papers by McCormick do touch on the subject. The first examines the zooarchaeological and documentary evidence for changes in the domestic fauna with the coming of the Anglo-Normans,[25] while the second provides an account of the evidence for the introduction and extinction of individual species to Ireland.[26] One outcome from these works is that both parks and fallow deer appear to be relatively uncommon in Ireland compared to England. This raises the questions that if a park was an essential manorial feature in England, and if the English manorial system was transposed to Ireland, then why are there so few records of high-medieval parks in Ireland? Furthermore, why are there so few fallow deer remains in Ireland and why did fallow deer ownership not filter down the social ladder? The answers to this question lie in chronology, landscape and politics and form a major theme within the present study.

This book concentrates on parks dating from the period 1169 to *c*.1350, but also discusses what happened to them in later periods. It has been limited to Anglo-Norman parks that are documented in primary sources of the time. The thematic and multidisciplinary approach combines a range of sources such as evidence from literature, folklore, place-names and art, as well as edited historical works and some original documents. This has complemented a programme of archaeological fieldwork and the review of a range of published and unpublished excavation reports and faunal reports. The fields of archaeology, history, literature studies and art history have traditionally operated independently of each other, however in this case the integration of these strands is essential in order to gain a rich understanding of the subject. Documentary and literary evidence are important since these provide a particular understanding of the time; and these sources can be integrated with archaeology to obtain a more holistic view.[27] Documents and literature of the high-medieval period were invariably created for specific purposes, by, or for, the elite. They present 'a truth' as it was perceived by the writer, rather than 'the truth', which varies depending on the perspective of the individual. In the past, as today, text was used 'in the production, negotiation and transformation of social relations',[28] so that the use of text to record the ownership of property such as a park, or the amounts of taxes owed on deer hides are examples of occasions when documents were used as a vehicle for social and economic control.

25 McCormick, 'The effect of the Anglo-Norman settlement on Ireland's wild and domesticated fauna' (1991), passim.   **26** McCormick, 'Early evidence for wild animals in Ireland' (1998), passim.   **27** Finan, 'Introduction: Moylurg and Lough Cé in the later Middle Ages' (2010), p. 11; O'Conor, 'Castle studies in Ireland: the way forward', 333.   **28** Moreland, *Archaeology and text* (2001), p. 31.

The development of new and refined methodological approaches has improved the potential for understanding past society, while the expansion of interest in later-medieval archaeology in Ireland has opened up a wider range of subjects for study. This book will draw on these influences and will attempt to integrate the various forms of evidence to examine the phenomenon of the park in high-medieval Ireland and to achieve a richer interpretation of the subject than would be possible using only a single approach.

CHAPTER TWO

Place and people

Medieval parks were essentially enclosed areas of land set aside for specific purposes and the documented high-medieval examples from Ireland range from just four acres to 913 acres in extent (Appendix 2). In England, the study of a much greater number of known examples has shown that there they ranged in size between 30 and 4,300 acres.[1] The highest status parks were used to confine deer, usually fallow deer, and as a result, parks are usually thought of as venues for keeping and hunting deer. This was not their only use, however, and evidence from England shows that they could have a range of purposes such as to graze cattle and sheep, grow crops, raise horses, supply timber for construction, supply wood for firewood and craftwork and provide a site for fish ponds and rabbit warrens.[2] The evidence to be presented from Ireland demonstrates that very often these other uses overshadowed their role as deer enclosures.

The modern English word 'park' comes from Old French (ninth to fourteenth century) and in this form the word *parke* could mean both an enclosure and a hunting territory.[3] Similarly, the Old English form of the word, *pearroc*, meant 'an enclosed plot of ground, a paddock, a field', so that it did not necessarily denote a deer park, but could instead refer to enclosures with a range of functions.[4] In turn, the Irish word *páirc* is a loan word from English, with a similar meaning.[5]

FORESTS, CHASES AND WARRENS

When discussing medieval parks, one should note the existence of a number of other related landscape features, and acknowledge that documentary evidence of these can sometimes assist with the task of identifying medieval parks. In modern usage the word 'forest' is almost synonymous with 'woodland', particularly with plantations of economically important trees. In later-medieval times, however, 'forest' had a very specific meaning. It referred to land in which the timber and

---

1 Cantor and Hatherly, 'The medieval parks of England', 73. **2** Rackham, *The history of the countryside*, p. 125. **3** Muir, *The new reading the landscape* (2000), pp 12, 17; Einhorn, *Old French: a concise handbook* (1974), p. 1. **4** Moorhouse, 'The medieval parks of Yorkshire: function, contents and chronology' (2007), pp 101–2. **5** MacBain, *An etymological dictionary of the Gaelic language* (1911).

9

3 Woodland at Dunamase, Co. Laois. Timber was a vital resource controlled through the management of forests and parks.

the hunting of the 'beasts of the forest', in particular the various species of deer and wild pigs, was reserved for the king. The modern usage has therefore retained the importance of the trees and their ownership, but the deer have been lost from the equation (fig. 3). When considered simply as a jurisdictional area within which hunting and timber production were tightly controlled, a later-medieval forest could include woodland, open heaths, farmland and even villages and incorporate both land held by the king and land held by his subjects.[6] These large areas were not fenced in; instead they were legally defined places that were subject to forest law, rather than common law. Any enclosure of land within the bounds of a forest, including for agriculture or for park formation, required royal permission. This definition of forest, *forestis* or *forestum*, as opposed to woodland, *boscum* or *silvis*, can cause problems when using calendared or translated texts, since some translators use the words interchangeably.[7] A further complication is that during later-medieval times 'forest' could also be used for areas of woodland

6 Cantor and Wilson, 'The medieval deer-parks of Dorset: II' (1963), 141; Cantor and Wilson, 'The medieval deer-parks of Dorset: III' (1964), 141–52; Rackham, *The history of the countryside*, p. 130; James, *A history of English forestry*, pp 3, 5; Watts, 'Wiltshire deer parks: an introductory survey' (1996), 88–98; Young, *The royal forests of medieval England*, pp 2–4, 16, 88.   7 For example, *PRC*, pp 29, 59.

held in demesne, again stressing the rights of the lord over the timber trees.[8] One
example of this is at Maynooth, Co. Kildare, where the 'forest' of Croghmore is
listed in the assignment of dower of 1283, and by 1540–1 it is described as '100
acres of wood and underwood called Crymore'.[9] A 'chase' or 'chace' was similar to
a forest but technically this should only be used where it was under the control of
a noble rather than the king, and the regulations concerning its operation could
vary depending on the circumstances.[10] Sometimes forest and chase were also
used interchangeably in the medieval period, so that there are references to royal
chases or to forests owned by the nobility.[11]

The word 'warren' had two meanings in the later-medieval period: a 'right of
free warren' meant that a landholder had the exclusive right to hunt the 'beasts
of the warren' on his manor and that others were forbidden by law to do so.
The 'beasts of the warren' included the hare, rabbit, fox, wild cat, badger,
wolf and squirrel. In addition, there were a number of 'birds of the warren'
including pheasant, partridge and woodcock, with plover and lark also included
occasionally.[12] The other meaning of the word 'warren' relates to an artificial
construction for rearing rabbits, also known as a 'coneygarth'.[13]

THE ORIGINS OF PARKS

The idea of confining wild animals in order to stage a hunt goes back at least
as far as Pharaonic Egypt, where pictorial evidence shows that temporary
constructions of nets and ditches were stocked with wild animals immediately
before a hunt. One of these temporary parks has been excavated at Soleb in
Nubia, modern Sudan, and has been dated to 1402–1364BC.[14] The earliest
written records of permanent hunting parks or 'paradises' (*par-de-su*) are much
later, dating to the sixth century BC. At this time Syrus the Great had a hunting
park at Sippar, on the banks of the Euphrates, in modern Iraq. On conquering
Mesopotamia, he gave his administrators permission to create and stock their
own parks in the newly annexed territory (fig. 4). His successors continued to
construct parks and when Mesopotamia and Persia were conquered by the
Muslims in the seventh century, the caliphate took on the trappings of the former
Persian rulers, including the concept of the hunting park.[15] Muslim Sicily was

8 Gilbert, *Hunting and hunting reserves in medieval Scotland* (1979), p. 19.   **9** *RBK*, no. 120; *CSL*, 142.
10 Cantor and Wilson, 'The medieval deer-parks of Dorset: III', 141; Grant, *The royal forests of England*
(1991), pp 30–1; James, *A history of English forestry*, p. 5; Cantor, 'Forests, chases, parks and warrens'
(1982), p. 70.   **11** Rackham, *The history of the countryside*, p. 131.   **12** James, *A history of English forestry*,
pp 6, 31, 39.   **13** Williamson, *Rabbits, warrens and archaeology* (2007), pp 12, 17.   **14** Allsen, *The royal
hunt in Eurasian history* (2006), p. 36.   **15** Ibid., pp 35–6; Fletcher, *Gardens of earthly delight*, pp 64–5.

4 Winged figure carrying a fallow deer, found at Nimrud, Iraq. From Austen Henry
Layard, *Monuments of Nineveh, from drawings made on the spot* (London, 1847),
pl. 35. Courtesy of the National Library of Ireland.

conquered by the Normans between 1060 and 1071, and the fashion for keeping fallow deer may have then been copied by the Normans and brought to north-west Europe.[16]

The concept of the park was also known in the Classical world, having spread from Asia to the Greeks and Romans, who maintained parks filled with a range of wild animals such as deer, wild pigs, wild goats and wild sheep. These could be extravagant features, the example owned by Quintus Hortensius at Laurentum, south of Rome, had an area of *c*.34 acres and contained a dining room from which guests could view animals that were summoned by blowing a horn.[17] These Roman parks, and the wild animals that they contained, spread across the empire and eventually reached Britain. There is zooarchaeological evidence to support this: for example, one study used strontium isotope analysis on the skeletal remains of a fallow deer from the Roman site of Fishbourne, Sussex.[18] Researchers were able to show that it had spent the early part of its life outside south-east England, but that it had been reared to maturity in the Fishbourne area, with a diet that demonstrated that it was probably confined within a garden or park.

The use and creation of parks continued during the post-Roman period. Charlemagne had a park containing 'multitudes of antlered stags', which can be considered as a deliberate imitation of Roman status symbols, and hence as a means of legitimising the new imperial power.[19] There is substantial evidence for the existence of reserved hunting grounds or 'hays' in Anglo-Saxon England, often with royal or ecclesiastical associations. The word *hay, haga, hage, hege* or *haia* is believed to have originally meant an impenetrable barrier of vegetation and to be related to the modern words 'hedge' and 'haw' as in 'hawthorn'. This meaning had evolved by the late eleventh century to mean a deer enclosure. Over thirty hays are identified in the Domesday Book, of which only nine were royal.[20] Until recently it was thought that few hays pre-dated the Norman Conquest and that they were not true parks.[21] However, it is now understood that many of them dated to the Anglo-Saxon period and that they were used in the same way as later parks.[22] By the thirteenth century, parks stocked with fallow deer were a

16 Brown, *The Norman conquest of Southern Italy and Sicily* (2003), p. 106; Fletcher, 'The rise of British deer parks: their raison d'être in a global and historical perspective' (2007), 36. **17** Jennison, *Animals for show and pleasure in ancient Rome* (2005), pp 133–6; Toynbee, *Animals in Roman life and art* (1973), p. 16. **18** Sykes et al., 'Tracking animals using strontium isotopes in teeth: the role of fallow deer (*Dama dama*) in Roman Britain' (2006), 948–59. **19** Allsen, *The royal hunt in Eurasian history*, p. 40; Andrén, 'Paradise lost: looking for deer parks in medieval Denmark and Sweden' (1997), p. 470. **20** Cantor, 'Forests, chases, parks and warrens', p. 76; Fletcher, 'The rise of British deer parks: their raison d'être in a global and historical perspective', 37–9; Hooke, 'Medieval forests and parks in southern and central England' (1998), p. 21; Liddiard, 'The deer parks of Domesday book' (2003), 4–23; Vera, *Grazing ecology and forest history* (2000), pp 159–62; Vera, 'The wood-pasture theory and the deer park: the grove – the origin of the deer park' (2007), 109–10. **21** Rackham, *The history of the countryside*, p. 123. **22** Liddiard, 'The deer parks

common feature of the manorial system in England. They were part of the aristocratic landscape but were moving down the social ladder and had become accessible to even minor nobility and knights.[23] Cantor and Hatherley suggested that there were at least 1,900 parks in England; whereas Rackham claimed that at their peak around the year 1300 there were approximately 3,200 examples, resulting in an average of one park for every 1,500 acres of woodland recorded in the Domesday Book.[24]

The remarkable number of parks created in later-medieval England was not matched in other European countries, but this does not mean that they were not created elsewhere or were not important. Parks are known from various locations, including Belgium, Germany, Italy, Denmark and Sweden, with one of the most spectacular being the park at Hesdin, France.[25] In general, parks elsewhere in Europe were similar in form and function to those found in England, but they never attained the levels of popularity found there. For example, in Scotland, Gilbert identified twenty-five royal and forty-nine baronial parks appearing in documentary sources between 1165 and 1512.[26] Up to the fifteenth century, private forests seem to have been favoured over enclosed parks in Scotland, implying that Gaelic-influenced cross-country drives or *par-force*-style chases had remained the preferred form of hunting. Very little work has been carried out on the parks of later-medieval Wales, but these are currently the subject of ongoing research.[27] There are approximately fifty recorded medieval parks, the majority of which are found in south Wales and the Marches, with fewer examples in the north of the country.[28] This may suggest that here also there was less emphasis on parkland hunting than in England, but it should also be noted that this may be an underestimate due to the presence of many liberties in Wales, where licences to empark would not have been required.[29] The geographical spread may also suggest that parks were generally a feature of Norman rather than native lordships. Given the popularity of parks in high-medieval England, and their existence in other neighbouring countries, the question then arises whether this was also the case in Ireland and, if so, then to what extent?

---

of Domesday book', 4–23; Vera, *Grazing ecology and forest history*, p. 160.   **23** Mileson, *Parks in medieval England*, p. 103.   **24** Cantor and Hatherly, 'The medieval parks of England', 71–85; Rackham, *The history of the countryside*, p. 123.   **25** Cummins, 'Veneurs s'en vont en Paradis: medieval hunting and the "natural" landscape' (2002), pp 47–8 ; Creighton, *Designs upon the land: elite landscapes of the Middle Ages* (2009), pp 148–9; Almond, *Medieval hunting* (2003), pp 141, 150; Andrén, 'Paradise lost: looking for deer parks in medieval Denmark and Sweden'; Taylor, *The Oxford companion to the garden* (2006), p. 457.   **26** Gilbert, *Hunting and hunting reserves in medieval Scotland*, pp 222, 356–9.   **27** Smith, 'Medieval parks, gardens and designed landscapes of north Wales and the Shropshire Marches' (2012), 4–6.   **28** Linnard, *Welsh woods and forests* (2000), p. 52; Rackham, *The history of the countryside*, pp 124–5.   **29** Stringer, 'States, liberties and communities in medieval Britain and Ireland (c.1100–1400)' (2008), map 1.

EVIDENCE FOR PARKS IN IRELAND

Documentary evidence

For this study, documentary evidence for high-medieval parks was identified by systematic searches of calendars and other transcriptions of later-medieval documents. One methodological limitation however, was the small number of extant Gaelic documents with detailed economic information. There are a substantial number of references to parks both as specific locations and as a concept.[30] In 1200, for example, the Knights Hospitaller received a charter of liberties that included freedom from works regarding parks,[31] and in a legal dispute in 1290 the Knights Templar produced a charter dating from the time of Henry III (reigned 1216–72) that gave similar rights to their order.[32] These rights did not necessarily mean that parks existed in areas that would have had an effect on the orders, but instead they refer generally to the concept of parks. Another example dates from 1234 when the justiciar, Maurice FitzGerald, was charged to look after the lands of the late Richard Marshal, earl of Pembroke and lord of Leinster, and 'to allow no waste, sale or spoil, in the lands, parks, woods or mines'.[33] Although there is documentary evidence to demonstrate that the earl did actually have parks, again this does not necessarily refer to specific parks, but instead is designed to ensure that all potential landscape resources are included in the instructions.

In total, there are over sixty references to at least forty-six specific parks in high-medieval Ireland, all of them in Anglo-Norman contexts, and these were most commonly found in inquisitions post-mortem, or in manorial extents.[34] Many of the parks may have been in use for decades prior to being recorded following the death of the lord and, given that not all deaths resulted in a surviving inquisition post-mortem, it is possible that some may have been in use for generations before being documented in a surviving record. One clear example of this delay is at Earlspark, Co. Galway, where the manor, castle and town were established in 1236 and charcoal in the mortar of the park wall has been radiocarbon dated to 1251–97.[35] Despite this, the first known record of the park does not occur until 1333, when it is recorded in an inquisition post-mortem following the murder of William de Burgh, earl of Ulster and lord of Connacht.[36]

Licences to empark are an important source of information about medieval parks in England, and have formed the basis of many regional surveys of parks. However, such licences can be unreliable since, strictly speaking, they were only

---

30 Appendices 1 and 2. **31** *CDI*, i, no. 123. **32** Ibid., iii, no. 666. **33** Ibid., i, no. 2111. **34** See Appendix 2. **35** UBA18087 2-σ. **36** *CIPM*, vii, Edw. III, no. 537; *IEMI*, no. 262.

5 Much of the ancient forest of Glencree is now modern forestry plantation.

necessary where a park was in or close to a royal forest, where the presence of a park could reduce the availability of deer in the forest.[37] Only one such licence is known from Ireland, dating to 1206–7.[38] In this case the archbishop of Dublin was granted the right to create a park and a deer-leap and was exempted from the duty of feeding foresters. This was in the manor of Kilmasantan (Kicopsentan), identified as being in the foothills of the mountains close to the Kildare–Dublin–Wicklow border.[39] This would have been close to the royal forest of Glencree (fig. 5), which lay immediately to the south-east and so the park would have required a royal licence due to its proximity to the forest. By comparison with England, there were few royal forests in Ireland, and so most park owners would not have needed to seek a licence. Furthermore, the majority of parks are located within the great liberties of Ireland, where the lord had the right to construct parks at will, without recourse to royal permission. There are some examples of tenants holding parks, but where these were within a liberty it would have been the permission of their lord that was required. Since few Irish later-medieval

37 Cantor, 'Forests, chases, parks and warrens', p. 75; James, *A history of English forestry*, p. 6.   38 *CDI*, i, no. 316.   39 Murphy and Potterton, *The Dublin region in the Middle Ages* (2010), p. 170.

manorial documents have survived, and even fewer have been calendared or published, it is not surprising that no licences granted by lords of liberties have been identified. It is therefore very likely that more parks held by the second tier of the Anglo-Norman settlers originally existed within these liberties.

Although only one licence to empark exists, two other similar documents have survived. The first of these is the application by Theobald Walter (Butler) as follows:

> 1299 March 16. Pleas at the Nanagh, before John Wogan, Chief Justiciar, on Monday in the Second Week of Lent.
>
> Tipperary. The petition was heard of Theobald le Butteiller that he might divert a highway which leads through the midst of his wood of the Nanagh, and prepare another road for it, below said wood towards the south, and maintain it at his own expense; and that he might enclose the wood, and make a park of it. The Sheriff was directed to summon a jury to make known whether it be to the damage of the king or of others that the king should grant this. And John son of Robert, Dionysius de Mariscis, Nich. Crok, Hugh son of Robert, Geoffrey Techeseye, Ph. Lagheles, Ric. de Mariscis, Ric. de Barwe, Ph. le Blund, Henry Golcfre, Rob. Goer ... Trauers, and Will. Shorthals, jurors, say that it would not damage any but those who dwell in Theobald's town of the Nanagh in the street below the castle towards the east, viz., Rob. son of David, and his neighbours dwelling in that street; and it is to their hurt if the way is diverted, because it would oblige them in going to their lands on the other side of the wood to make a circuit of four furlongs. And they estimate their damage at 40s.[40]

The 'highway which leads through the midst of his wood of the Nanagh' probably ran north-east from the castle, and Gwynn and Gleeson suggested that the road that was to be constructed to the south of the park was the Dublin Road/Thomas MacDonagh Street.[41] This would mean that residents 'below the castle towards the east' would need to detour around the park rather than pass through it to reach lands to the north (fig. 45).

This plea before the chief justiciar can be considered as a form of planning permission to re-route the road around Theobald's proposed park at Nenagh. The majority of documented Irish parks were constructed within the liberties or palatine lordships, but Nenagh was then in the county of Tipperary, which did

---

40 *CJRI*, i, p. 234; Murphy and O'Conor, 'Castles and deer parks in Anglo-Norman Ireland'; Gwynn and Gleeson, *A history of the diocese of Killaloe* (1962), p. 88.   41 Gwynn and Gleeson, *A history of the diocese of Killaloe*, p. 88.

not become a liberty until 1328. There is no evidence for the location of a royal forest in the vicinity, suggesting that Theobald Walter (Butler) had no requirement to obtain permission for a park. Instead, it is quite possible that for political reasons he wished to be seen to be publicly and officially creating a park at this time of rising tensions between the crown and the Gaelic population. Moreover, his petition is primarily concerned with diverting the highway, rather than the actual park construction. Permission was needed to divert the royal road (*via regia*), which was defined in English law as 'a royal highway which is always open, which no one can close or divert with walls he has erected, which leads into a city or fortress or castle or royal town'.[42] Generally, at this time, the law as it applied in England was deemed to be valid in Ireland, except in particular cases where legislation might be modified to suit the circumstances.[43] This may have influenced Theobald's decision to seek permission to realign the road as there was certainly precedent for legal action. In 1130, in Newark, England, the bishop's reeve had been fined for diverting a road without permission.[44] Theobald may therefore have been concerned that to go ahead with his park construction without approval would potentially leave him open to royal disfavour. A century earlier than at Nenagh, in 1228 Walter de Ridelisford sought and received royal permission to 'divert outside his park of Garnenan, a way which passes through its middle',[45] and although no further details are given in the source, it is likely that similar reasoning can be applied since in this case the park was already in existence when the request was made.

Of the forty-six documented parks in Ireland, the general location of forty-two is clear from the documentary source, while the locations of the remainder are known at a more general level (fig. 6). The documented parks were mainly in Leinster, and the majority were either in the modern counties of Dublin and Wicklow, or within the great liberties of Ireland. They generally lay, therefore, within the main area of Anglo-Norman settlement and there is also a cluster of documented parks in Co. Cork, together with a few examples in more westerly areas. There are three examples in Galway: Earlspark at Loughrea, which was held by the powerful de Burgh family; Kilcorban, close to Tynagh, which was also in de Burgh lands but in the adjacent medieval cantred of Muntremolynan; and Ardrahan, which was held by the de Clares, who also held Baliduwil in Co. Kerry. It is notable that there are only three documented parks west of the River Shannon, but again they are in Anglo-Norman heartlands. The other outlier is at Adare, Co. Limerick, which was held by the FitzGeralds, earls of Kildare. They

42 *Leges*, p. 80, 3a.   **43** Orpen, *Ireland under the Normans, 1169–1333* (1911–20), iv, pp 41–4. **44** Cooper, 'The king's four highways: legal fiction meets fictional law' (2000), 357.   **45** *CDI*, i, no. 1641; Murphy and O'Conor, 'Castles and deer parks in Anglo-Norman Ireland'; Gwynn and Gleeson, *A history of the diocese of Killaloe*, p. 88.

	Legend
●	Park location well defined
●	Park location approximate
▨	Liberties c.1250
▢	Counties

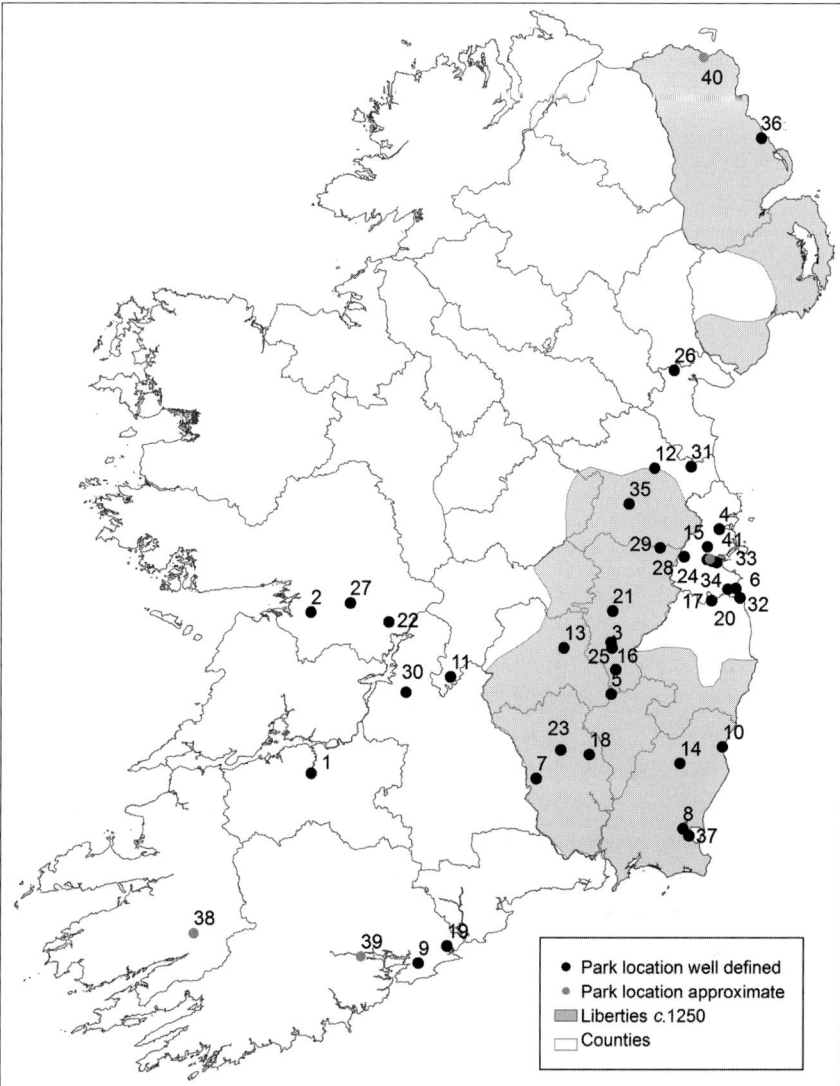

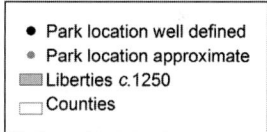

No. Park location well defined
1. Adare
2. Ardraghin (Ardrahan)
3. Arscol (Ardscull)
4. Ballykeene, Swords
5. Balydonegan (Dunganstown)
6. Bray
7. Callan (2)
8. Carrick
9. Cloyne
10. Curtun (Courtown)
11. Donkeryn (Dunkerrin)
12. Donmowe (Dunmoe)
13. Dunamase
14. Ferns
15. Fynglas (Finglas) (2)
16. Garnenan (Kilkea)
17. Glencree
18. Gowran
19. Inchiquin (3)
20. Kilcopsentan (Kilmasantan)
21. Kildare
22. Kilkarban (Kilcorban)
23. Kilkenny
24. Kilmaynan (Kilmainham)
25. Kylka (Kilkea)
26. Le Roche
27. Loughrea
28. Lucan
29. Maynooth
30. Nenagh
31. Platin
32. Senekyll (Shankill)(2)
33. Shanballymore (Baggotrath)
34. St Sepulchre's Colonia (divers)
35. Trim
36. Villa de Hacket (Ballyhacket)
37. Wexford

No. Park location approximate
38. Baliduwil, Co. Kerry
39. Co. Cork
40. Pouloc, Ulster
41. Welshtown, Dublin

6 Locations of documented high-medieval parks. Liberties after Keith Stringer, 'States, liberties and communities in medieval Britain and Ireland, c.1100–1400' (2008).

had their caput at Maynooth, Co. Kildare, the site of another documented park. Notably, none of the parks identified so far is in areas held by Gaelic lords in the period *c.*1300 so that, contrary to the assertions of Weir, there is at present no evidence for Gaelic lords constructing parks in the high-medieval period.[46] This does not mean that they did not do so, but that there is no evidence for this practice at the moment. As Chapter 7 will demonstrate, however, Gaelic lords who gained control over lands containing parks seem to have retained them intact and continued to use them for timber and grazing. It is only much later though that there is currently any evidence for the creation of enclosed parks for deer spreading into Gaelic-held lands; for example at Leamaneh, Co. Clare, where the park is believed to date to the seventeenth century.[47]

Place-name evidence

There are, quite remarkably, 776 townlands in Ireland with 'park' as an element in the name (fig. 7a). The element 'park' is found in all counties and comes in a number of guises, ranging from townlands simply called 'Park' to those that give details of function such as Woodpark, of which there are fourteen examples, Calfpark or, commonly, Deerpark. Many place-names also incorporate the names of landowning families, such as Frenchpark, Co. Galway.[48] This already large total does not include field names and names of blocks of land that straddle more than one modern townland. For example, the 'Park of Maynooth' is shown on maps until the late eighteenth century, and incorporated the modern townlands of Crewhill, Mariavilla and part of the townland of Maynooth itself.[49] These denominations of larger and smaller 'park' lands cannot easily be identified without detailed local study and so their frequency is difficult to determine. The general element 'park' combined with other words is so common that it is of little use in identifying undocumented high-medieval examples, but it can be useful where contemporary sources indicate a park in a particular area. For example, Earlspark lies 2km south-east of Loughrea, Co. Galway, and fieldwork there demonstrated that this was the location of the medieval park. This means that for places with 'park' as an element in the name, the local history and the origin of any supplementary name element need to be carefully considered.

Narrowing the focus to townlands called 'Deerpark', there are 91 examples, rising to 112 when townlands incorporating the phrase into a longer name are included (fig. 7b). Taking county size into consideration, the densest concentration of 'Deerpark' townlands is in Wicklow, followed by Waterford, Clare and Longford. When the locations of documented parks are combined with the

46 Weir, 'Deer parks of Clare', 54–5.   47 Reetz, 'The elite landscape of Leamaneh Castle, County Clare' (2003), pp 82–95.   48 Broderick, 'The IreAtlas townland database' (1999).   49 Taylor, 'A map of the

**All 'park' townlands
per 1,000km2   n=776**

● Park location well defined
○ Park location approximate

Up to 5.00
5.01 - 10.00
10.01 - 15.00
15.01 - 20.00
20.01 - 25.00
>25

**'Deerpark' townlands
per 1,000km2   n=112**

● Park location well defined
○ Park location approximate

0
0.01 - 0.75
0.76 - 1.50
1.51 - 2.25
2.26 - 3.00
3.01 - 3.75
>3.75

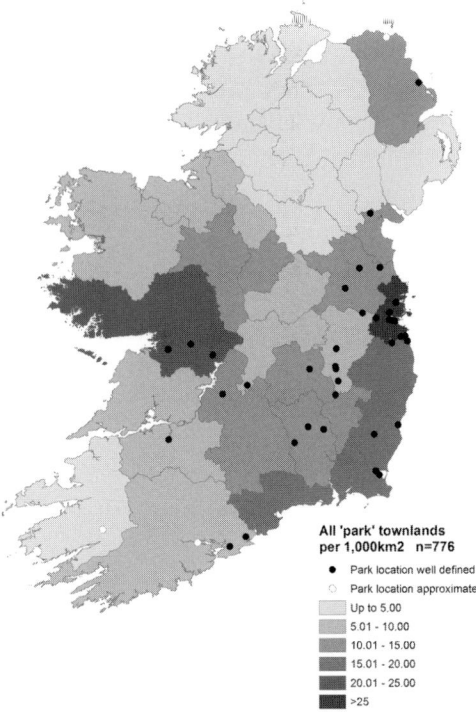

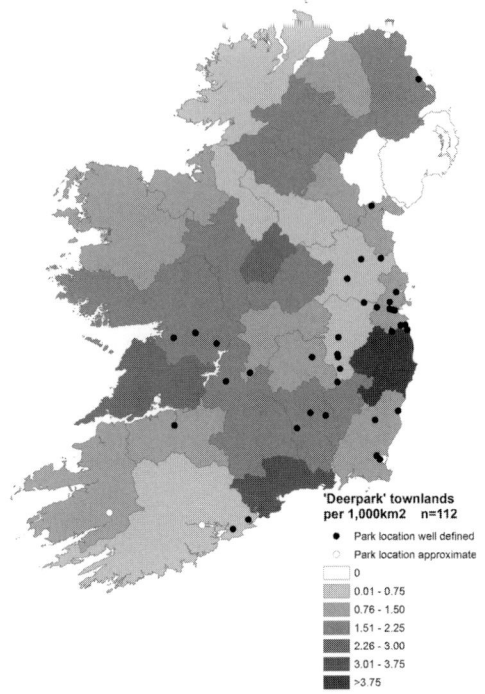

7 County densities of
the townland names
   a. -park,
   b. Deerpark, and
   c. Park.

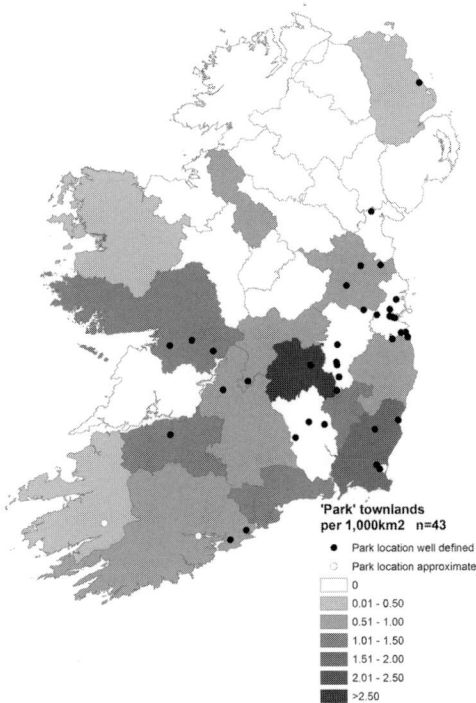

**'Park' townlands
per 1,000km2   n=43**

● Park location well defined
○ Park location approximate

0
0.01 - 0.50
0.51 - 1.00
1.01 - 1.50
1.51 - 2.00
2.01 - 2.50
>2.50

townland name information, it becomes apparent that there is no automatic connection between the place-name evidence and a high-medieval park and the place-name is widespread in modern counties that were outside Anglo-Norman control in the high-medieval period. In fact, none of the contemporary medieval sources use this term, so that the evidence strongly suggests that the name 'Deerpark' is associated with one of the later waves of park-making in the late-medieval or post-medieval periods. One caveat is that in some cases the site of a high-medieval park may have been reused for a late-medieval or post-medieval deer park. This means that sites with the name 'Deerpark' should not be automatically discounted as possibly having an origin in the high-medieval period. For example, the high-medieval park at Balydonegan is likely to have been located in the modern townland of Dunganstown, *c.*4km north of Carlow town. In the eighteenth century the townland of Oakpark Demesne was laid out to partially overlie what had become known by the seventeenth century as Painestown, Ducanston and Durkanswood, and on the first-edition OS map an area called 'Deerpark' was marked in the eastern portion of Oakpark townland.[50]

Narrowing the focus further still, there are forty-three townlands simply called 'Park', or where 'Park' is appended only by geographical qualifiers such as 'Upper', or 'West' (fig. 7c). When county size is taken into consideration, Laois has by far the densest concentration, with Wexford, Limerick and Galway also well represented. This place-name is much more regional, being focused in the south and west, with a single example from Antrim being the only townland of this name in the entire province of Ulster. The townland name 'Park' on its own does seem to have a closer connection with the presence of a high-medieval park than either a general 'park' element or with 'Deerpark', since the geographical spread of counties yielding these place-names and documented parks is similar. Furthermore, and very importantly, several of the physically identified high-medieval parks have the name 'Park' attached to them. The Park of Maynooth was shown on maps until the late eighteenth century and the name continued in use into the nineteenth century.[51] At Carrick, Co. Wexford, part of the high-medieval park still has the townland name 'Park', as does the townland of 'Park or Dunamase' in Co. Laois. Overall, although this suggests that the place-name 'Park' is the most reliable of the place-name evidence for a medieval park, it will not identify all parks of this period, and some townlands with this name may be later features.

---

county of Kildare' (1783).   **50** Petty, 'Down survey parish maps' (*c.*1656); First-edition, 6-inch to the mile maps (1837–42); Lewis, *A topographical dictionary of Ireland* (1837), i, p. 262.   **51** Taylor, 'A map of the county of Kildare'; *DEP*, 28 Jan. 1804; OS name books.

PARK CREATION AND OWNERSHIP

The documented parks were owned by the crown, the Church and various private individuals and families. The level of detail given in the sources varies considerably; sometimes it is mentioned only incidentally, whereas at other times the records give details of the location or provide evidence of its size or function.

The crown

By contrast with England, where the crown held large numbers of parks, only one park in Ireland was recorded as the property of the crown. This sole example was at Glencree, Co. Wicklow, within the royal forest of the same name, and it is extremely well documented, because most of the extant later-medieval documents are correspondence to and from the royal court.[52] The lack of royal interest in emparkment in Ireland can probably be explained by the almost entire absence of the king from Ireland throughout the whole later-medieval period. Instead, the park at Glencree probably operated as a livestock store, providing live deer and venison for gifts to favoured subjects or to be used in great feasts at Dublin Castle, the royal centre of government in Ireland.

There are a number of references to the park and forest at Glencree, with over twenty references to the forest of Glencree, which mainly relate to timber or wood, although some refer to pannage or deer. As regards the park, in 1242 '20 bucks and 40 does [were] to be taken alive and transmitted to Ireland, to stock a park of the K. there'.[53] While this park is unnamed, it is probably referring to Glencree, since this is the only known royal park and since only two years later the park is mentioned by name. This is in 1244 when '60 does and 20 bucks [were] to be taken alive in the K.'s parks nearest to the port of Chester, to be sent to the port of Dalkey, Ireland, and delivered to the K.'s treasurer of Dublin, to stock the K.'s park of Glencry'.[54] This means that a total of one hundred does and forty bucks appear to have been sent to Ireland over the course of just three years. These two large-scale transfers may mark the initial creation and stocking of the park, with the females providing breeding stock and the majority of the males destined as gifts and for the table. Certainly by 1251 the park was sufficiently established that the king could gift the archbishop of Dublin with seven does and four bucks, presumably to stock his own park.[55]

There is then a break in references to the park, which is not mentioned again until January 1279/80, when John de Walhope was gifted with seven oak trees fit

---

52 *CDI*, i, nos 2580, 2671, 3123; ii, no. 1633; Murphy and O'Conor, 'Castles and deer parks in Anglo-Norman Ireland'; Le Fanu, 'The royal forest of Glencree', 268–80.   **53** *CDI*, i, no. 2580; Murphy and O'Conor, 'Castles and deer parks in Anglo-Norman Ireland'.   **54** *CDI*, i, no. 2670; Murphy and O'Conor, 'Castles and deer parks in Anglo-Norman Ireland'.   **55** *CDI*, i, no. 3123; Murphy and

for timber.[56] Timber was wood used for the structural parts of buildings such as the supporting beams, whereas underwood was the term used for smaller branches and twigs that were used for firewood or for making smaller items. This gap in the records may suggest that the park fell out of use for stocking deer between the 1250s and 1270s, but interestingly it is not until 1282 that the first reference to the 'forest' or 'wood' of Glencree is made. This is despite the evidence for the archbishop of Dublin seeking a licence to empark at his nearby park of Kilmasantan (Kicopsentan) in 1206–7, which would suggest that the forest was extant by this time.[57] By the 1290s there is evidence for fallow deer in the forest of Glencree, but no further mention of the park. The park may have been out of use and the deer may have roamed freely in the forest, or more likely the words *park* and *forest* were used interchangeably. In 1290 the queen set up timber works in the forests of Glencree and Newcastle to supply building materials for her castle at Haverford West in Wales, and the records show that considerable quantities of timber were harvested from these sites.[58] After this there are no further references to the park, and the latest reference to the forest is in 1305, when a forester is documented.[59] There was increasing instability in the Uí Briúin Cualann region in the early fourteenth century,[60] so that it is likely that the park and forest essentially became obsolete at this time when the land came under the control of Gaelic lords.[61]

The Church

Officially, the Church disapproved of clerical involvement in hunting, but nevertheless it often took place.[62] In the light of this official disapproval, it may seem surprising that the largest number of documented parks were owned by the archbishops of Dublin, although this is likely to be an accident of survival, since the Church was a keen record-keeper. However, it may also accurately reflect an ecclesiastical interest in park-making and it is important to remember that parks had many uses apart from deer keeping, and that the archbishop did not need to be a hunter himself in order to want access to venison for consumption. On the contrary, evidence from England suggests that much of the venison consumed at table was killed by professional parkers rather than by elite hunters.[63] Nevertheless,

---

O'Conor, 'Castles and deer parks in Anglo-Norman Ireland'.   **56** *CDI*, ii, no. 1633.   **57** *CDI*, i, no. 316; Murphy and O'Conor, 'Castles and deer parks in Anglo-Norman Ireland'.   **58** *CDI*, iii, nos 641, 741, 769, 796.   **59** *CJRI*, ii, membrane 36; Le Fanu, 'The royal forest of Glencree', 276.   **60** Frame, 'English officials and Irish chiefs in the fourteenth century' (1975), 748–77.   **61** Price, 'Powerscourt and the territory of Fercullen' (1953), 117–32; Fitzgerald, 'The manor and castle of Powerscourt, County Wicklow, in the sixteenth century, formerly a possession of the earls of Kildare' (1909–11), 127–39.   **62** Cummins, *The hound and the hawk: the art of medieval hunting* (1988), p. 10; Thiebaux, 'The mediaeval chase' (1967), 260–74.   **63** Almond, *Medieval hunting*, pp 18–19.

8 Ferns Cathedral, Co. Wexford. The bishop of Ferns held 'wild cattle' in his nearby park.

in both England and Ireland many clergy did take part in hunting despite official disapproval. Most high-ranking clergy such as bishops and abbots were from noble families and so had been trained in the aristocratic arts from boyhood. There is even a record of the abbot and monks of St Mary's Abbey in Dublin being accused of poaching in the royal forest.[64]

The archbishop of Dublin is recorded as having parks at Finglas (Fynglas), Kilmasantan (Kicopsentan), Shankill (Senekyll), St Sepulchre's (Colonia) and Welshtown.[65] Some of these contained domestic livestock, but the park at Kilmasantan was specifically constructed with deer in mind, having a deer-leap fitted to attract animals in from the wild. This interest in keeping captive deer is demonstrated by evidence for the archbishop receiving royal gifts of fallow deer, which could be used to stock a park.[66] The bishops of Cloyne and of Ferns are also documented as having parks at their caputs, although in these cases deer are not referred to (fig. 8).[67] The Knights of the Hospital of St John of Jerusalem,

64 *CSMA*, 4, 136–7. 65 *CAAR*, pp 170–2, 173, 195; *CDI*, i, no. 316; ii, no. 1281; Murphy and O'Conor, 'Castles and deer parks in Anglo-Norman Ireland'. 66 *CDI*, i, no. 3123. 67 *CDI*, ii, no. 297;

known as the Hospitallers, had a park at Kilmainham, Co. Dublin, and although it is not clear whether this contained deer, one of the parkers recorded there was also responsible for the 'waters' of the manor, presumably the fishponds and weirs, which suggests that this was a park for game rather than for domestic animals.[68]

The de Burgh family

The de Burghs, who were the earls of Ulster and lords of Connacht, first came to Ireland early in the Anglo-Norman conquest and, from 1236 onwards, had their caput at Loughrea, in Connacht, while also holding extensive lands in Munster and Ulster. As such, they were among the leading families in Anglo-Norman Ireland.[69] There are documentary references to their parks at Loughrea and Kilcorban (Kylkarban), both Co. Galway, and Balydonegan, Co. Carlow.[70] In 1250 and 1251 Walter de Burgh was given four stags and four does from the king's Irish forest of Slescho/Slefco.[71] Although these records do not state that these were to stock a park, this is very likely, given the number of animals and that they included both sexes, so providing a breeding herd.

The park at Loughrea is mentioned in an inquisition post-mortem following the death of William de Burgh. This was held at Athenry on 18 October 1333, and detailed lands in the cantred of Monewagh and the manor and castle of Loughrea. While only an outline was calendared, further details of the extent were published by Knox and by Murphy and O'Conor.[72] Both of these included information on the park, which measured seven carucates. Knox equated this to the modern townland of Earlspark, although he did not conduct any fieldwork to confirm this. Substantial remains of the park exist there to this day, with a mortared stone wall surrounding the townland.[73]

Loughrea and the nearby park are described or shown in various forms on a number of historical maps and post-medieval documents, in particular the *Books of survey and distribution* and the *Inquisitions of Galway*, and Petty's county map of Galway from the *Hiberniae Delineatio* provides good detail of the area (fig. 9). A particular feature of this map is the presence of trees in 'The Parke', suggesting that this was still at least partly wooded at the time of the survey in the 1650s.

PRC, p. 13.   **68** *Registrum de Kilmainham*, p. 8.   **69** Orpen, *Ireland under the Normans, 1169–1333*, ii, pp 146–7; iii, pp 191–2.   **70** *CJRI*, ii, pp 136, 314; *CIPM*, vii, Edw. III, no. 537; *IEMI*, nos 251, 262; Gibbons and Clarke, 'Deer parks', 4–5; Murphy and O'Conor, 'Castles and deer parks in Anglo-Norman Ireland'.   **71** *CDI*, i, nos 3076, 3197.   **72** *CIPM*, vii, Edw. III, no. 537; *IEMI*, no. 262; Knox, 'Occupation of Connaught by the Anglo-Normans after AD1237' (1902), 134; Murphy and O'Conor, 'Castles and deer parks in Anglo-Norman Ireland', 69.   **73** Beglane, 'Theatre of power: the Anglo-Norman park at Earlspark, Co. Galway, Ireland' (2014), passim.

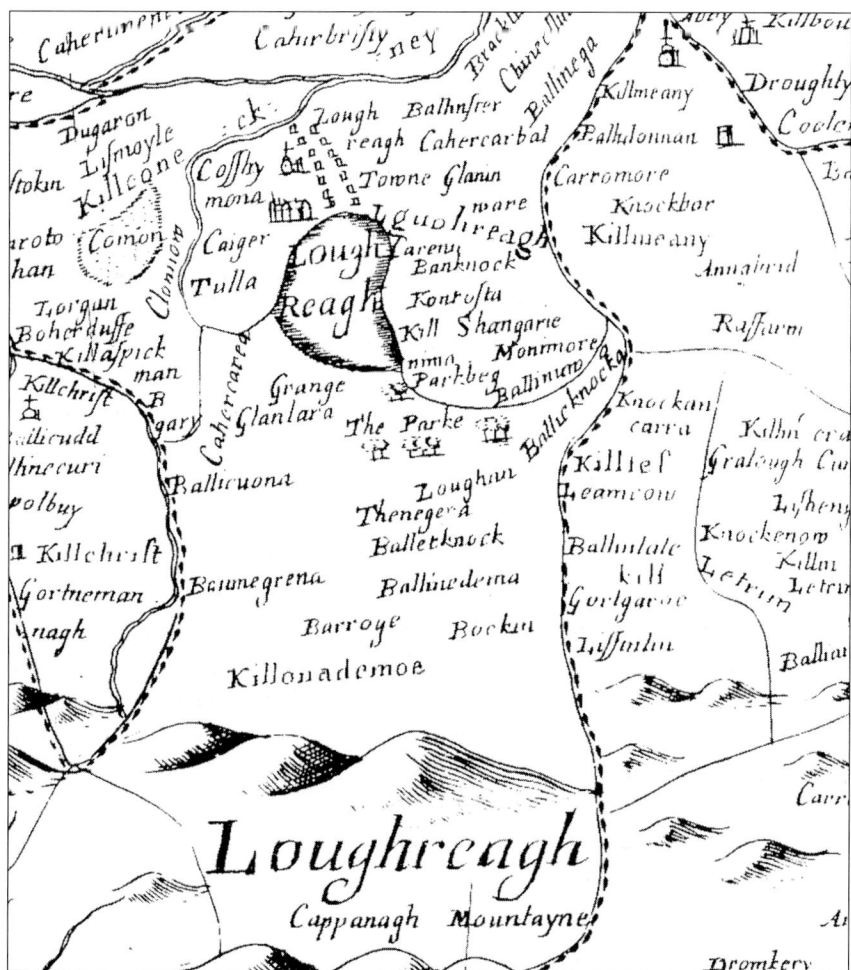

9 'The Parke' at Loughrea, Co. Galway, on William Petty's map of Galway. Courtesy of the National Library of Ireland.

The land of Balydonegan (modern Dunganstown), Co. Carlow, lies slightly to the north of Carlow town and was originally part of the lands of the earl marshal. In the partition of Leinster, it passed to Matilda Marshal and hence to the Bigods, earls of Norfolk, being acquired by the de Burghs at some point probably prior to 1279.[74] The park is first mentioned in 1305, and so may have been created in the time of either the Marshals, the de Burghs or, less likely, the Bigods.

74 Murphy and O'Conor, 'Castles and deer parks in Anglo-Norman Ireland', 59; Orpen, *Ireland under the Normans, 1169–1333*, iii, pp 81–2.

The Marshal family and descendants

A number of the references to parks can be traced to William, earl marshal the younger, and his collateral descendants. The king gave twenty does from Cheddar, England, to William in 1225, and it was stated that these were to bring to Ireland, which suggests that they were to stock a park.[75] Parks are documented at Wexford Castle and at Carrick, Co. Wexford, and there is zooarchaeological evidence from the nearby Ferrycarrig Castle, which is situated just north of Wexford town, where excavation yielded six fragments of fallow deer bones.[76] A park was also recorded at Dunamase, which was subsequently held by the de Mortimers, having been inherited through the female line from the Marshal, and again fallow deer remains have been found at this castle.[77] Finally, the aforementioned park at Balydonegan, Co. Carlow, may originally date to the period in which Marshal held Carlow or to the subsequent ownership by the Bigods or the de Burghs.

A park is first referred to at Carrick in the charter of disafforestation of the Forests of Ross and Taghmon, written at some time between 1231 and 1234. This charter states:

> Now of the forest around Tauchmune I have deforested outside the metes
> and bounds hereunder-written, that is to say, from the place where the river
> which flows between the castle of Karrich [and] the park [into] the Slaney,
> and by that river ascending to my mill on that river …[78]

No mention is made of the park in the inquisition held on the death of Joan (Munchensy) de Valence in 1307, but this does include a reference to 'two carucates and 20 acres of appurtenant land in demesne worth 60s. a year'.[79] This suggests that the area in demesne was *c.*260–90 acres, depending on the size of the local acre,[80] and the surveyed park boundary encloses 308 statute acres. A later inquisition in 1323–4 on the death of Aymer de Valence included a value of £2 for 'two carucates arable and pasture in demesne', presumably the same lands.[81] There are no further references to the park at Carrick until post-medieval times, when it is frequently documented as being let out to tenants.[82] The park must have been constructed by one of the two William Marshals in the period between 1189 and 1231x4, as it is unlikely to have been created during the short period in which Strongbow held the land, or during the minority of Isabella, his

---

75 *CDI*, i, no. 1323.   76 McCormick, 'The mammal bones from Ferrycarrig, Co. Wexford' (n.d.), passim.   77 Butler, 'Preliminary report on the animal bones from Dunamase, Co. Laois, 93E150: 1994 season' (1995), passim.   78 *CERM*, 56.   79 *IEMI*, no. 228.   80 Bennett, 'Preliminary archaeological excavations at Ferrycarrig ringwork, Newtown td, Co. Wexford' (1984–5), 30; MacCotter, *Medieval Ireland: territorial, political and economic divisions* (2008), p. 25.   81 *IEMI*, no. 228.   82 For example, Hore, *History of the town and county of Wexford* (1900–11), v, p. 246.

10 The strategically positioned Anglo-Norman ringwork at Carrick, Co. Wexford, was topped with a replica round tower, *c.*1800.

daughter. Furthermore, since the stone castles at Carrick and Wexford were probably constructed by one of the two Williams, it is likely that the park was created at the same time or shortly after these (fig. 10). The park seems to have been put to ordinary agricultural use by the time of Joan de Valence's death in 1307, so that it had a lifespan of not more than a century in its primary function. Nevertheless, the place-name has remained as a reminder of the original concept of the manor.

There is also firm documentary evidence for a park at Wexford itself. In 1324, in the inquisition following the death of Aymer de Valence, the demesne of Wexford Castle was recorded as having a park of sixty acres, which contained oak trees and was used for pasturing cattle.[83] Furthermore, in the assignment of dower to Mary, his wife, on 6 December 1324 it is noted that Mary was to receive a number of properties including a third part of the park.[84] The park at Wexford continues to be referred to throughout the medieval and post-medieval periods, and is consistently stated as being about sixty acres. It was located in the

---

83 *IEMI*, no. 228; Murphy and O'Conor, 'Castles and deer parks in Anglo-Norman Ireland'. **84** *IEMI*, no. 237; *CIPM*, vi, Edw. II, nos 339–40.

area of Townparks, close to the castle, which can be identified as it is bounded on one side by 'Laffaed',[85] the street known as 'Faigh' at the time of William Petty's map in 1657, 'The Feagh' on the first-edition map and as 'The Faythe' today. It is likely, however, that the post-medieval name 'Townparks' is entirely unrelated to the high-medieval park, except in the sense that it was open land that had not been built on. There are fifty-seven townlands in Ireland incorporating the name 'Townparks'[86] including the one at Maynooth, and in that particular case, Horner[87] stated that this name was applied in the eighteenth century for grazing land given to new residents of the town, which would fit with this being a previously undeveloped area of ground.

The other possible Marshal park is at Dunamase, Co. Laois. In 1282–3 an inquisition was carried out following the death of Roger de Mortimer. At this time the jurors noted that

> Roger held 2 carucates, 73 acres and a stang of arable land in demesne in the manor and honour of Dunamase in the tenement of Leix, which extend at £10 8s. 10d. a year at 8d. an acre ... The mountain pasture and an emparked pasture extend at 33s. 4d. a year.[88]

This '2 carucates, 73 acres and a stang' gives an area of 313 acres, which is surprisingly close to the modern townland size of 338 acres at the townland of 'Park or Dunamase' and which also includes the 12.9 acres of the Rock of Dunamase itself (fig. 11). It strongly suggests that this townland was the demesne land and there is archaeological evidence for a bank around the townland so that it was *in parco* or enclosed. The mention of the value of pasture raises the issue of whether there was a second park used for grazing, or whether part of the demesne was used in this way. If a value of 4d. per acre is assumed for this category of land, then the total acreage of the mountain and park pasture would be about one hundred statute acres. Given that mountain pasture is likely to be extensive rather than small scale, any second park must have been small, so that it is much more likely that a portion of the demesne park was being used for pasture rather than that there was a second park. One possibility is that the rough ground immediately around the rock itself functioned as the 'emparked pasture', while the better land to the west of this was the '2 carucates, 73 acres and a stang' referred to. This would suggest that any emparked area given over to deer was relatively small. Fallow deer remains were found during the excavation of Dunamase Castle, which supports the evidence for them being kept in this area,

85 *CIRCLE*, PR 1 Rich., no. 11.   **86** Broderick, 'The IreAtlas townland database'.   **87** Horner, *Irish historic towns atlas, 7: Maynooth* (1995), p. 3.   **88** *IEMI*, no. 54; Murphy and O'Conor, 'Castles and deer

11 The Rock of Dunamase provides a dramatic backdrop for the park below.

but as only two out of eighty-two deer bones could be identified as fallow rather than red deer this could mean simply that one dead fallow deer carcass was brought to the castle, rather than the live animals being kept there.[89]

The FitzGerald family

The FitzGeralds, earls of Kildare, were extremely powerful members of the Anglo-Norman nobility in Ireland.[90] Parks owned by the earls of Kildare are documented at the family caput of Maynooth, as well as at Kildare and at Adare, Co. Limerick (Appendix 2). There are also references to Maurice FitzGerald receiving gifts of deer in England between 1244 and 1251.[91] These may be deer for export to stock the Irish parks, and so may indicate the date at which the park at Maynooth was established.

There is reference to a park at Maynooth in the assignment of dower to Lady Joanna de Burgh in 1328, following the death of her husband Thomas FitzGerald,

parks in Anglo-Norman Ireland'. **89** Butler, 'Animal bones from Dunamase, Co. Laois, 93E150', passim. **90** Orpen, *Ireland under the Normans, 1169–1333*, iii, pp 111–14. **91** *CDI*, i, nos 2701, 3104, 3144.

12 The Anglo-Norman keep at Maynooth Castle, Co. Kildare, from the east. This was the caput of the powerful FitzGerald dynasty.

second earl of Kildare and justiciar of Ireland. An unpublished translation of the assignment of dower was kindly supplied by Margaret Murphy:

> Park: Assigned in dower of the park that is the third part of two parts next to the dower of Lady Blanche ... It is assigned to the said Joanna in her dower free ingress and egress by the gates, ways and footpaths of the park from any part of the park to drive [or possibly hunt] all her animals ...[92]

The location of the park is hinted at in the descriptions of the various aspects of the manor. Another document, possibly also from 1328, is an extent of the manor. This states that the

> Lympitisfeld contains 20 acres and a half and one stang and a half ... Crenegele alias Cravile now in the park contains 36 acres ... Moriceisfeld contains 13 acres and 1 stang.[93]

92 *RBK*, no. 120, trans. M. Murphy.   93 *RBK*, no. 119, trans. present author.

There is also an undated later-medieval reference to a tenant who was to have the right to cut wood in certain circumstances from woodland outside the park of Maynooth.[94] In addition to the documentary evidence, twenty-eight fallow deer bone fragments were found during the excavation of Maynooth Castle (fig. 12), demonstrating that fallow deer were kept nearby.[95]

The de Clare family

In an inquisition dated 1321 there is a reference to three parks, including a wood called le Park at Inchiquin, Co. Cork. This inquisition was convened to determine the lands held by Thomas FitzRichard de Clare on his death in 1287, and the park is again detailed on the death of his grandson Giles de Badlesmere in 1348.[96] Prior to *c.*1275 the manor of Inchiquin and the vill of Youghal had been in the possession of Maurice FitzMaurice FitzGerald. They were given to Thomas FitzRichard de Clare on his marriage to Maurice's daughter and prospective heiress Juliana. Maurice was one of the FitzGerald barons of Offaly, and his son was created earl of Kildare.[97] Again, the date of construction of the park is unclear so that it may date from the time of the FitzGeralds or from the time of the de Clares. There is also a park at Ardrahin (Ardrahan), Co. Galway, mentioned in the inquisition of 1321 (Appendix 2). In an earlier inquisition in 1288, Thomas de Clare is listed as holding a four-acre park at Baliduwil, however the Ardrahan park is not listed, and of course the Inchiquin parks would not have been de Clare possessions at that time.[98]

Joan, countess of Gloucester and Hertford, was a daughter of Edward I who married Gilbert de Clare.[99] Gilbert was the earl of Gloucester, and elder brother to Thomas de Clare. At the time of her death in 1307, her lands included a park at Callan, Co. Kilkenny (fig. 13), inherited from her husband.[100]

The Butler family

The Butlers, earls of Ormond, were also among the most important of the Anglo-Norman families in Ireland, with the founder of the family, Theobald Walter (Butler) (d. 1205–6), being the brother of Hubert, who was the archbishop of Canterbury as well as the justiciar and lord chancellor of England.[101] As well as the park at Nenagh, Co. Tipperary, documented in 1299, there are records of parks at Dunkerrin (Donkeryn), Co. Offaly, in 1305 and Gowran, Co. Kilkenny,

94 *RPH, Antiquissime dorso*, no. 41.3.   **95** Murray, 'Faunal remains from Maynooth Castle' (n.d.), passim. **96** *CIPM*, ix, Edw. III, no. 119; *IEMI*, nos 205, 207, 291; Murphy and O'Conor, 'Castles and deer parks in Anglo-Norman Ireland'.   **97** Orpen, *Ireland under the Normans, 1169–1333*, iv, pp 66, 129.   **98** *CDI*, iii, no. 459.   **99** Orpen, *Ireland under the Normans, 1169–1333*, iii, pp 94–5.   **100** *CDI*, v, no. 659; *IEMI*, no. 154.   **101** Gwynn and Gleeson, *A history of the diocese of Killaloe*, p. 175.   **102** Gleeson, 'The castle and manor of Nenagh' (1936), 248–9, 251, 253; *RBO*, nos 14, 91.   **103** *CJRI*, i, p. 234.   **104** St

in 1306.[102] The only documentary reference to the park at Nenagh is the court case described above in which the fifth Theobald Walter (Butler) sought to have a road realigned so that it did not pass through his new park.[103]

The de Ridelisford family and descendants

Three or possibly four parks were associated with the de Ridelisfords and their descendant Christiana de Mariscis or de Marisco. Christiana was a granddaughter of Walter de Ridelisford, and on this side of her lineage was a descendant of Henry I. Her father's family, the de Mariscis, were not aristocratic, but were also well connected, being descended from a nephew of Richard de Clare, also known as Strongbow.[104] The documented parks were at Bray, Garnenan, Kilkea (Kylka) and Courtown (Curtun).[105] Walter de Ridelisford was one of the earliest Anglo-Normans to come to Ireland and in 1173 he was given the manor of Bray by Strongbow.[106] In 1228 de Ridelisford sought royal permission to 'divert outside his park of Garnenan, a way which passes through its middle'.[107] Murphy and O'Conor suggested that this was in Wicklow, but, St John Brooks located 'Carvenagh' or 'Garnenagh' in the parish of Kilkea, Co. Kildare.[108] There is also a mention of a park at Kilkea in 1284, so these may refer to two parks within the parish or to a single park.[109] In 1280–1 a 'coveria' or preserve is recorded on the lands formerly belonging to Christiana de Mariscis at Courtown (Curtun) in Co. Wexford.[110] This may refer to a park for deer or to an area of chase.

The de Lacy family

It is unclear whether the de Lacy family held any parks, although given their status it is likely that they did. There was a park documented at Trim (fig. 14) from 1388 onwards, during the time that it was held by the de Mortimers; they had obtained Trim from the de Lacys who held the liberty of Trim, however, so that if the park originated at an earlier date than it was first recorded, it was probably created by the de Lacys.

Other owners

In the case of the remaining parks, many come from a lower tier in society, but still relate to substantial figures in the community. All of these individuals held only one recorded park and it is notable that in many cases the parks are

John Brooks, 'The family of Marisco' (1932), 22–38; Webb, *A compendium of Irish biography: comprising sketches of distinguished Irishmen, and of eminent persons connected with Ireland by office or by their writings* (1878), p. 134.   **105** *CDI*, i, no. 1641; ii, nos 1801, 2340; Murphy and O'Conor, 'Castles and deer parks in Anglo-Norman Ireland'.   **106** Lewis, *A topographical dictionary of Ireland*, i, p. 221.   **107** *CDI*, i, no. 1641.   **108** Murphy and O'Conor, 'Castles and deer parks in Anglo-Norman Ireland', 67; St John Brooks, 'The de Ridelesfords' (1951), 124.   **109** *CDI*, ii, no. 2340.   **110** *CDI*, ii, no. 1801.

13 The motte at Callan, Co. Kilkenny, was held by Joan, countess of Gloucester and Hereford, at the time of her death.

14 Trim Castle and the Yellow Steeple, Co. Meath. Trim was the largest Anglo-Norman castle in Ireland, with construction of the stone keep beginning *c.*1176.

mentioned in relation to cattle being pastured, emparked or stolen rather than to deer being kept in them. This means that there were probably many other small, non-hunting parks owned by the second and third tiers of society and used as enclosed pasture.

The park at Kilkenny is not referred to until 1375, when William Ilger, who had been appointed constable of the castle by Alice, widow of Hugh le Despenser, sold on the constableship to William Lumbard.[111] Despite this, it is likely that the park was created in the early thirteenth century, when William, earl marshal, first built Kilkenny Castle.

Robert Baggot was a knight, and the founder of the Carmelite order in Ireland, who had a 'small park' at Shanballymore or Baggotrath, Dublin in *c.*1274 (fig. 15).[112] In 1279 John, son of John Bisset, had a park at Villa de Hacket (Ballyhackett), Co. Antrim,[113] and William FitzWarin held a park at Pouloc, also in Ulster, in 1282.[114] William de Mohun had a park at Ardscull (Arscol), Co. Kildare, which in 1282 was worth 13*s.* 4*d.*[115] At Lucan, Roesia de Peche and her husband John Hanstede held the manor and park in 1299.[116] While the de Peche family were not titled, they did hold their lands directly from the crown and an ancestor of Roesia, Richard, had been bishop of Lichfield in the twelfth century.[117] At Platin, Co. Meath, animals were illegally impounded in a park held by William de la Ryuere in 1305.[118] In 1306 Geoffrey Savage (Sauuage) was recorded as holding a park at Ballykene, Swords, Co. Dublin.[119] Thomas Cod

111 *COD*, ii, no. 201.   112 *CAAR*, p. 146.   113 *IEMI*, no. 36.   114 *CDI*, ii, no. 1918.   115 *IEMI*, no. 46.   116 *CJRI*, i, p. 222; Murphy and O'Conor, 'Castles and deer parks in Anglo-Norman Ireland'. 117 Elrington Ball, *A history of the county of Dublin*, 4 (1906), pp 36–7; Lewis, *A topographical dictionary of Ireland*, pp 321–2.   118 *CJRI*, ii, p. 18.   119 *CJRI*, ii, p. 326.

15 Baggotrath Castle, from Francis Grose, *The antiquities of Ireland: the first volume* (London, 1791), pl. 8. Courtesy of the National Library of Ireland.

had a park in Co. Cork and in 1311 it is recorded that cattle were stolen from the park.[120] Theobald de Verdun held the castle at Castleroche, Co. Louth, and in 1378 this was recorded as having a small plot called the park.[121] A park rented by a tenant is referred to in the dower of Margaret, widow of John Darcy in Dunmoe (Donmowe), Co. Meath, in 1415.[122]

***

In summary, documentary evidence for high-medieval parks is mainly, but not exclusively restricted to the first tier of Anglo-Norman society. Some great magnates had several parks in their various manors, but the numbers of parks held by each magnate did not reach the figures found in England, where, for example, the earls of Lancaster had forty-six parks while the bishop of Winchester owned twenty-three.[123]

---

120 *CJRI*, iii, p. 200. **121** *CIRCLE*, PR 2 Rich. II, no. 38. **122** *IEMI*, nos 347, 348. **123** Cantor, 'Forests, chases, parks and warrens', p. 76.

CHRONOLOGY

The earliest recorded individual park belonged to the archbishop of Dublin at Kilmasantan in 1207. Records were searched to the early fifteenth century, and the last new parks to be recorded in this timeframe were Trim, which is first mentioned in 1388, although it was clearly already well established by this time, and the tenanted park held by Margaret Darcy in 1415. There is a notable peak of parks being first documented between 1270 and 1339 (fig. 16). The parks were mainly recorded in manorial extents, in inquisitions post-mortem and in the judiciary rolls. This means that when they were first documented, most had already been in existence for some time and were a 'going concern'. On an individual basis it is difficult to determine how long they had been in use, but on a national scale some trends are apparent. The giving of royal gifts of fallow deer to Anglo-Norman lords with Irish lands begins in earnest in the 1220s and peaks in the 1250s. Since a park was needed in order to keep fallow deer, this suggests that many parks were being developed during this period. Furthermore, the evidence from Glencree suggests that in the 1240s the king recognised the need for a stock of fallow deer in Ireland and created a park in which to maintain them.[124] This would have provided a ready stock of animals for royal gifts to loyal subjects, without the inconvenience and cost of shipping them from England on each occasion. Notably the 1250s were also the decade when grants of free warren peaked in Ireland. This idea that there was a considerable time lag between construction and documentation of parks is also supported by evidence from some of the documented parks. By contrast, Mileson has shown a much wider spread of park construction dates in England and Wales.[125] Using licences to empark as an indicator of the dates of park construction, he found that parks were created at relatively steady rates through the decades of the thirteenth and early fourteenth centuries, but with a peak in park creation between the 1320s and 1360s. After this, emparkment continued, but at a slower rate, declining to very few examples by the mid-fifteenth century. The peak of park creation in England is therefore at least thirty and possibly fifty or sixty years after the peak in Ireland, and the reasons for this are explored in the next chapter.

The clearest example of the chronology of a park is that of Earlspark, Loughrea, Co. Galway. The castle and town were founded in 1236 as part of the conquest of Connacht,[126] and a radiocarbon date of AD1251–97 was obtained from charcoal in the mortar of the park wall.[127] There are also historical

---

124 *CDI*, i, nos 2580, 2670.   **125** Mileson, *Parks in medieval England* (2009), p. 128.   **126** Orpen, *Ireland under the Normans, 1169–1333*, iii, p. 191.   **127** UBA-18087 2σ, Calibration data set: intcal09.14c.

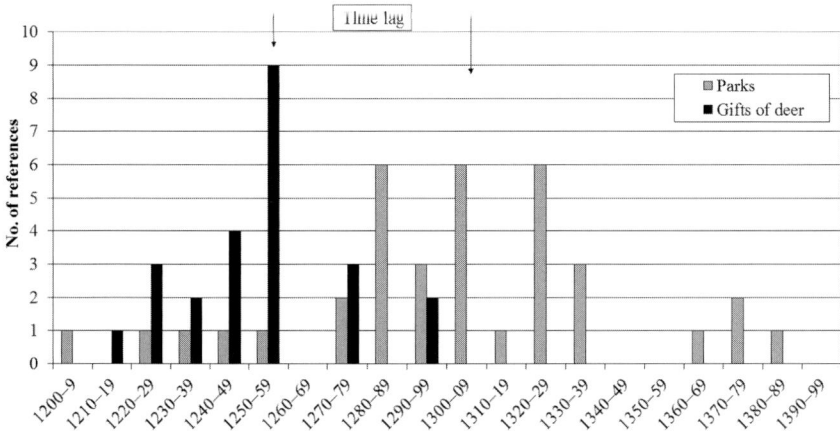

16 First documented references to particular parks collated with documented references to red and fallow deer being given as gifts.

references to deer being gifted to Walter de Burgh in 1250 and 1251.[128] Loughrea was the caput of the de Burghs at that time, so that logic would suggest that the gifts of deer should have been destined for there. This implies that construction took place around this time, about fifteen years after the conquest of Connacht by the de Burghs and the founding of the town. By this time it is likely that the castle and town defences were complete, and other less critical features of the manor could be developed. Notably, however, the park was not documented until an inquisition post-mortem in 1333.[129] Two Marshal parks were located at Dunamase, Co. Laois, and at Carrick, Co. Wexford. Again, there is reference to William, earl marshal the younger, receiving a royal gift of deer in 1225, but whereas the park at Carrick is referred to shortly afterwards, in 1231x4,[130] the first record of the park at Dunamase is not until 1282–3.[131] This raises the possibility that the park at Dunamase was an early thirteenth-century creation that was not recorded until later. Finally, Maynooth was the caput of the FitzGerald family from the late twelfth century, so this is the most likely location for the first and premier park in their holdings. Despite this, the park is not recorded until the very late date of 1328,[132] although Maurice FitzGerald received gifts of fallow deer in 1244, 1250–1 and 1251,[133] which suggests that the park should have been in existence at this time.

128 *CDI*, i, nos 3076, 3197.   129 *CIPM*, vii, Edw. III, no. 537; *IEMI*, no. 262.   130 *CERM*, 36. 131 *CDI*, ii, no. 2028; *IEMI*, no. 54; Murphy and O'Conor, 'Castles and deer parks in Anglo-Norman Ireland'.   132 *RBK*, no. 120.   133 *CDI*, i, nos 2701, 3104, 3144.

As a result, the peak of emparkment is likely to have been much earlier than the year in which the parks are first recorded, giving a main construction window of, say, 1220–60, with some parks developed before and after this date. This is one to two generations after the initial formation of the manors and building of the castles, particularly the stone castles. It is tempting to suggest that, having achieved economic prosperity, this was the time at which landowners could turn their attentions to less immediate concerns. They could commit money and resources to emparking areas of existing demesne land, which may have been earmarked for a park from the initial laying out of the lands of the manor.

Documentary references to previously unmentioned parks tail off in the fourteenth century, with few new parks being recorded from 1340 onwards. If the average of a sixty-year lag between construction and documentation is true, then it suggests that very few parks were built in the late thirteenth and fourteenth centuries in Ireland. The restricted date range for park construction in later-medieval Ireland, coupled with the documentary evidence for the types of manor on which parks were located, suggests that the vast majority of high-medieval parks will be found in manors that have a late twelfth- or early thirteenth-century stone castle, ringwork or motte at their core. Sites at which the first recorded stone castle is a tower house are unlikely to yield a high-medieval park, although a park may have been constructed beside these in one of the later waves of park-building.

CONCLUSION

The documentary evidence gives a picture of a range of parks varying from the large, such as Earlspark, Co. Galway, at 913 statute acres, to the very small, such as Baliduwil, Co. Kerry, at four medieval acres. They seem to have been constructed mainly in the early to mid-thirteenth century, when the Anglo-Norman colony was in its heyday, once the manors were established and profitable. There is evidence for deer being imported to Ireland to stock the parks of the great magnates, but in the case of many smaller parks, deer are not referred to. There was evidently a desire among the Anglo-Norman elite to empark lands, and this brings us on to a close examination of the function and form of high-medieval parks in Ireland.

CHAPTER THREE

Parks for hunting

Some of the fundamental questions to be asked about high-medieval parks in Ireland are, firstly, what was their function and, secondly, was this the same as in other countries such as England, or did it differ, and if so, how? The starting point must therefore be the evidence from overseas, as this can provide a basis for comparison. Parks in England are arguably the most relevant comparison since the Anglo-Norman landholders in Ireland had origins in Norman-controlled parts of Wales and England, and many of the major landholders among them also held considerable estates there.

English medieval parks are inextricably linked with deer, especially fallow deer, and there is evidence to show the importance of venison and hunting in English elite culture.[1] Many English parks were used to retain fallow deer but they also had a range of other functions. It is necessary therefore to examine whether Irish parks follow a similar pattern, with evidence indicating a range of uses for different parks and with some parks performing a number of functions either simultaneously or at different times. The archaeological, documentary and cartographic evidence can be explored in order to investigate the functions of parks relating to the keeping and hunting of deer and the more obviously economic functions, which will be examined in the next chapter.

THE DEER

Regardless of all other possible functions, parks in England have become inextricably linked to fallow deer. However, some scholars have stated that, due to their limited area, parks were of little use for actual hunting and instead functioned mainly as live larders for venison, as pasturage and as sources of timber.[2] Bond and Tiller saw the purpose of the later-medieval Woodstock Park as fundamentally a mundane source of venison, with the recreational use of the park for hunting being important but the landscape setting being incidental.[3] In support of this, they note the orders for two hundred does in 1250 and for a

---

1 For example, Mileson, *Parks in medieval England*, pp 29–35. **2** For example, Rackham, *The history of the countryside*, p. 125; Bond and Tiller, *Blenheim: landscape for a palace* (1997), p. 25; Franklin, 'Thornbury woodlands and deer parks, pt 1: the earl of Gloucester's deer parks' (1989), 164, 166.

further one hundred in 1298, which were to be killed, salted down and dispatched elsewhere for the use of the royal household. Despite these mundane activities, there are many records of monarchs, aristocrats and ecclesiastics being involved in parkland hunts and in 1415 the bishop of Winchester received a gift of a bow and arrows specifically for use in his parks.[4] This linkage of parks with deer, coupled with the herds of ornamental deer kept in the post-medieval and modern landscaped parks, means that, in current perception, 'parks' and 'deer parks' have become synonymous with each other.

There were two species of deer found in medieval Ireland: red and fallow. Red deer (*Cervus elaphus*) have been present in Ireland since at least the Neolithic, when they were probably introduced by people; however, there is some evidence that they may be a genuinely native species that survived in Ireland since the post-Glacial period. By contrast, fallow deer (*Dama dama*) were introduced to Ireland by the Anglo-Normans and do not appear in the archaeological record prior to this.[5] In red deer the male is a stag or a hart, the female is a hind and juveniles are calves. By contrast, in fallow deer the male is a buck, the female is a doe and juveniles are fawns.

For reasons outlined by Fletcher,[6] fallow deer were more suited to being maintained in a park environment and the evidence suggests that the majority of English parks were stocked with this species;[7] both in England and in Ireland royal gifts were a common source of deer to stock or restock a park.[8] Males were usually hunted between June and September when their body fat levels were at their highest, while females were usually hunted from late November to mid-February,[9] and based on figures from parks in Cornwall and at Havering in Essex, a park owner could expect a venison yield of approximately one eleventh of his stock per annum.[10] Sixteenth-century stocking densities at Woodstock may have been as high as 2,000–3,000 animals on *c.*1,500 acres,[11] but probably a maximum of one individual per acre was a more feasible and sustainable figure, depending on the terrain and ground cover.

The type of hunting and the species of deer hunted depended on the location in which the hunt took place. Various later-medieval hunting manuals survive and, although none is of Irish origin, they can nevertheless provide an insight into the potential methods employed by Anglo-Norman hunters.[12] In medieval

3 Bond and Tiller, *Blenheim*, p. 25.   4 Mileson, 'The importance of parks in fifteenth-century society' (2005), p. 27.   5 Woodman et al., 'The Irish Quaternary fauna project' (1997), 129–59; McCormick, 'Early evidence for wild animals in Ireland'; Carden et al., 'Phylogeographic, ancient DNA, fossil and morphometric analyses reveal ancient and modern introductions of a large mammal: the complex case of red deer (*Cervus elaphus*) in Ireland' (2012), 74–84.   6 Fletcher, *Gardens of earthly delight*, pp 97–103.   7 Rackham, *The history of the countryside*, p. 125; Watts, 'Wiltshire deer parks: an introductory survey', 92.   8 Birrell, 'Deer and deer farming in medieval England' (1992), 120–1.   9 Ibid., 122–3.   10 Birrell, 'Deer and deer farming in medieval England', 125.   11 Bond and Tiller, *Blenheim*, p. 25.   12 *Livre de chasse*,

Europe, red deer were considered to be the noblest quarry and were tightly bound into a complex symbolism, with royal, religious and erotic connotations.[13] As a result, *par force* hunting of red deer was considered to be the highest and most noble form of hunting. This involved selecting a single animal, then tracking it using a scenting dog called a lymer, before chasing it using greyhounds. This method needed a large area such as unenclosed countryside, and possibly the very largest parks, since the aim was for the men and dogs to be challenged by the hunt.[14] It was a highly ritualised method of hunting, involving the performance of specific actions by specific people at specific times.[15]

The 'drive' or 'ambush' and its variation, 'bow and stable' hunting, could be carried out in the wider countryside, but was also much more suitable than *par force* hunting for confined spaces such as parks and, furthermore, it was much less strenuous for the hunters. It could be employed for a range of species including both red and fallow deer. In this method, archers or spearmen positioned themselves in a suitable area towards which the deer were driven by human beaters, with or without hounds to assist them.[16] Parks of several hundred acres would have been eminently suitable for carrying out 'bow and stable' hunting, in which a relatively small group of beaters and dogs could drive a modest number of deer towards the archers waiting in their 'stables' or hides.[17] It is unlikely that any worthwhile drive could take place within the confines of smaller parks of say fifty or sixty acres; however, in Ireland there is little evidence for deer being maintained in these small parks, which seem to have functioned more as sources of wood and for cattle pasture. In England by contrast, where fallow deer were common in parks of all grades, smaller parks were probably used as live larders to maintain deer for slaughter and consumption, with coursing and stalking on foot also feasible.[18] Bow and stable hunting was considered by the French to be poor sport, but the *Master of game*, written in England in the early fifteenth century, devotes an entire chapter to this form of hunting, reflecting the relative importance of parks in England compared to France, where there were much larger areas of unenclosed land and *par force* continued to be the main form of hunting throughout the later-medieval period.[19]

passim; *Master of game*, passim; BSA, passim; *Livre du Roy Modus*, passim.   **13** Cummins, *The hound and the hawk: the art of medieval hunting*, pp 68–72, 78; Fletcher, *Gardens of earthly delight*, pp 123, 127; Stuhmiller, *The hunt in romance and the hunt as romance* (2005), pp 132, 202–3.   **14** Cummins, *The hound and the hawk: the art of medieval hunting*, pp 32–46; Almond, *Medieval hunting*, pp 73–5. **15** Cummins, *The hound and the hawk: the art of medieval hunting*, pp 32–46, 72; Beglane, 'Deer in medieval Ireland: preliminary evidence from Kilteasheen, Co. Roscommon' (2010), pp 150–2. **16** Cummins, *The hound and the hawk: the art of medieval hunting*, pp 47–67; Gilbert, *Hunting and hunting reserves in medieval Scotland*, pp 52–5; Beglane, 'Deer in medieval Ireland: preliminary evidence from Kilteasheen, Co. Roscommon', pp 150–2.   **17** Cummins, *The hound and the hawk: the art of medieval hunting*, pp 48–9, 53–5.   **18** Fletcher, *Gardens of earthly delight*, p. 105; Mileson, *Parks in medieval England*, p. 30.   **19** Mileson, *Parks in medieval England*, p. 32; *Master of game*, pp 188–200.

Although hunting was primarily an aristocratic activity, there was also a requirement for additional fresh venison for the table and for live deer to be given as gifts, and so the aristocracy often employed professional huntsmen to supply these. Venison was an important gift to be provided to the lord's peers and subordinates as well as to high-ranking members of the clergy.[20] This leads to the third and final method of hunting, which was to trap the deer. Deer could be driven into nets or fences, thereby allowing live deer to be captured and either transported elsewhere or killed at leisure.[21] In 1282–3 and 1283–4 there were two documented occasions on which nets were bought and sent to the royal castle at Roscommon, one of which cost £1 11s. 6d., but unfortunately the records do not show whether these were for hunting or for fishing.[22] Trapping deer was considered by both the English and the French to be ignoble and unsuitable for aristocratic hunting. For example, the late fourteenth-century French aristocrat Gaston Phoebus believed that driving deer into nets to kill them was 'in reality the work of a fat and aged man, who wants not to work'.[23] Instead this technique would mainly have been used by professional huntsmen who needed an efficient, functional method to obtain live deer and venison.[24] Interestingly, however, there is literary evidence to suggest that this method was considered honourable among Gaelic hunters and was used as part of a drive.[25]

Deer could also be caught on spikes, in leg traps or in pit fall traps, such as the one described at Balydonegan, Co. Carlow.[26] These are likely to have been lower-status attempts to obtain venison, and could also have been used by poachers. Leg traps had a long history and, for example, a deer caught in a trap is shown on the ninth-century high cross at Banagher, Co. Offaly, and an archaeological example found at Prumplestown Lower, Co. Kildare, has been dated to the early medieval period.[27] A pit trap excavated at Garryduff Bog, Co. Galway, was radiocarbon dated to AD1410–1650.[28] The trap contained the remains of a red deer that had fallen through a covering of leafy branches and brushwood into a pit below and had then died there.

---

20 Kelly, *Early Irish farming: a study based mainly on the law-texts of the 7th and 8th centuries AD* (2000), p. 279; Cummins, *The hound and the hawk: the art of medieval hunting*, pp 235, 260–5; Murphy and O'Conor, 'Castles and deer parks in Anglo-Norman Ireland'; Gilbert, *Hunting and hunting reserves in medieval Scotland*, p. 57; *CDI*, i, nos 3076, 3123. **21** Gilbert, *Hunting and hunting reserves in medieval Scotland*, p. 54; Kelly, *Early Irish farming: a study based mainly on the law-texts of the 7th and 8th centuries AD*, p. 277. **22** *IEP*, pp 81, 100. **23** *Livre de chasse*, p. 60. **24** Gilbert, *Hunting and hunting reserves in medieval Scotland*, p. 57; Cummins, *The hound and the hawk: the art of medieval hunting*, p. 235. **25** Kelly, *Early Irish farming: a study based mainly on the law texts of the 7th and 8th centuries AD*, p. 277. **26** *CJRI*, ii, p. 136. **27** Kelly, *Early Irish farming: a study based mainly on the law-texts of the 7th and 8th centuries AD*, p. 280; Long, 'Ancient hunting in County Kildare' (2008), 38. **28** NMS, 'Excavations database'.

DOCUMENTARY EVIDENCE

The documentary evidence for deer in high-medieval Ireland comes from two main sources: firstly, records of deer being given as gifts or being present on particular properties, and secondly deer skins or antlers listed in taxation documents such as murage and pavage grants. The latter are of little importance in this discussion and will not be dealt with further. Deer are recorded in a number of documents, particularly in the first half of the thirteenth century (fig. 17). Many of the examples specifically detail live deer that were to be caught and transported to Ireland, or refer to deer already in Ireland. In some cases they relate to gifts of venison in England or permission to hunt deer while in England; however, it is not always clear whether these were for transport back to Ireland or for use there, so all of these references have been included where they relate to individuals with extensive Irish landholdings.

References to deer as royal gifts reach a peak in the 1250s, but then almost entirely disappear. In many cases only 'deer' has been calendared by the editors, without differentiating the species or sex, but where the species is given, these are usually fallow deer, since 'bucks' or 'does' are referred to rather than 'stags' or 'hinds'. This is unsurprising, because 'wild' red deer were unlikely to be housed in parks or given as live gifts, whereas fallow deer were commonly kept in parks and so were available for gift-giving.[29] Occasionally, editors have calendared 'does and

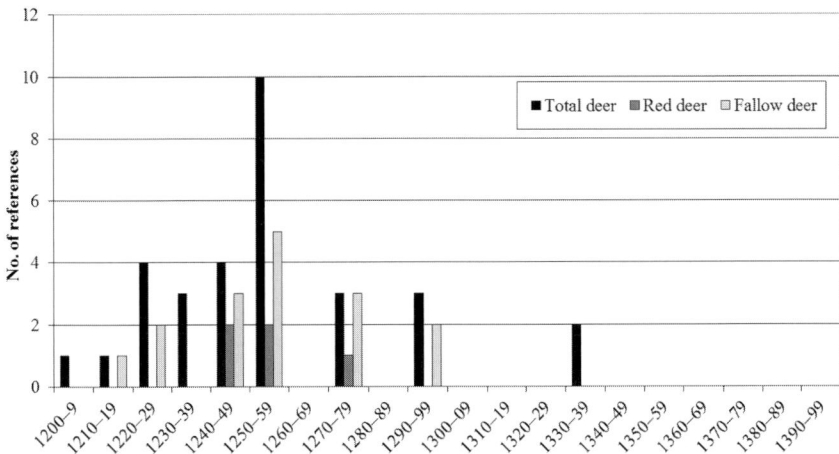

17 Summary of references to deer/venison being given as gifts to Irish elite or mentioned as being in particular locations.

29 Birrell, 'Deer and deer farming in medieval England', 126.

stags', which suggests confusion over the terminology when translating from the Latin documents, as it is unlikely that mixed species were being gifted. As a result, Figure 17 probably underestimates the proportion of fallow deer, and hence a 'total deer' column is also provided, which probably more closely reflects the records of fallow deer.[30] Once in Ireland, fallow deer would have been considered unusual and valuable, so that they would certainly have been kept within enclosed parks rather than being allowed to roam the open countryside and risk becoming prey to poachers and wolves.[31] Documentary evidence for the presence of fallow deer should therefore provide indirect but very definite evidence for parks.

The earliest mention of deer of any species in an Anglo-Norman legal document from Ireland dates to *c.*1185, when Alard son of William received grants of various lands along with 'hunting of stag, doe, pig, hare, wolf and rabbit in said lands' – in essence a grant of free chase.[32] This, however, is a general legal reference, rather than relating to actual deer. Stags and does are listed in the document, but this should not be considered to relate to male red deer and female fallow deer, which would not be a logical grouping. Undoubtedly, the editor used doe instead of hind to refer to female red deer and at this early date Alard was entitled to hunt both the male and female of this wild species (fig. 18).

As noted, in 1207 John, archbishop of Dublin, requested permission to construct a park and deer-leap at Kilmasantan.[33] The earliest record of fallow deer mentioned in connection with Ireland dates to 1213 and relates to his successor:

> Mandate to the keepers of the see of Coventry, to cause Henry archbishop of Dublin to have 30 fallow deer of the K.'s gift in the park of Brewood, and to lend him aid in taking them.[34]

Unfortunately, this reference does not categorically state that the deer were to be transported to Ireland, so that they could have been brought to lands in England, but it is likely that they were imported since the archbishop had been recently appointed and so would have been setting up his household at that time. Contrary to McCormick, and Chapman and Chapman, who state that the earliest evidence for fallow deer actually coming to Ireland was the delivery of eighty fallow deer from Chester to Glencree in 1244, there are earlier references.[35]

---

30 This study relied on calendared documents and although in some cases the originals have since been destroyed, it would be possible and worthwhile for others to be re-examined by a scholar with the necessary skills.   31 Murphy and O'Conor, 'Castles and deer parks in Anglo-Norman Ireland', 79; Sykes, *The Norman conquest: a zooarchaeological perspective* (2007), p. 68.   32 *COD*, i, no. 7.   33 *CDI*, i, no. 316. 34 *CDI*, i, no. 477.   35 McCormick, 'The effect of the Anglo-Norman settlement on Ireland's wild and domesticated fauna', p. 49; McCormick, 'Early evidence for wild animals in Ireland', p. 360; Chapman and

18 Red deer. The antlered stag protects his harem of hinds. © Can Stock Photo Inc./Veneratio.

In 1225, William, earl marshal received twenty does from the King's Forest of Cheddar specifically 'to convey them to Ireland'[36] and in 1242 the justiciar of Chester was ordered to send sixty fallow deer 'to stock the king's park in Ireland'.[37]

The number and type of individuals with extensive Irish interests receiving gifts of deer or venison from the king were very restricted and were limited to senior ecclesiastical figures and a number of influential landholders. Some of these gifts appear to have been for sport and consumption in England rather than breeding stock for transport to Ireland, and so are of little significance in an examination of Irish parks. However, gifts of venison and the opportunity to hunt on the king's lands were particularly highly regarded in the medieval period, and therefore these are also worth noting as signs of royal approval of individuals:[38]

Archbishops and bishops:
• Henry, archbishop of Dublin, 1213 (thirty fallow from Brewood), 1225 (two does for Christmas, Oxfordshire)[39]

Chapman, *Fallow deer* (1997), p. 57.   **36** *CDI*, i, no. 1323.   **37** *CDI*, i, no. 2580.   **38** Birrell, 'Deer and deer farming in medieval England', 112–26.   **39** *CDI*, i, nos 477, 1336.

- Luke, archbishop of Dublin, Apr. and Oct. 1234 (five deer from Bardfield and five from Wychwood), 1251 (seven does and four bucks from Glencree)[40]
- Hugh, bishop of Ossory, 1253 (five stags from Decies)[41]
- John, archbishop of Dublin, 1291 (twelve fallow from Windsor)[42]

Magnates:
- William, earl marshal, 1225 (twenty does from Cheddar to bring to Ireland)[43]
- Geoffrey de Marisco, 1226 (venison while waiting for wind at Bristol)[44]
- Maurice FitzGerald, justiciar of Ireland, 1240 (twelve deer and two stags from Havering), 1244 (four stags, six fallow from Wirral), 1250–1 (twelve deer from Selwood) and 1251 (twelve deer from Bradenstock)[45]
- Walter de Burgh, 1250 and 1251 (four does and four stags from forest of Slefco/Slescho)[46]
- John FitzGeoffrey, justiciar of Ireland, 1251 (three bucks from forest of Dean), 1254 (fifteen deer – well cured)[47]
- Roger de Mortuo Mari (Mortimer), 1275 (four does from forest of Pember), 1275 (twenty-four bucks and does from the park and forest of Duddely), 1279 (two harts and ten bucks from the forest of Dene)[48]
- Eustace le Poer, 1296 (six male and six female from Glencree)[49]

As noted, Glencree is the only known royal park in Ireland, and it lay within the forest of Glencree. As such it could have provided fallow deer and potentially red deer. In 1242 fallow deer were sent to an unnamed royal park in Ireland, presumably Glencree.[50] In 1244 a further consignment of sixty does and twenty bucks was sent to Glencree via Dalkey;[51] these animals evidently thrived since some were given as gifts in 1251.[52] By 1296 their descendants may have prospered sufficiently to be allowed to range over the forest since in this year Eustace le Poer was granted fallow deer from the 'Forest of Glencree', although it is also possible that they were actually sourced from the park within the forest.[53] The English kings rarely visited Ireland and hence would have had little use for a hunting park, so it is likely that the park at Glencree was a 'live larder' that provided deer for gifts and venison for feasting.

---

40 *CDI*, i, nos 2214, 3123; Murphy and O'Conor, 'Castles and deer parks in Anglo-Norman Ireland'.
41 *CDI*, ii, no. 241. 42 *CDI*, iii, no. 1014. 43 *CDI*, i, no. 1323. 44 *CDI*, i, no. 1421. 45 *CDI*, i, nos 2486, 2701, 3104, 3144. 46 Ibid., i, nos 3076, 3197. 47 Ibid., i, nos 3173, 3175; ii, no. 394.
48 *CCR*, Edw. I, ii, pp 149, 214, 536. 49 *CDI*, iv, no. 352; Murphy and O'Conor, 'Castles and deer parks in Anglo-Norman Ireland'. 50 *CDI*, i, no. 2580; Murphy and O'Conor, 'Castles and deer parks in Anglo-Norman Ireland'. 51 *CDI*, i, no. 2671; Murphy and O'Conor, 'Castles and deer parks in Anglo-Norman Ireland'. 52 *CDI*, i, no. 3123; Murphy and O'Conor, 'Castles and deer parks in Anglo-Norman Ireland'.

The archbishops of Dublin were evidently well favoured with royal deer. Based on the number of fallow deer and the fact that the archbishop was to have help in taking them, the reference from 1213 suggests that they were to be taken alive and transported elsewhere, rather than killed for sport or venison. Henry was appointed archbishop of Dublin in 1212 and justiciar of Ireland in 1213.[54] Since we have documentary evidence of a park being constructed for deer around 1207,[55] and another associated with bishop's palace of Colonia, St Sepulchre's, in 1226,[56] it is not unreasonable to suggest that the deer were to be transported to Ireland. This supposition is strengthened as the grant was made shortly after Henry's appointment, so it is likely that this was part of the setting up of the archbishop's household. The park at Kilmasantan was evidently designed to keep deer since it had a deer-leap, and the number and sex of the deer supplied at various times to the archbishops of Dublin show that at least one of their parks was stocked with deer. Apart from the numbers of deer involved, one way of determining whether they were for sport and consumption or for breeding stock is the sex of the animals involved. Stocking a park or forest with breeding animals requires that the majority of individuals should be female, so maximising the potential increase. By contrast, males were primarily used for meat since only one buck is needed to service a number of does.[57] Henry is likely to have stocked his parks using the thirty fallow deer brought from Brewood and it seems probable that the eleven deer from Glencree given to Luke supplemented their descendants. It is unlikely that the twelve deer mentioned in December 1291 were sent to Ireland, since by this time Archbishop John had resigned his post in Ireland and after March 1291 had travelled to England on royal business.[58]

One particular recipient of royal favour is Eustace le Poer, who received a grant of six male and six female deer from Glencree in 1296.[59] Based on these constituting a reasonable number of both males and females, these are also likely to have been breeding stock. Only four days previously he received a grant of free warren in his demesne lands of Ughtertur in Co. Waterford, Nerny (Nurney), Co. Carlow, and Obrun in Co. Dublin.[60] This was extended in 1301–2 to various demesne lands in Waterford, Tipperary, Kilkenny, Carlow, Kildare and Connacht,[61] and again in 1304 he received a grant of free chase for his demesne lands of Slefto, Ireland.[62] Le Fanu suggested that le Poer moved the fallow deer to Slefto,[63]

53 *CDI*, iv, no. 352; Murphy and O'Conor, 'Castles and deer parks in Anglo-Norman Ireland'. **54** Murphy, 'Henry of London (d. 1228)' (2004), p. 212. **55** *CDI*, i, no. 316; Murphy and O'Conor, 'Castles and deer parks in Anglo-Norman Ireland'. **56** *CAAR*, pp 170–2; Murphy and O'Conor, 'Castles and deer parks in Anglo-Norman Ireland'. **57** Chapman and Chapman, *Fallow deer*, pp 133, 159. **58** Lee, *Dictionary of national biography*, l (1897), p. 274. **59** *CDI*, iv, no. 352; Murphy and O'Conor, 'Castles and deer parks in Anglo-Norman Ireland'. **60** *CDI*, iv, no. 347. **61** *CDI*, v, no. 6. **62** *CDI*, v, no. 331. **63** Le Fanu, 'The royal forest of Glencree', 270.

although, given the timing in relation to his grant of free warren, it may be more likely that the deer were destined for an undocumented park in Ughtertur, Nurney or Obrun. As with the other recipients of royal favour, le Poer was an important subject and although he was not a member of the titled classes, he had been a member of the parliament of 1295.[64] He also held his lands directly of the king, and his ancestor Robert le Poer had accompanied Henry II on his expedition to Ireland, receiving extensive grants in Waterford as his reward.[65]

In addition to gifts of deer, they are also documented as being present in particular locations. As well as the royal deer documented in the park and forest of Glencree, they are recorded in the forests of Decies, Slescho/Slefco and Dublin.[66] The archbishopric of Dublin is recorded as having parks containing deer in 1206–7, 1350 and 1373–4.[67] Richard de Burgh, the 'Red Earl', had deer in his park at Balydonegan in 1305, while in 1333 his grandson William, the 'Brown Earl', had parks stocked with deer at Balydonegan and Loughrea.[68] There are also deer or, to be precise, animals that were either 'hunted' or 'driven', in the park at Maynooth in 1328, and by 1540–1 and 1585 deer are specifically recorded there.[69]

ZOOARCHAEOLOGICAL EVIDENCE

Turning to the zooarchaeological evidence, fallow deer remains have been found at a number of medieval castle sites in Ireland and in many cases these can be correlated with the presence of a nearby documented park (fig. 19).[70] Deer bones, including those of fallow deer, have also been found at urban sites, probably having been deposited due to poaching activities but also due to the use of bone and antler as an important raw material in craft working. The correlation of castles, parks and fallow deer is to be expected, since initially this species would have been rare and exotic and so would have been maintained in an enclosed area to prevent poaching and the effects of predators such as wolves.

The present whereabouts of the various zooarchaeological assemblages with reported fallow deer was ascertained, and, where possible, the relevant bones were re-examined by the author to confirm the identification of this species. Male

---

64 Ibid.   **65** Leslie, *Dictionary of national biography*, 66 (1885), p. 15.   **66** *CDI*, i, nos 925, 926, 927, 930, 932, 933, 1531, 2671, 3076, 3197, 3213; ii, nos 241; iv, no. 352; *CSMA*, nos 1, 118a.   **67** *CDI*, i, no. 316; *CPR*, Edw. III, viii, 590; xv, 309.   **68** *CJRI*, ii, p. 136; *CIPM*, vii, Edw. III, nos 372, 375; *IEMI*, nos 251, 262; Murphy and O'Conor, 'Castles and deer parks in Anglo-Norman Ireland'; Knox, 'Occupation of Connaught by the Anglo-Normans after AD1237', 132–8; Gibbons and Clarke, 'Deer parks', 4–5.   **69** *RBK*, no. 120, trans. M. Murphy; *CSL*, pp 132–3; *CICB*, pp 318–19.   **70** Beglane, 'Deer and identity in medieval Ireland', passim.

19 Fallow deer herd. The palmated antlers and spotted coat are characteristic of this species.
© Roger Sargent Wildlife Photography.

fallow deer are similar in size and form to female red deer, while female fallow deer can be the size of large sheep, and deer and sheep bones are somewhat similar in form.[71] These factors, coupled with the relative rarity of the species in Ireland, and a general lack of examples in comparative reference collections held by specialists, particularly in the past, mean that on re-examination a number of examples were reclassified as being from other species. Unfortunately, however, many of the assemblages have been disposed of since they were analysed, or access was not possible and so they could not be reviewed. In these cases, any fallow deer recorded were deemed to have been correctly identified. The current list of castle sites that have yielded fallow deer remains is: Carrickmines Castle, Co. Dublin; Dunamase Castle, Co. Laois; Ferns Castle, Co. Wexford; Ferrycarrig Castle, Co. Wexford; Greencastle, Co. Down; Maynooth Castle, Co. Kildare and Trim Castle, Co. Meath. On re-examination of bones from Carlow Castle, these were re-classified to other species, so that this site has to be removed from the list

71 Lister, 'The morphological distinction between bones and teeth of fallow deer (*Dama dama*) and red deer (*Cervus elaphus*)' (1996), 119–43; Schmid, *Atlas of animal bones* (1972), passim.

of fallow deer sites despite the documented presence of a park at nearby Balydonegan.[72] Of the castles yielding fallow deer remains, there are documented parks at Dunamase, Ferrycarrig, Maynooth and Trim. At Ferns there is no record of a park belonging to the castle; however, the bishop of Ferns is known to have had a park on his nearby holdings.[73] In addition, excavations at Tintern Abbey yielded this species, the first example of fallow deer found at an ecclesiastical site in Ireland.[74] Denham reported that fallow deer remains had been found in a medieval context at Carrickfin, Co. Donegal,[75] but a review of the original report produced by McCormick showed that red, not fallow, deer were present on this rural site.[76]

While fallow deer have been found at seven castle sites in Ireland, red and fallow deer as a whole constitute approximately 1 per cent only of the mammal bones from Irish castle excavations, and, of these, fallow deer make up just under a quarter (23 per cent).[77] By contrast, in England for the twelfth to fourteenth centuries approximately 8 per cent of the mammal bones found on elite sites were deer bones, with fallow deer making up 59 per cent.[78] Furthermore, looking at edible wild species overall, these are over five times more common at English elite sites (13 per cent) than at Irish castles (2.3 per cent).

Venison therefore provided only a small proportion of the meat consumed even at the high-status Irish sites. For example, at Greencastle, Co. Down, only 6 per cent of the meat came from venison in Phase 3, the main occupation phase of the castle.[79] This suggests that the significance of venison was in its symbolic value as an elite foodstuff rather than as an important component of the diet. Nevertheless, this seemingly small percentage was important, with the proportion of wild mammal bones from excavations of castle sites being of the order of five times higher than from excavations of rural non-elite sites and more than twice the levels found at ecclesiastical and urban sites.[80]

Fallow deer had the advantage of being smaller and more manageable than red deer and so were the species of choice for the English park. After initial importation to England, their numbers increased there and they became the dominant species.[81] Interestingly, they are present in Norman Britain at an earlier date than in mainland western Europe, suggesting that they were brought directly

---

72 O'Conor, 'The origins of Carlow Castle' (1997), 13–16.   **73** *CDI*, ii, no. 297.   **74** McCormick, 'Appendix IV: the faunal remains' (2010), p. 228.   **75** Denham, 'Animal exploitation in medieval Ireland' (2008).   **76** McCormick, 'The animal bones from Carrickfin, Co. Donegal' (n.d.), passim.   **77** Beglane, 'The social significance of game in the diet of later-medieval Ireland' (2015), 1–30.   **78** Sykes, *The Norman conquest: a zooarchaeological perspective*, app. 1; Beglane, 'The social significance of game in the diet of later-medieval Ireland'.   **79** Beglane, 'Deer and identity in medieval Ireland', p. 79.   **80** Beglane, 'The social significance of game in the diet of later-medieval Ireland'.   **81** Rackham, *The history of the countryside*, p. 133; Sykes, *The Norman conquest: a zooarchaeological perspective*, pp 66–8.

from their native distribution in the eastern Mediterranean rather than via Normandy or the Norman colony of Sicily.[82] The situation in Ireland is somewhat more complex. Based on the relatively small number of bones and the restricted number of sites at which they have been found, there is a perception that fallow deer are rare in the Irish archaeological record. Nevertheless, we have seen that they constitute almost one quarter of all the deer bones identified from later-medieval castles, so that while they are unusual overall, they are relatively common among deer bones from castles. In the samples in which this species was present, the total of seventy-two fallow deer bones was complemented by 126 red deer bones, with the remainder not identified to species.[83] Dunamase Castle was the largest assemblage reviewed, and in this case 10,966 animal bones were identified over the course of four years of excavation. This had the largest sample of deer bones, at eighty-nine, but only two of these were fallow deer. Excluding this site, the new total of seventy fallow deer bones was complemented by only thirty-nine red deer bones, giving a ratio of 1.8 fallow deer bones to every red deer bone, while Sykes found a ratio of *c*.1.9 for the same two species at elite sites in England.[84] The evidence therefore suggests that, with the exception of Dunamase, if fallow deer were available at a particular castle, then they were usually dominant over red deer remains. Furthermore, this suggests that although fallow deer were much less prevalent than in England, where they were available, similar patterns of consumption generally occurred and that they were utilised preferentially to red deer.

INTEGRATING THE EVIDENCE

Overall, the evidence suggests that both parks and fallow deer were relatively uncommon in Ireland compared to England. The forty-six documented parks in Ireland are a very small number compared to the figure of between 1,900 and 3,200 in England.[85] The zooarchaeological evidence shows that fallow deer, and hence parks containing deer, were present only in a restricted range of locations in Ireland, whereas in England they were very common. Similarly, there was a density of 1.1 forests per 1,000km² in England, which contrasts strongly with only 0.16 forests per 1,000km² in Ireland.[86] So, if a park stocked with deer was an

---

82 Sykes and Carden, 'Were fallow deer spotted (OE *pohha/ *pocca) in Anglo-Saxon England? Reviewing the evidence for *Dama dama dama* in early medieval Europe' (2011), 139–62. **83** Beglane, 'The social significance of game in the diet of later-medieval Ireland', tab. 2. **84** Sykes, *The Norman conquest: a zooarchaeological perspective*, p. 67. **85** Cantor and Hatherly, 'The medieval parks of England', 71–85; Rackham, *The history of the countryside*, p. 123. **86** Beglane, 'Parks and deer-hunting: evidence from medieval Ireland' (2012), pp 113–14.

essential manorial feature in England, and if the English manorial system was transposed to Ireland, then why are there so few records of high-medieval parks in Ireland? Furthermore, why do there seem to be so few fallow deer remains in Ireland? And why is there currently no evidence for the Gaelic elite constructing parks for deer in the high-medieval period?

It could be argued that the lack of evidence for parks in Ireland is due to poor survival of later-medieval documents, a problem that has frequently been noted by researchers examining a variety of aspects of this period.[87] Possible reasons include the Four Courts' fire in 1922, which destroyed many original documents, the existence of many liberties in Ireland, the records of which have rarely survived, and the relative lack of forests in Ireland so that licences to empark were rarely needed. However, the suggestion that the lack of documented fallow deer is due to poor record survival is not borne out by the later-medieval zooarchaeo-logical evidence, which shows a restricted range of sites yielding fallow deer remains.[88] Since a park would have been necessary to keep fallow deer, their restricted distribution suggests that there was only a small number of true 'deer parks' in Ireland, although this does not limit the potential number of parks with other functions.

The zooarchaeological results also suggest much less emphasis than in England on elite hunting of truly wild species such as red deer and hare.[89] Despite this, however, the results do demonstrate that wild animal bones in general, and deer bones in particular, are much more common on castle sites in Ireland than on other site types. This confirms that hunting was an activity of the elite in Ireland and that they considered it important to hunt and to consume venison, albeit less often than their cousins in England. In high-medieval Ireland, deer were present in the wider countryside and within parks. As a result of the restrictions on who could hunt, certainly in the Anglo-Norman areas, the great majority of legitimate deer hunting was carried out by the elite or by their employees, with very little legitimate hunting seemingly undertaken by the peasants. The conclusion from this is that while parks in Ireland were important as a venue for keeping deer, they must also have had other functions.

ANGLO-NORMAN CONCEPTS OF HUNTING AND PARKS

A number of elements of an elite package were necessary for a magnate belonging to the highest echelon in European society.[90] These included a range of manors,

---

87 For example, Barry, *The archaeology of medieval Ireland*, p. 2.   **88** Beglane, 'The social significance of game in the diet of later-medieval Ireland'.   **89** Ibid.   **90** Liddiard, *Landscapes of lordship* (2000), p. 51;

each having a suitable fortified castle and sufficient agricultural land. The manors provided resources for the household and surpluses for sale. Mills, fishponds and rabbit warrens, as well as markets and towns, were key aspects of the manorial system. Hunting was a vital element of aristocratic society and, particularly in England, this was symbolised by the ownership of a park stocked with deer. It is likely that the original aim of the Anglo-Norman colonists was to transport English ideas of the castle, manor and landscape directly into Ireland. As a number of researchers have noted, until very recently little work had been carried out on later-medieval settlement patterns in Ireland.[91] As a result, where there was a lack of data, researchers have assumed that this theoretical plan actually took place and that what held in England was also true for Ireland, a problem also highlighted by Oram in relation to setlement in medieval Scotland.[92] While the aim was probably to set up the manorial system in a similar format to that seen in England and Europe, with villages clustered around a central castle and parish church, this did not always occur,[93] and whereas there were up to three thousand parks in England, in Ireland there are records of only forty-six, and zooarchaeological evidence suggests that this is likely to be a true reflection of the situation. The reasons for the differences are complex but can be considered in two categories: the landscape and the political situation, although these are inevitably intertwined.

The Irish landscape was physically and legally very different to that of England, which was relatively crowded compared with many other European countries, including Ireland. As a result of population growth, there was a need for additional agricultural land in twelfth-century England; hence, by the thirteenth century land was at a premium in parts of England, so that there was a move to assart forest and clear ground for agriculture.[94] This led to a pressure on woodland and on uncultivated land, so that by 1500 only 10 per cent of England was woodland, compared to approximately one third of the land area of Germany.[95] Because of the high proportion of royal forest and the pressure on agricultural land, English landowners had an incentive to create parks to provide themselves with access to timber and to venison.[96] Hence, while medieval parks

Bailey, *The English manor, c.1200–1500* (2002), pp 2–5; O'Conor, *The archaeology of medieval rural settlement in Ireland*, pp 26–38; Liddiard, *Castles in context: power symbolism and landscape* (2005), pp 100–19; O'Conor, 'Medieval rural settlement in Munster', passim. **91** Barry, *The archaeology of medieval Ireland*, pp 1–2; Barry, 'Rural settlement in medieval Ireland' (2000), p. 112; O'Conor, *The archaeology of medieval rural settlement in Ireland*, pp 9, 14. **92** Oram, 'Castles, concepts and contexts: castle studies in Scotland in retrospect and prospect', 355. **93** Barry, 'Rural settlement in medieval Ireland', pp 113–14. **94** Campbell, *English seigniorial agriculture, 1250–1450* (2000), p. 388; Gardiner, 'The quantification of assarted land in mid- and late twelfth-century England' (2009), 165–86. **95** Wickham, *Land and power: studies in Italian and European social history, 400–1200* (1994), pp 169, 174. **96** Mileson, *Parks in medieval*

are known from many European countries, they reached their apogée in England.[97] As such, it is important to realise that in a European context England can be considered to be the exception rather than the rule in the creation of large numbers of parks.

In Anglo-Norman Ireland, these pressures were much less. The very limited areas of royal forest coupled with the presence of the liberties meant that whereas in England even the great magnates were restricted in where they could hunt, in Ireland this tier of society had open access to hunting in their liberties and lands.[98] In the late twelfth century, although arable agriculture was a significant feature of the landscape, there was a greater emphasis on pastoral uses of the land than in England,[99] there was no shortage of timber, there was plenty of undivided land on which hunting could take place without affecting arable agriculture and there were generally no royal restrictions on hunting red deer. Parks were expensive to build and to maintain, and so there was little incentive for a lord to create them in large numbers and, where they were created, they were not always stocked with deer. Only at Dunamase, Ferns, Ferrycarrig, Maynooth and Trim is there zooarchaeological evidence of fallow deer remains at a castle that can be associated with a documented park nearby. The consumption of venison was symbolic of lordship and aristocracy, regardless of species. When compared to England, the low proportions of deer bones in the Irish faunal assemblages demonstrate that venison was not an essential part of the diet in terms of its calorific content; instead, this meat was consumed on particular occasions, in order to make a statement about the status of the host. Hunting red deer was more strenuous and was more highly regarded from both a physical and a symbolic perspective than hunting fallow deer in parks, but where fallow deer were kept their availability meant that venison could be served more often and on demand. Thus, red deer continued to be the species available at the majority of elite sites, but where there were fallow deer, for example at Maynooth and at Trim, they usually became the dominant species. As a result, with fallow deer less common than in England, and red deer hunting more accessible due to a less controlled landscape, there was less need to construct parks to retain deer, and hence fewer parks to be found.

The political and military situation in Ireland was also very different to that in England. By the thirteenth century, England had a generally peaceful countryside, with its wars usually fought overseas. English castles and their surroundings were therefore designed to be aesthetically pleasing while retaining defensive features.[100] Castles in Ireland have long been interpreted as primarily military

England, pp 58–9.   **97** Ibid., p. 32.   **98** Hartland, 'The liberties of Ireland in the reign of Edward I' (2008), passim.   **99** *Topographia*, 34–5.   **100** For example, Liddiard, *Castles in context: power symbolism*

structures,[101] although this view is changing. McNeill identified that domestic comfort and the expression of power and domination were more important than military might in the design of Irish castles.[102] In particular, he commented on Trim, where the design of the keep made it poorly defensible, yet highly comfortable and impressive to visitors.[103] Later he noted the importance of the ability to view the landscape from the roof of a castle in psychologically controlling and dominating the landscape.[104] O'Keeffe also saw Irish castles as primarily designed for display, and expanded outwards from this to consider the landscape in which castles sat, and the view from the exterior of the castles, seeing these as features that displayed power, domination and status.[105] Nevertheless, O'Conor, while recognising the importance of aesthetics and display, disagreed and believed that when properly analysed these places can be shown to have serious defences.[106] In his opinion, this fits the documentary evidence, which shows that many of these castles were under constant pressure from the Irish. An example of this is Roscommon Castle. McNeill believed that this castle was built for display and comfort, arguing that it lacks serious defences.[107] However, Murphy and O'Conor found the site to be militarily capable, with concentric defence and carefully designed arrowloops.[108] These were necessary since the castle came under attack no fewer than ten times between 1270 and 1360, when it eventually succumbed to Gaelic forces.[109]

While Anglo-Norman Ireland was modelled on England, the importance of warfare in thirteenth- and fourteenth-century Ireland had a significant effect on the activities and material culture of the Anglo-Normans. Hunting was an essential part of the training for war of a young nobleman in the south of England, and subsequently he would have maintained his skills and fitness through this activity.[110] There was less need for this in Ireland, where the elite would undoubtedly be involved in real skirmishes and battles on a relatively regular basis. For example, in the frontier region of the lordship of Meath, in what is now Longford, O'Conor and Parker showed that the colony was under constant pressure from the Irish of Connacht and Ulster as well as from the local Irish septs.[111] Despite McNeill's and O'Keeffe's views,[112] it would seem that this

and landscape, pp 6–11; O'Conor, 'Castle studies in Ireland: the way forward', 329–39. **101** For example, Leask, 'Irish castles, 1180–1310', passim; Leask, *Irish castles and castellated houses* (1977), pp 5, 13–24; Sweetman, *Medieval castles of Ireland*, pp 33, 41, 105. **102** McNeill, *Castles in Ireland*, pp 230, 235. **103** Ibid., p. 52. **104** McNeill, 'The view from the top', 122–7. **105** O'Keeffe, 'Concepts of "castle" and the construction of identity in medieval and post-medieval Ireland', 69–88; O'Keeffe, 'Were there designed landscapes in medieval Ireland?', 52–68. **106** O'Conor, 'Castle studies in Ireland: the way forward', 329–39. **107** McNeill, *Castles in Ireland*, pp 165–6. **108** Murphy and O'Conor, *Roscommon Castle: a visitor's guide* (2008), pp 13–19, 21–4, 38. **109** O'Conor, 'Castle studies in Ireland: the way forward', 329–39. **110** *Master of game*, pp 12–13. **111** O'Conor and Parker, 'Anglo-Norman settlement in Co. Longford' (2010), passim. **112** McNeill, *Castles in Ireland*, pp 165–6; O'Keeffe, 'Concepts of

was reflective of most frontier areas during the thirteenth and fourteenth centuries, especially from *c.*1250 onwards.[113] This is probably the reason for the overall lower levels of wild species found at Irish castle excavations compared to their English equivalents. While hunting was an important pastime for both Anglo-Normans in Ireland and their English cousins, it took on a greater significance in the settled lands of southern and central England than in the more unstable lands of Ireland. However, when hunting did take place in Ireland, red deer were an accessible quarry. Compared to emparked fallow deer, these gave a more energetic cross-country hunt, so providing considerably better physical and skills training for warfare. Again, this would have reduced the incentive to create and maintain parks stocked with fallow deer.

A third area in which Ireland and England can be seen to differ is in the timing of emparkment, discussed in Chapter 2. The documentary evidence for parks and the introduction of fallow deer stocks to Ireland, coupled with radiocarbon dating evidence, tentatively suggest a peak of park creation for the period *c.*1220–60, with the parks being documented somewhat later, as a result of them being recorded mainly in extents and inquisitions post-mortem. This is significantly earlier than in England, where the peak is 1320–69.[114] In both countries, the first wave of emparkment would have been at the highest level of society, and over time this gradually moved down the social ladder. By the time park-building in England was becoming widespread as a result of being accessible to the gentry and minor aristocracy, the Anglo-Norman colony in Ireland was in retreat, and many ostensibly Anglo-Norman families were taking on Gaelic customs.[115] As a result, in fourteenth-century Ireland, instead of becoming more common, park building and the keeping of fallow deer became less accessible and few new parks were created, and by *c.*1600 Fynes Moryson knew of only two parks in Ireland that contained deer.[116]

McNeill identified that in the early years of the Anglo-Norman colony there was a heavy financial input in developing the castles and manors, with the quality of the buildings being notably fine.[117] The money for this is likely to have been invested in a speculative way, using resources from the English lands held by the lords. After 1220, however, he sees a decline in the quality of construction and design, which he linked to disappointing financial returns from the Irish estates.

"castle" and the construction of identity in medieval and post-medieval Ireland', 69–88; O'Keeffe, 'Were there designed landscapes in medieval Ireland?', 52–68.   **113** Lydon, 'A land at war' (1987), pp 240–1; Lydon, 'The impact of the Bruce invasion, 1315–27', pp 286–7; Watt, 'Gaelic polity and cultural identity' (1987), p. 344; Watt, 'The Anglo-Irish colony under strain, 1327–99', pp 366–7; Smyth, *Celtic Leinster* (1982), p. 105.   **114** Mileson, *Parks in medieval England*, fig. 19.   **115** Watt, 'The Anglo-Irish colony under strain, 1327–99', p. 352; Nicholls, *Gaelic and gaelicized Ireland in the Middle Ages* (2003), pp 14–21.   **116** *Itinerary*, iv, pp 193–4.   **117** McNeill, *Castles in Ireland*, pp 230–1.

If this was the case, then it provides a further reason for the relative lack of parks in Ireland. While the very highest echelons of Anglo-Norman society created parks at their major manors in the period *c.*1220–60, they may have held back on enclosing parks at more peripheral castles, where there was little to be gained from the large expenditure involved. Similarly, for the second tier of Anglo-Norman settlers, the emparkment of demesne lands may not have been a financially viable option, so that they did not create parks within even their principal manors.

Finally, the issue of absenteeism was important, particularly for the most powerful aristocrats. Some Anglo-Norman families were resident in Ireland and notable examples of these include the de Burghs in Connacht and Ulster, who held Earlspark at Loughrea, and the FitzGeralds in Leinster, who held Maynooth. These families had their primary lands and influence in Ireland and were committed to close management of their manors. This can be seen in the impressive nature of the park at Earlspark and the longevity of the park of Maynooth, which survived until it was directly replaced by the landscaped park surrounding Carton House. Other parks were in manors that became less central to the interests of their owners. After the death of the last earl marshal, the partition of Leinster led to the inheritance of much of the province by a number of female heirs, and these lands were then passed to the families of their husbands.[118] The result was that in many cases the inherited manors were of relatively minor significance to their owners, whose focus was on their English lands and English politics. The parks at Dunamase, Co. Laois, and Carrick, Co. Wexford, come into this category. In the later thirteenth and early fourteenth centuries Dunamase was held by the de Mortimer family, who also held substantial lands in Wales and in England,[119] and furthermore, the castle and lands were then lost to the O'Mores *c.*1330.[120] The lands around Carrick, Co. Wexford, passed through a number of hands: the de Munchensys, the de Valences, the Hastings and the Talbots. Finally, in 1537 Wexford was one of the areas taken into royal hands due to continued absenteeism by the owners.[121] It has already been stressed that in addition to being used to retain deer, parks were important for timber and for pasture. In the case of an absentee lord, the timber and pasture would have continued to be integral to the maintenance and profitability of the manors. By contrast, for a manor rarely visited by the lord, there would have been little or no

---

118 Otway-Ruthven, *A history of medieval Ireland* (1968), p. 100; Hore, *History of the town and county of Wexford*, v, pp 41–2. **119** *CIPM*, ii, Edw. I, no. 446; Murphy and O'Conor, 'Castles and deer parks in Anglo-Norman Ireland'. **120** Carey, 'The end of the Gaelic political order: the O'More lordship of Laois, 1536–1603' (1999), pp 216–17; Fitzgerald, 'Historical notes on the O'Mores and their territory of Leix, to the end of the sixteenth century' (1909), 25; Hodkinson, 'A summary of recent work at the Rock of Dunamase, Co. Laois' (2003), p. 43. **121** Hadden, 'The origin and development of Wexford town, pt 4'

incentive to continue to stock a park with deer or to develop new hunting parks. These were therefore the most likely to be disparked by default. This did not need to be a formal process, but there would have been little incentive to maintain security features such as high palings or lodges. Instead, once deer stocks had been exhausted, they would have gradually reverted to 'ordinary' demesne pasture and woodland, while still being called 'parks'. And hence, by the start of the seventeenth century Moryson could note the lack of deer parks and of fallow deer in Ireland, and comment specifically on the rarity of venison on the menu.[122]

GAELIC CONCEPTS OF HUNTING AND PARKS

While the attitudes to hunting of the Anglo-Normans in Ireland were different to those of their cousins in England, they were also distinct from those of the Gaelic aristocracy. The most significant of these differences was the maintenance of enclosed fallow deer and deer parks by the Anglo-Normans, a fashion that was not adopted by the Gaelic elite. There is absolutely no evidence at present that Gaelic lords constructed parks for deer in the high-medieval period. They did not construct any of the documented high-medieval parks and, similarly, no fallow deer remains have been found at any Gaelic site. For example, there was no evidence for fallow deer at the historically attested O'Neill settlement on Island McHugh, Co. Down,[123] and fallow deer reported by Denham from Carrickfin, Co. Donegal,[124] were found, on review of the original report, to be red deer.[125] Instead, all later-medieval fallow deer remains in Ireland have been found at Anglo-Norman sites or in urban assemblages. This difference of approach is likely to relate to the different understanding of landscape, land ownership, lordship and male identity between the two cultural groups.

There is a very great lack of published and unpublished excavation and faunal reports for Gaelic Ireland, and this does place a caveat on the results. There are a number of reasons for this lack; firstly, much of the development work during the Celtic Tiger years was carried out in the east and south of the country, in areas formerly under Anglo-Norman control. For example, the NRA detail sixty-nine excavations carried out under their remit in Meath, but only eleven in Donegal.[126] Secondly, soil conditions in the Gaelic west tend to be more acidic, resulting in poorer survival of bone from these areas and hence leading to smaller, less well-preserved assemblages.[127] It could therefore be argued that the lack of

(1970–1), 10. **122** *Itinerary*, iv, pp 193–4. **123** Denham, 'Animal exploitation in medieval Ireland'. **124** Ibid. **125** McCormick, 'The animal bones from Carrickfin, Co. Donegal', passim. **126** NRA, 'NRA archaeological database' (2011). **127** Mitchell and Ryan, *Reading the Irish landscape* (1998), p. 308.

fallow deer remains in Gaelic areas is due to a dearth of faunal reports or poor bone survival. However, while future excavation may yield fallow deer remains from these areas, other strands of evidence suggest that this is unlikely. From a methodological standpoint, zooarchaeological data discussed here has come from thirteen separate zooarchaeologists who between them have probably analysed *c.*90 per cent of the assemblages recovered in the last two decades in Ireland.[128] In addition, requests to the Irish Zooarchaeological Working Group (IZWG) and the ZOOARCH Internet forum did not yield any further incidences of fallow deer. This suggests that the vast majority of fallow deer bones that have been zooarchaeologically analysed were included in the data collated.

The literary evidence suggests that in Gaelic Ireland cross-country hunting was the method of choice. For example, both the *Duanaire Finn*, dating to the late twelfth century, and the *Acallam na Senórach*, dated to the early thirteenth century, predominantly describe large-scale drives across open country, or sometimes a single animal being sought in a manner similar to *par force* hunting.[129]

Prior to the Anglo-Norman invasion, Ireland was relatively lightly populated compared to England, and the Anglo-Normans perceived this to be a problem throughout the later-medieval period, with tenants being at a premium.[130] It has already been argued that in Anglo-Norman areas of Ireland lack of pressure on land-usage meant that there was less need for parks to retain deer compared to England. In the western parts of Ireland, where Gaelic settlement predominated, this could be argued to be even more significant. The land was generally of poorer quality than in the Anglo-Norman east and, as a result, a mainly pastoral economy was more suited to these areas.[131] This lower proportion of arable agriculture means that relatively large areas of unenclosed countryside would have been available for cross-country hunting similar to that described in the literary texts.

Cross-country hunting was a useful preparation for warfare for a number of reasons. Firstly, it developed the physical fitness and horse-riding skills necessary to move through the land. Secondly, by hunting regularly the lord and his followers would develop an intimate knowledge of the local landscape, becoming familiar with the route-ways, valleys, rivers, woods and other natural features that could be utilised for attack or retreat. Thirdly, following on from the previous point, any enemy incursions or changes would soon be noticed if places were visited regularly. There were differences in the way that the Anglo-Norman and Gaelic forces used the landscape in times of war, with a detailed knowledge of the

128 Beglane, 'Deer and identity in medieval Ireland', passim; Beglane, 'The social significance of game in the diet of later-medieval Ireland'. **129** *Duanaire Finn; Acallam na Senórach.* **130** Simms, 'Warfare in the medieval Gaelic lordships' (1975), 98–108; Glasscock, 'Land and people, *c.*1300' (1987), p. 226. **131** O'Conor, *The archaeology of medieval rural settlement in Ireland*, p. 98; Glasscock, 'Land and people,

landscape being particularly important for the tactics employed by the Gaelic warriors.[132] When under attack they used natural features to force pitched battles at chosen strategic locations, such as passes or river fords and then if these were not successful they retreated into the woods, bogs and mountains with their cattle and began a campaign of guerrilla warfare.[133] This suited a pastoral economy in which much of the wealth was held in mobile form, being herds of cattle rather than masonry structures. The classic example of this use of the landscape is the famous image of the lightly armoured Art McMurrough emerging from a hidden valley to meet the heavily armoured Thomas, earl of Gloucester (fig. 20).[134] In the event of an attack, an expensive castle, or indeed a park, would be a potential liability rather than an asset. It would need to be defended and, if it was taken, then this would result in financial, territorial and psychological loss.

An essential element in the manorial system in England and elsewhere, including in Anglo-Norman Ireland, was the timber or masonry castle, exemplified by Hen Domen and by Trim respectively.[135] By contrast, during the high-medieval period, the Gaelic elite rarely built what contemporaries and modern scholars consider to be castles in this sense, although from the late fourteenth century onwards there was a change in their outlook and they did adopt the use of tower houses.[136] Instead, there is increasing evidence for the continued use of crannogs, ringforts and cashels and for the introduction of moated sites as a form of lordly residence.[137] The Rock of Lough Cé, Co. Roscommon, was the stronghold of the McDermotts from the twelfth century through to the seventeenth century. This family were second only to the O'Conors in the Gaelic hierarchy of Connacht and so would have had the resources to construct castles if they chose to do so,[138] and they were probably responsible for the foundation of the nearby Boyle Abbey, which is noted for its fine stone architecture.[139] The Rock of Lough Cé contains what has been described as a 'super-cashel', with 4m-high, mortared stone walls in a defensive location on a semi-artificial island in the lake.[140] However, unlike contemporary

---

*c.*1300', pp 225–6.　**132** O'Conor, *The archaeology of medieval rural settlement in Ireland*, pp 98–100. **133** Ibid.; Nicholls, 'Gaelic society and economy in the high Middle Ages' (1987), p. 404; O'Conor, 'Gaelic lordly settlement in 13th- and 14th-century Ireland' (2005), p. 218.　**134** *Histoire du roy.* **135** Liddiard, *Landscapes of lordship*, p. 51; Bailey, *The English manor, c.1200–1500*, pp 2–5; O'Conor, *The archaeology of medieval rural settlement in Ireland*, pp 26–38; Liddiard, *Castles in context: power symbolism and landscape*, pp 100–19; O'Conor, 'Medieval rural settlement in Munster'.　**136** O'Conor, *The archaeology of medieval rural settlement in Ireland*, pp 75–7; Nicholls, 'Gaelic society and economy in the high Middle Ages', pp 404–6; McNeill, *Castles in Ireland*, p. 164; O'Conor, 'Gaelic lordly settlement in 13th- and 14th-century Ireland', pp 213–15.　**137** FitzPatrick, 'Native enclosed settlement and the problem of the Irish "ring-fort"' (2009), 271–307; Brady and O'Conor, 'The later-medieval use of crannogs in Ireland' (2005), 127–36.　**138** O'Conor et al., 'The Rock of Lough Cé, Co. Roscomman' (2010), pp 17–20, 34.　**139** Moss, 'Romanesque sculpture in north Roscommon' (2010), passim. **140** O'Conor et al., 'The Rock of Lough Cé, Co. Roscomman', pp 21–4, 37.

20 Art MacMorrough meets Thomas, earl of Gloucester (*c.*1399). © The British Library
Board. Harley MS 1319, fo. 9r.

Anglo-Norman, English and European castles, it lacked features such as 'flanking
towers, battlements, a gatehouse or arrow-loops'.[141] Similarly, *c.*1300 at Cloonfree,
Co. Roscommon, Aodh O'Conor built a moated site rather than a masonry castle
as his principal royal residence.[142] In Anglo-Norman areas this site type would be
more usually associated with middle-ranking settlers than with the head of a
powerful dynasty.

A number of reasons have been put forward for why few stone castles were
built by the Gaelic elite during the high-medieval period. The first of these is the
method of inheritance. Gaelic lordships and kingships did not use primogeniture;
instead, a new leader was elected from within the extended family group or
derbfine, the descendents of a common great-grandfather.[143] While a son could
inherit, it was also possible for distant cousins, nephews or brothers of the
previous ruler to be selected. As a result, there was little incentive for a king or
lord to invest money and resources in building a stone castle that would not
necessarily be inherited by his son. By contrast, commissioning a fine abbey or
church would imbue its patron with an air of godliness and virtue, and on death,
would ensure a speedy entry into heaven.

141 Ibid., p. 33.   **142** Finan and O'Conor, 'The moated site at Cloonfree, Co. Roscommon' (2002),
72–87.   **143** O'Conor, 'Gaelic lordly settlement in 13th- and 14th-century Ireland', passim; Nicholls,
'Gaelic society and economy in the high Middle Ages', pp 423–4; Nicholls, *Gaelic and gaelicized Ireland in*

A second reason for lack of stone castles was the periodic redistribution of land within the kin group. The process as it operated in the high-medieval period is poorly understood, but evidence from the sixteenth century does exist.[144] Essentially, much of the land was owned by the kin group rather than the individual and was redistributed between the males on a regular basis. In the sixteenth century this could be as often as each year, or it could be on the death of one of the co-heirs. As a result, families would regularly move from one portion of land to another, and again this would have been a disincentive to costly building programmes.

It has already been shown that Anglo-Norman parks date to one or even two generations after the construction of the stone castles, so that even for the incoming Anglo-Normans the park was of secondary importance. By extension, if Gaelic lords did not construct elaborate castles of stone or even timber as their primary residences, it can be seen to be highly unlikely that they would construct other elements of the Anglo-Norman elite landscape such as a park to enclose fallow deer. By the late fourteenth and fifteenth centuries, when Gaelic lords were building tower houses and developing more nucleated settlement, the evidence suggests that few new parks were being created even in the Anglo-Norman heartlands.

Bourdieu's concepts of economic, social and cultural capital can be used to examine the way in which Gaelic lords showed their status.[145] In Gaelic Ireland, status was not demonstrated through the ownership of castles and parks but instead was tightly bound to genealogy and family lineage. Election to leadership was open only to members of the *derbfine*, hence demonstrating a link to one's ancestors was extremely important. The inauguration rituals went beyond this by using prehistoric monuments and landscapes to link kingship to the distant past and to mythological heroes.[146] Patronage of the Church also increased the social capital of the elite patron, recording his name for posterity and demonstrating his piety.[147] Feasting was important in obtaining social capital by making alliances, rewarding good service and setting up cycles of obligation.[148] This also allowed the lord to demonstrate his patronage of the arts by employing musicians and poets who, in turn, would create poems and songs in honour of the patron.[149]

---

the *Middle Ages*, pp 9, 29. **144** O'Conor, 'Gaelic lordly settlement in 13th- and 14th-century Ireland', p. 217; Nicholls, 'Gaelic society and economy in the high Middle Ages', pp 432–3; Nicholls, *Gaelic and gaelicized Ireland in the Middle Ages*, pp 69–73. **145** Bourdieu, *Distinction: a social critique of the judgement of taste* (1984), passim; Bourdieu, 'The forms of capital' (2008), passim. **146** FitzPatrick, *Royal inauguration in Gaelic Ireland* (2004), pp 52, 99; Watt, 'Gaelic polity and cultural identity', p. 319; Duffy et al. (eds), *Gaelic Ireland, c.1250–c.1650* (2001), p. 41. **147** For example, Nugent, 'The dynamics of parish formation in high-medieval and late-medieval Clare' (2006), pp 188–9. **148** O'Sullivan, *Hospitality in medieval Ireland, 900–1500* (2004), p. 85. **149** Ibid., pp 237–9; Simms, 'Native sources for

21 Wall painting of a stag being chased by a hound at Clare Abbey, Co. Mayo. © Christoph Oldenbourg.

Gift-giving to one's peers and followers performed a similar function to hospitality, again creating cycles of obligation and binding clients to the lord.[150] Economic capital was not usually held in the form of elaborate castles, instead cattle and horses were perceived as wealth: cattle could be used as currency to pay rents and fines, while horses were often used as high-status gifts.[151] Cattle-raiding was therefore a vital part of the way in which Gaelic lords gained and maintained power and as a result, a successful lord or king would maintain large herds.[152] Hence, military prowess and the leadership skills to be able to call on large numbers of followers were the forms of cultural capital necessary to be successful in raiding and warfare.[153]

For the Gaelic lords, hunting was an opportunity to display their social capital and to reinforce the bonds of gift-giving, hospitality and clientship, while simultaneously training followers for raiding and warfare. While the lack of faunal reports for this section of later-medieval society is a problem, other strands of evidence can be called into play. Iconographic evidence is an important source, and interestingly the hunting scenes that survive from medieval Ireland are all either from the early medieval period or are Gaelic representations from a period slightly later than the scope of this book. Nevertheless, they are valuable as so few art works from medieval Ireland are extant.

There are a number of images of individual deer being hunted. Most notable are the wall and ceiling paintings in a Gaelic context in the abbey church at Clare

Gaelic settlement: the house poems' (2001), passim.　**150** O'Sullivan, *Hospitality in medieval Ireland, 900–1500*, p. 242.　**151** Watt, 'Gaelic polity and cultural identity', pp 329–31.　**152** Ibid.; O'Conor, 'Gaelic lordly settlement in 13th- and 14th-century Ireland', p. 216.　**153** O'Conor, 'Gaelic lordly settlement in

22 Now-destroyed painted hunting scene at Urlan More Castle, Co. Clare. © Karena Morton.

23 Wall painting at Holycross Abbey, Co. Tipperary, depicting a stag, a hound and three
huntsmen. From H.S. Crawford, 'Mural paintings in Holy Cross Abbey', *JRSAI* (1915),
pl. xiv. Courtesy of the Royal Society of Antiquaries of Ireland.

Island, Co. Mayo.[154] These probably date to the first half of the fifteenth century
and, as well as hunting scenes, they include musicians, herdsmen, mythical
creatures and St Michael.[155] One focal image at this site is a large painting of a
stag being chased by a hound, which is positioned on the north wall above a
decorative tomb niche (fig. 21).[156] There are also hunting scenes on the ceilings:
notable are an image of a stag being attacked by three hounds, and that of a
halting or standing stag being confronted by a hunter with his hound on a

13th- and 14th-century Ireland', p. 219. **154** Morton and Oldenbourg, 'Catalogue of the wall paintings'
(2005), pp 61–95. **155** Ibid., pp 118–19, 61–95. **156** Ibid., pp 62–3.

24 Hunting scene from Ardamullivan Castle, Co. Galway, showing a stag chased by a
mounted huntsman and his hound. © Rory Sherlock.

sliplead.[157] The ceiling also includes scenes of hawking, and of using hounds to
chase hares, as well as other images in which dogs appear.

At Urlan More Castle, Co. Clare, a fifteenth-century Gaelic tower house that
collapsed in 1999, there was a painted hunting scene (fig. 22).[158] This showed a
stag being brought down by two hounds, one of which was wearing a collar. At
Holycross Abbey, Co. Tipperary, which was founded by Donagh O'Brien
although was later in the patronage of the earls of Ormond, a fifteenth-century
wall painting depicts a stag lying behind a tree, while a huntsman with a dog
approaches and blows his horn. Two further figures, both carrying bows and
arrows, approach from behind the huntsman (fig. 23).[159] Finally, a decorated
fireplace lintel from the sixteenth-century O'Shaughnessy tower house at
Ardamullivan, Co. Galway, shows a scene in which a rider and his hound chase a
stag. This hunter has thrown a spear and has a sword in his scabbard (fig. 24).[160]
The stag has many religious and moral symbolisms and it is likely that it is in this
context, as well as from an aesthetic perspective, that these images should be seen.

Scenes in which a stag or a group of animals that include deer are chased by
hunters and/or hounds are relatively common on early medieval Irish high crosses
and, where groups of animals are shown, these suggest 'drives'.[161] The *Acallam na
Senórach*, which also comes from a Gaelic context, probably dates to the first
decade of the thirteenth century and is an important source of evidence regarding

157 Ibid., pp 82, 90, 107. **158** Ibid., pp 106–7; Gleeson, 'Drawing of a hunting scene, Urlan Castle, Co.
Clare' (1936), 193. **159** Crawford, 'Mural paintings in Holy Cross Abbey' (1915), 149–50, pl. xiv;
Morton, 'Iconography and dating of the wall paintings', pp 106–7. **160** Morton, 'Iconography and
dating of the wall paintings', p. 100. **161** Soderberg, 'Wild cattle: red deer in the religious texts,

hunting in the early and later-medieval periods and regarding perceptions of hunting at the time of its composition.[162] This includes a description of a hunt by Bran, son of a king of Munster, in which his method of hunting is unfavourably compared with that formerly practised by the *fianna*:

> 'Well now, Bran', said Caílte, 'what is your method of hunting?' 'We surround a hill or a mound or a high, level wood with our hounds, our servants and warriors and spend the whole day chasing the game. At times we kill some game, but at other times it gets away'. On hearing this, Caílte, in the presence of Patrick, wept tearfully and sorrowfully until both his shirt and his chest were wet.[163]

It is likely that this hunt was a 'drive'. The Old Irish *timchell*, meaning 'going around, surrounding' passed into Lowland Scots as *tinchell* meaning a beater in a deer drive.[164] In this case Caílte is likely to have wept because by his standards a hunt in which all the game escaped would be considered a very inferior attempt at hunting. By comparison, in the large-scale hunts of his own time hundreds of animals were successfully slaughtered.[165] Furthermore, as hunting was a symbol of masculinity, a man who was not a successful hunter could not be considered a noble warrior.

Gilbert identified that the drive was the most important of the methods employed in medieval Scotland and he considers that its use in early medieval Ireland is supported by literary evidence such as the *Duanaire Finn*.[166] This text contains material dating from the late twelfth century onwards, but describes events occurring in the time of Fionn Mac Cumhaill.[167] The tales therefore relate to Gaelic Ireland, and many are on the theme of hunting. These often note the slaughter of large numbers of animals, suggesting drives rather than *par force* hunts, although on occasion individual stags or boars were also selected as the quarry. The deer drives were conducted using spears and dogs that were coupled in pairs.[168] One particular tale, *The Chase of Sliabh Truim*, clearly describes a drive, in which individuals, with tethered pairs of hounds,

> were spread over every glen: stout was our strain against the hills; two by two on each slope … There was many a cry of deer and boar on the mountain, of those that fell by the chase: from the spoils of herds and

iconography and archaeology of early medieval Ireland' (2004), 174.   **162** *Acallam na Senórach*, xli.   **163** *Acallam na Senórach*, 28–9.   **164** Kelly, *Early Irish farming: a study based mainly on the law-texts of the 7th and 8th centuries AD*, p. 277.   **165** *Duanaire Finn*, i, pp 130–1.   **166** Gilbert, *Hunting and hunting reserves in medieval Scotland*, p. 52.   **167** *Acallam na Senórach*, xli–xlii.   **168** *Duanaire Finn*, i, pp xlv–xlvi, 113, 124, 141–4, 180–2, 187–9.

hounds blood abounded on the slope … No deer went east or west, nor boar of all that were alive on the mountain, not one of them all but was killed by the good pack fierce in attack.[169]

Recently, FitzPatrick has examined place-name and archaeological evidence for a continuation of this use of the open countryside into the later-medieval period and has connected the word *formaoil* or *formáel* with a round-topped hill used as a 'mound of chase' or *dumha selga* within former Gaelic hunting grounds, and has noted that these are often in isolated or upland areas.[170] Drives in open country would have been significant events, requiring complex organisation to provide sufficient people and dogs to move the deer. This implies that these were events of particularly high status, where power was conspicuously demonstrated by the ability to control large numbers of individuals and the death of potentially hundreds of animals in one hunting day.[171]

In summary, a Gaelic lord held his position by demonstrating the everlasting and timeless nature of his lordship by means of his lineage and his links to the past. This was backed up by military prowess, patronage of the Church and the arts, and the ability to maintain large numbers of clients, all of which required a level of economic success to underpin them. The lack of large-scale castles and elite landscape features in the Anglo-Norman fashion, including parks containing fallow deer, should not, therefore, be considered as a lack of status but as a different way of demonstrating that status. The ability to organise large-scale hunts traversing open countryside rather than possession of a park holding fallow deer would have been an essential feature in demonstrating and maintaining that elite status.

PARKS FOR HUNTING

The initially small numbers of fallow deer would have necessitated them being kept in parks as valuable exotica, and the documentary evidence does show that many of those individuals given royal gifts of deer had parks. Down stressed the difference between later-medieval pasture parks and hunting parks, considering them to be two separate phenomena.[172] However, detailed study of the documentary and archaeological evidence for parks and fallow deer suggests a continuum. At one end of the scale were aristocratic parks stocked with deer, to which only the most powerful could aspire. Simultaneously, these landowners

---

169 *Duanaire Finn*, i, pp 187–90.   **170** FitzPatrick, '*Formaoil na Fiann*: hunting preserves and assembly places in Gaelic Ireland' (2013), 95–118.   **171** *Duanaire Finn*, i, pp 130–1; Cummins, *The hound and the hawk: the art of medieval hunting*, p. 49.   **172** Down, 'Colonial society and economy' (1987), p. 477.

also had parks on their manors that did not hold any deer, as did their less-powerful relatives, neighbours and tenants, and due to the circumstances prevailing in Ireland fallow deer ownership never filtered down to the second tier of society. Thus, in the top stratum parks were undoubtedly more common, but they did not always contain deer. Deer in the park were an aspiration for those with royal favour, since these status symbols were often received as gifts from the king. This is reflected in the terminology used, as later-medieval documents, both in Ireland and in England, always refer to 'parks' rather than 'deer parks'. As Chapter 2 showed, the cartographic evidence supports this, suggesting that the term 'deer park' in place-names is of post-medieval origin.

Surprisingly, there are only five parks where deer are specifically referred to as being present: Balydonegan, Co. Carlow; Glencree, Co. Wicklow; Kilmasantan, Co. Dublin; Loughrea, Co. Galway and Maynooth, Co. Kildare. Of these, two were held by the de Burghs, earls of Ulster, one by the FitzGeralds, earls of Kildare, one by the archbishop of Dublin and one by the king. There is also zooarchaeological evidence to support the presence of fallow deer in the vicinity of Carrickmines Castle, Co. Dublin, Dunamase Castle, Co. Laois, Ferns Castle, Co. Wexford, Ferrycarrig Castle, Co. Wexford, Greencastle, Co. Down, Maynooth Castle, Co. Kildare, Trim Castle, Co. Meath, and Tintern Abbey, Co. Wexford, providing indirect evidence of parks close to these sites, and in most of these cases there is also documentary evidence of a park in the vicinity. Overall, though, these are restricted lists, clearly demonstrating that the holders of parks with deer were a highly exclusive group.

Timber, pasturage and pannage had a definite economic value but, by contrast, grazing deer instead of cattle was uneconomic. The value of venison could not, however, be measured in money, or in the calories contained in the meat, but instead venison – fallow deer venison in particular – was perceived as valuable currency in the social capital that it provided.[173] Because venison could not usually be bought, it could generally only be served after a successful hunt, and in areas of royal forest, free warren and free chase and in liberties there were restrictions on who could legally hunt and where. By contrast, having deer in a park would have been highly desirable for an Anglo-Norman landholder. The major advantage was that the meat was available 'on demand' and this easy access without having to undertake a hunt is likely to have been one of the important considerations when parks were originally created at the *capita* of major lords, such as the FitzGeralds at Maynooth and the de Burghs at Loughrea. A supply of fallow deer may have been less critical at smaller manors within the holdings of

---

173 Birrell, 'Deer and deer farming in medieval England', 114–15.

the great magnates, since these would have been managed by officials, and would rarely have been occupied by the lord.

Venison was, by its nature, a high-status meat,[174] and hunting for red deer was a noble pursuit with important symbolic connotations. In Ireland, however, red deer were relatively common in the countryside, so that serving red deer venison would have marked a host as being from the elite class, but it would not have marked him as being exceptional. By contrast, since fallow deer remains in Ireland are linked with the first tier of society, this suggests that the ability to serve 'exotic' fallow deer venison would have demonstrated an even higher status, adding further to the prestige of the host. For the king and his administration, venison was essential for providing entertainment at Dublin and other royal castles. It was also important to have a source of deer to give as gifts to high-ranking officials and to favourites, such as Eustace le Poer and the archbishop of Dublin.[175] The royal park at Glencree seems to have operated in this way; it was relatively far from a major castle, but being situated in the royal forest it was secure and could be effectively managed as a live larder.

Fallow deer did not become ubiquitous as they did in England, as by 1603 Moryson notes that both parks and deer were rare in Ireland.[176] By contrast, he had commented on the situation in England where 'every gentleman of five hundreth or a thousand pounds rent by the yeere hath a parke for them inclosed with pales of wood for two or three miles compasse'.[177] The reasons for this difference are complex. In both cases, hunting, the ownership of parks and the keeping of fallow deer were perceived as aristocratic activities that should be aspired to. In Ireland, the accessibility of the more symbolically important red deer and the higher intensity of the red deer hunt, as well as an initial relative lack of parks resulted in the continued overall dominance of red deer over fallow deer. This was generally true, except at those *capita* where fallow deer were well established in parks held by the very highest tier of the elite. By the fourteenth century the Anglo-Norman colony was in retreat, the manors had not fulfilled their early economic promise and many were held by absentee lords who were more concerned with their English lands. In addition, many resident Anglo-Norman families had become increasingly gaelicised, taking on Irish customs and habits. As a consequence, over the high-medieval period, even major families may have developed only one or two hunting parks, with potentially other parks to retain domestic animals. Similarly, the second tier of Anglo-Norman landholders had not invested in a status symbol that they could not afford to maintain and which would serve little practical purpose given the accessibility of wild venison.

---

174 Ibid., 112–26. **175** *CDI*, i, no. 3123; iv, no. 352. **176** *Itinerary*, iv, pp 193–4. **177** Ibid., pp 168–9.

In both countries hunting was used as physical training and as a leisure activity, but whereas in England considerable time could be devoted to this, in Ireland the nature of frontier society was such that this was an occasional pastime rather than a regular event.

Red deer hunting was more accessible to the Anglo-Norman lords in Ireland than in England, and this form of hunting continued to be important to them as they became embedded into the Irish landscape, providing training in military manoeuvres and horse-riding, in order to counter the threat of Gaelic attacks. For Gaelic lords, who were skilled in cattle-raiding and who also needed to be able to move fast over considerable distances to undertake the style of warfare at which they excelled, red deer hunting was also an appropriate form of training and provided other social and cultural benefits. Coupled with the lack of what their contemporaries and modern scholars would consider to be castles, there was no impetus for them to create parks stocked with fallow deer. Red deer were symbolic of wildness, nobility and honour and to hunt these over large swathes of countryside was a reflection of elite identity and power for both cultural groups. Fallow deer and deer parks had little symbolic or practical value for the Gaelic lords. Instead, they would have been linked to Anglo-Norman symbols of lordship such as manorial settlement, arable agriculture and the development of masonry castles.

CONCLUSION

While it is clear that fallow deer, hunting, parks and the manor were inextricably linked in the minds of the English elite, the situation in Ireland was more complex. Ongoing warfare and skirmishing meant that hunting and venison were less significant in Anglo-Norman Ireland than in English society. In this, the Anglo-Normans were different to their English cousins, and yet they did not take on Gaelic customs either. Instead, they forged a new paradigm in which parks with fallow deer were a status symbol only of the premier tier of magnates, and not a realistic aspiration for a middle-ranking nobleman. Many Irish parks had other functions, which will be examined in the next chapter.

CHAPTER FOUR

Parks as economic units

If keeping deer was not the primary aim of the majority of high-medieval parks in Ireland, then what other practical functions could they have performed? Cantor has highlighted the economic importance of parks, arguing that these could be a profitable source of income,[1] and there is substantive evidence to show that English parks were commonly used as a source of timber, underwood and coppiced wood, firewood and charcoal, pannage (allowing pigs to root for acorns and beech nuts), agistment (pasturage), turbary (peat cutting for fuel) and mining. They could have fruit trees, rabbit warrens, fish ponds, dovecotes, beehives, stud farms and even areas of tillage within their bounds.[2] This chapter examines the evidence for these uses of parks in Ireland.

PASTURE AND ENCLOSURE OF ANIMALS

One difficulty with examining the use of a park for pasture or for corralling domestic animals is that it is archaeologically invisible. Whereas fallow deer bones at a castle are likely to be indicative of a nearby park containing deer, cattle bones from the same site could have come from any number of enclosed or unenclosed locations in the vicinity. We must therefore rely entirely on the documentary evidence in order to examine this function of parks.

A number of sources refer to monetary values of parks for pasture, pannage or specifically for 'herbage', which was the sale of the pasture rights. This clearly demonstrates that these parks had an economic value over and above any deer that may have been kept within them. In 1282 at Dunamase, Co. Laois, there is reference to a mountain pasture and emparked pasture which together were worth the substantial sum of 33s. 4d. per annum.[3] In 1284 the park at Kilkea (Kylka), Co. Kildare, was yielding 40s. in herbage and pasture as well as 3s. in pannage,[4] while in 1333 profits from pasturage and underwood at William de

---

1 Cantor, 'Forests, chases, parks and warrens', pp 77–8. **2** Franklin, 'Thornbury woodlands and deer parks, pt 1: the earl of Gloucester's deer parks', 159; Cantor, 'Forests, chases, parks and warrens', pp 77–8; Cantor and Hatherly, 'The medieval parks of England', 80–1; Watts, 'Wiltshire deer parks: an introductory survey', 90; Watts, 'Some Wiltshire deer parks' (1998), 94; Creighton, *Castles and landscapes* (2002), pp 190–1. **3** *CDI*, ii, no. 2028; *IEMI*, no. 54; Murphy and O'Conor, 'Castles and deer parks in Anglo-Norman Ireland'. **4** *CDI*, ii, no. 2340.

Burgh's park at Balydonegan, Co. Carlow, amounted to a much more modest 8*s.* per year.[5] There were three parks at Inchiquin, Co. Cork, one of which is referred to in 1348 as having sixty acres, with the pasture there being worth 5*s.* per year 'not in underwood or in any other profits', so giving a value of 1*d.* per acre.[6]

It is notable that the rents achieved are highly variable and a number of factors are likely to have been at play. Firstly, the size of the park was an obvious factor in determining its value. The quality of the land could also vary, with good grazing being more valuable than rough mountain pasture. Demand was also a factor and land close to Dublin was then, as now, the most valuable and so higher rents could be charged. Furthermore, as enclosed demesne land, lords probably preferred to keep parks for their own use, and as a result, they sometimes only rented out small parcels within the park. For example, at Callan, Co. Kilkenny, 'herbage' in the park was worth 2*s.* for the period March to September 1350, but this related to only part of the park, as one and a half acres were 'in the lady's hands' – held by Joan, countess of Gloucester and Hertford, who also retained control over an unspecified portion of the 'New Park'.[7] Parks were also not immune to the effects of economic and military disruption. In 1326 a thirty-acre archiepiscopal park at Shankill, Co. Dublin, had no value in herbage or the sale of underwood 'on account of war', while a four-acre park similarly had 'no value for want of beasts'.[8] Also in archiepiscopal hands at Finglas, Co. Dublin, was a twenty-four-acre park worth nothing, and a seventy-one-acre park with grazing worth only 2*s.*[9] Similarly, two years earlier in 1324, the sixty-acre park with oak trees associated with Wexford Castle had a value of nothing, 'save for the pasturing of animals'.[10] This suggests that no monetary gain was derived from the park and that it was herds associated with the castle that were being kept there. Circumstances could change, however, as by 1375/6 the pasture there was worth 13*s.* 4*d.*, giving a value of approximately 4*d.* per acre.[11]

In some cases cattle or other animals are specifically referred to in the parks. Some of these were animals owned by the lord, while others belonged to tenants. The bishop of Ferns had a park containing 'wild cattle'.[12] Their coat colour is not stated, but many of these wild parkland cattle were white and a number of herds have existed until relatively recently, with some, such as the famous Chillingham herd from Northumberland, surviving as feral herds to the present day (fig. 25).[13] White cattle with red ears are a common theme within Irish and Welsh heroic tales and they also feature in early law tracts; there are also records of them being

5 *IEMI*, no. 251.   6 *CIPM*, ix, Edw. III, no. 119; *IEMI*, no. 291.   7 *Handbook*, pp 302–3.   8 *CAAR*, p. 195.   9 Ibid., p. 173; Murphy and O'Conor, 'Castles and deer parks in Anglo-Norman Ireland'. 10 *IEMI*, no. 228; Murphy and O'Conor, 'Castles and deer parks in Anglo-Norman Ireland'.   11 *IEMI*, no. 339.   12 *CDI*, ii, no. 297.   13 Visscher et al., 'A viable herd of genetically uniform cattle' (2001), 303.

25 Chillingham bull: white with rusty-red ears. © Stephen Hall.

given as a gift to the queen of England in 1211; an episode that emphasises the value placed on this genetically controlled feature. In mythology they have been associated with the Otherworld, being seen as fairy cattle in the *Táin Bó Fráich* and associated with the Morrigan in the *Táin Bó Cúailnge*.[14] Wild, or technically feral, park cattle were therefore valuable, high-status animals, with a colour that could only be maintained by genetic isolation, and being the owner of a herd of these prestigious animals would have reflected well on the bishop of Ferns, showing him to be a man of substance. By complete contrast, on a much more mundane level, the small park at Baliduwil, Co. Kerry, was specifically noted to be 'good for oxen', suggesting lush grassland to feed working animals.[15]

Many of the references to domestic animals in parks are as a result of legal cases and can provide an insight into high-medieval society. In 1282 a major disagreement had flared up between William FitzWarin and Richard de Burgh, earl of Ulster. As a result, de Burgh's men destroyed much of FitzWarin's property in Ulster and, acting on de Burgh's orders, John de Say, sheriff of Thuyscard, which was the northern part of the modern Co. Antrim, 'broke into said William's park of Pouloc, and set free the beasts of William's tenants there, which

14 Henning, '*Bos Primigenius* in Britain; or, Why do fairy cows have red ears?' (2002), 71. 15 *CDI*, iii, no. 459.

William had caused to be caught for his return'.[16] Interestingly, this suggests that William's tenants paid their rent in livestock rather than in money. Furthermore, since the cattle had been 'caught', it suggests that outside the park the cattle ranged freely in their grazing areas rather than being closely herded and brought back nightly to an enclosure. It is also notable that de Say deliberately targeted the park, which would have had economic consequences for FitzWarin but, as Chapter 6 will show in more detail, would also have been considered as an insult and an attack on his status.

In 1305, Richard, son of Robert, went to the court in Dunshaughlin, Co. Meath, to seek an 'assise of novel disseisin'. This was an attempt to recover two hundred acres and a messuage, or house, at Platin, Co. Meath, which he alleged had been taken from him illegally by William de la Ryuere. The property originally belonged to Richard, but as a result of an earlier court case it had been granted by the king's court to William de la Cornere, who had then enfeoffed de la Ryuere with the land; in other words, he had granted it to him in return for service. However, de la Ryuere had not waited for the king's sergeant to obtain the lands for him, but instead had taken matters into his own hands and 'seized the tenements … took herbage and other issues and imparked the beasts', and as a result of this pre-emptive and illegal action the lands were returned to Richard.[17] Again, this provides an insight. Firstly, either there was a park at the lands under dispute or de la Ryuere had access to a park relatively nearby in which he could enclose the stock. De la Ryuere was evidently on his way up in the world, and managed to obtain a number of properties of a similar size in the same general area. He died in May 1317, and at that time held land of Theobald de Verdun in Moymorty (now Mosney) and other places in Meath and Uriel.[18] He also held a messuage and half a carucate of land at Gaffney, near Duleek, Co. Meath, and *c.*1300 he had paid twenty marks of silver for another half carucate of land 'with the appurtenances' in nearby Duleek.[19] All his properties were therefore of a modest size, although in total they formed a substantial landholding. Since in all cases it is likely that some of the land of each property was used for open-field agriculture and for the peasant workforce, it suggests that the park in which the beasts were impounded was relatively small, maybe twenty to sixty acres.

Another example of a legal case was in Cork in 1311 where a number of members of the Tyntagel family were tried and acquitted of acting in collusion with Clement Cornwaleys and Nicholas and Richard Bryttoun. The group were accused of the theft of eleven cows from a park belonging to a Thomas Cod.[20]

---

16 *CDI*, ii, no. 1918; McNeill, *Anglo-Norman Ulster: the history and archaeology of an Irish barony, 1177–1400* (1980), pp 31, 99. **17** *CJRI*, ii, p. 18. **18** *RDKPRI*, xxxxii, 18. **19** James Mills and M.J. McEnery (eds), *Calendar of the Gormanston register* (Dublin, 1916), p. 50. **20** *CJRI*, iii, p. 200.

This is a clear example of a modest park, held by someone with a modest herd of cattle, which Thomas had unsuccessfully attempted to maintain in a secure location. A park could also be used as a secure location by a lord; for example, as a pound in which to keep animals confiscated from tenants. In 1298 at Leys, then part of Kildare, John le Clerk of the Litel Rath and Thomas Gowel were charged but acquitted of breaking a park owned by William de Vescy in order to remove six affers or draught horses that had been impounded by the sergeant, William de Graunt, in lieu of debts.[21] Draught horses were used to pull carts, plough fields and draw harrows, so they were valuable animals, without which agricultural production would soon grind to a halt.[22] By impounding them, the sergeant would maximise his chances of extracting the money owed by the tenant.

In 1306 at Ballykene or Ballykone at Swords, Co. Dublin, there was a dispute between Geoffrey Savage (Sauuage) and Geoffrey and John de Brandewode regarding animals being impounded in Savage's park, which ultimately led to Savage being assaulted with a sword.[23] A *hibernicus* (Irishman) called Geoffrey McWyther was in the service of Geoffrey de Brandewode but left his service without permission, and with his wife, household and animals arrived on the lands belonging to Savage, seeking his 'protection and defence'. Savage agreed to this, and McWyther's animals, consisting of three cows, two heifers, four calves, thirty sheep and six affers or draught horses, were placed in the park for safe-keeping. Savage and the de Brandewodes had an ongoing dislike of each other so when the de Brandewodes arrived at Savage's lands and tried to take McWyther's animals from the park and reclaim their tenant, matters got out of hand. John de Brandewode drew his sword on Savage 'and would have slain him if he had not been rescued by the aid of Jordan Laual and Hugh Maghan'. The court decided that John de Brandewode was guilty of assault and imprisoned and fined him. It was also noted, however, that Savage had lied to the court about his reasons for having the animals in his park, originally claiming that they had been grazing his lands without permission so that he was forced to impound them. In reality he had actually allowed McWyther to empark them, so that McWyther could illegally leave de Brandewode's service. Therefore, although the assault charge had been found in his favour, Savage received no compensation 'but be in mercy for false claim'.

All of these examples demonstrate the importance of parks in retaining animals, particularly cattle and horses, and in providing pasture. The pasture could be a source of income for the manor, or it could be used for animals belonging to a landholder or his retainers and tenants. A landholder could also

---

21 Ibid., i, p. 200.   **22** McCormick, 'Archaeology: the horse in early Ireland' (2005), p. 23.   **23** *CJRI*, ii, p. 326.

use his park to impound animals belonging to his tenants, so preventing them from accessing their beasts until, for example, debts were paid. Archaeological evidence for impounding animals is virtually impossible to obtain, however place-name evidence can be useful. At Earlspark, Loughrea, Co. Galway, there is a field known locally as the 'pound field'.[24] It is sited within the interior of the park and it may well be that this was formerly the location of a secure compound in which to hold animals. Parks were also useful to provide protection from thieves, and were probably generally successful in this, as it was only when the thieves succeeded that they came to attention in the courts.

TIMBER AND WOODLAND

The trees and shrubs within a park were valuable resources that were directly under the control of the park owner. There were various classifications of wood-based resources. 'Timber' was the most valuable, consisting essentially of the trunks of trees over twenty years old, which could be used for major structural purposes. These were often oak, but ash and elm were also classified as timber trees. By contrast, 'wood' was any smaller material, including boughs of large trees as well as 'underwood', which specifically referred to wood from young trees, coppices, pollards and bushes.[25]

Trees had to be managed using a variety of techniques in order to extract repeated and economic harvests of timber and wood from them. Coppicing was commonly used, this was where a tree such as ash, willow, oak or hazel was cut to the base, as a result of which it then rapidly sent up shoots that could be left for a number of years until they reached a suitable thickness, at which point these 'poles' were cut for use.[26] Coppices were vulnerable to browsing by cattle, sheep and deer so an alternative in wood pasture was to pollard trees. In this case, the trunk was cut across, typically at two to four metres above ground so that it that was out of the reach of stock, in effect creating an overhead coppice. Pollarding had the advantage that the tree was less susceptible to damage from browsing animals, but on the other hand it was much more labour intensive than a normal coppice to manage and to crop (fig. 26).[27]

Wood products were used in a variety of ways. Timber was used for the main structural members in the construction of buildings, large-scale machinery and ships. The majority of wood was used as firewood or for charcoal production.

24 Michael 'Micky' Murphy, Loughrea, pers. comm.   **25** James, *An historical dictionary of forestry and woodland terms* (1991), pp 191, 200; Rackham, *The history of the countryside*, p. 67.   **26** Rackham, *The history of the countryside*, p. 65.   **27** Rackham, *The history of the countryside*, pp 66–7.

26 Pollarded willows. Browsing animals could not reach the valuable crop of willow poles used in basketry and hurdle-making. © Can Stock Photo Inc./Ivonne Wierink.

Underwood poles were made into items such as scaffolds, hurdles, fencing, ploughs, domestic tools, furniture, musical instruments and small-scale machinery such as looms.[28] The effective management of woodlands was therefore important to ensure continued profitability and a yield of materials that were suitable for use. As a result, park boundaries needed to be maintained in order to prevent theft of timber and wood and to deter unauthorised grazing. Certainly in the fourteenth century, when many Anglo-Norman manors were coming under pressure from the Gaelic advance, revenues were limited or even non-existent. For example, in 1321 there was an inquisition post-mortem to value the manor of Ardrahan (Ardraghin), Co. Galway, after the death of Thomas fitz Richard de Clare. In general, the manor was in poor condition with no standing buildings and only a ruined tower, although some of the land was still in use. The inquisition stated that 'the wood there had previously been emparked, but is now open and contains 100 acres of brush and thicket worth nothing in profits'.[29] The manor had another six hundred acres of woodland, but this too was worthless. Even in the east of the country there were problems. For example, at Shankill, Co. Dublin, in 1326 the thirty-acre archiepiscopal park was described as a park of oaks and thorns but it had no value for herbage or underwood 'on account of

28 Munby, 'Wood', pp 389–404. 29 IEMI, no. 204.

war'.[30] By contrast with these tales of woe, at Callan, Co. Kilkenny, in 1307 wood from within this park was only worth 6s. 8d., whereas for the period March to September 1350, the herbage in the park had a value of only 2s., but the wood was worth 27s. 2d.[31] This suggests that in the intervening time there had been substantial investment of time and resources in developing areas of well-managed trees and shrubs that could be profitably exploited. This also reflects the balance to be struck between having sufficient grazing land for animals and having access to raw materials for craftwork and construction. Another example of this is the sixty-acre park at Inchiquin, Co. Cork, which in 1348 was worth 5s. for pasture but had no value for underwood, the two evidently being incompatible in that particular park.[32] By contrast, the tiny four-acre park at Baliduwil was 'good for oxen and for osiers for carts', and was worth 12d. per year.[33] Osiers are a type of willow often used for basketry and wickerwork,[34] so this apparent incompatibility within such a small acreage may suggest that the trees were pollarded rather than coppiced, in order that grazing and wood production could co-exist within such a confined space. While underwood and animals did not mix well, full-sized 'standard' trees, which were used for timber, were compatible with grazing once they had reached a sufficient size that they would not be damaged by stock. This seems to have been the case at the sixty-acre park associated with Wexford Castle, which in 1324 contained oak trees and was also used for pasturing cattle.[35]

As with gifts of deer or venison, gifts of timber were highly valued, and in the case of royal gifts these could be used to demonstrate royal favour. Glencree is the only known royal park in Ireland, and it lay within the forest of Glencree, so it is not always clear whether documentary sources are referring to the forest or to the park. Nevertheless, in 1279/80 John de Walhope received a royal gift of '7 oak trees fit for timber' specifically from the park.[36] As well as timber, John was rewarded for his loyal service to the king with three and a half carucates of land in various locations.[37] We can imagine his pride as he was able to point out his hall, constructed with 'royal' timber. Gifts of timber could also be used to demonstrate piety; for example, in 1472 a parliament held at Naas granted:

> to the abbot and convent of the house of our blessed lady of Trim, and their successors, two watermills in Trim, with the weirs, fisheries &c., trees in the park of Trim, and services of the villeins of the manor for the ordering, establishing, repairing and continuance of a perpetual waxlight, from day to day and night to night, burning before the image of our Blessed Lady ...[38]

30 *CAAR*, p. 195.   31 *Handbook*, pp 302–3.   32 *CIPM*, ix, Edw. III, no. 119; *IEMI*, no. 291.   33 *CDI*, iii, no. 459.   34 Collins Dictionary, *Collins pocket English dictionary* (1981).   35 *IEMI*, no. 228; Murphy and O'Conor, 'Castles and deer parks in Anglo-Norman Ireland'.   36 *CDI*, ii, no. 1633.   37 Ibid., nos 1466, 1613, 1625, 1626.   38 *Statute of Kilkenny*, p. 51n.

The gift of trees from the park would have been a valuable resource for the abbot and convent to draw upon, providing access to materials for construction as well as underwood, which was needed on an ongoing basis.

Theft of timber and wood by criminals or by those with a political motive or personal grudge could also be significant and is mentioned in a number of medieval documents. During vacancies in the see, the archbishopric of Dublin lost timber, underwood and many other valuables to thieves at a number of locations in 1350 and again in 1373–4.[39] The 1305 court case referred to in Chapter 1 of this volume is another example, in which William Waspayl

> entered the park [at Balydonegan, and belonging to Richard de Burgh] and ascended the oaks and other trees, and cut the branches and carried them to William's manor; and there they were burned, and otherwise expended in his service, with William's assent.[40]

Since wood and timber were essential raw materials, a ready supply was needed by everyone, and tenants had specified rights to wood from within the manor for particular purposes. These rights were called 'estovers', with the more common examples being *firebote* – the right to take firewood, *haybote* – the right to take wood for fencing, *housebote* – the right to take wood for building, and *ploughbote* – the right to take wood for making ploughs. Often the location in which these rights could be exercised was specified as, for example, in an undated later-medieval reference to a tenant who was to have reasonable estovers, housebote and haybote from woodland outside the park of Maynooth.[41] In the thirteenth century the archbishop of Dublin had extensive private forests. On his lands a tenant was entitled to haybote and housebote, provided it was cut 'in view' of the foresters.[42] In some cases a tenant or a family member could have rights within the park itself. A notable case is one of an assize of novel disseisin at Lucan in 1299 where Hugh de la Felde and his wife Alianora complained to the court that they had been disseised (dispossessed) of 6*d.* of rent, one third of a fishery, a share of two mills and 'reasonable estovers for housebote and hayebote in the park of Lyuekan', all of which Alianora had received as a dower. In answer to these charges, the defendants, who included Roesia de Peche and her husband John Hanstede, said that 'a certain moor was assigned to Alianora for all her dower coming to her from the park, except she should have hoops, rods and hafts in the park for her ploughs'. Eventually, Hugh and Alianora withdrew the

---

39 *CPR*, Edw. III, viii, 590; xv, 309.   **40** *CJRI*, ii, p. 136; Murphy and O'Conor, 'Castles and deer parks in Anglo-Norman Ireland'; Gibbons and Clarke, 'Deer parks', 4–5.   **41** *RPH*, Antiquissime Dorso no. 41. 3.
42 For example, *CAAR*, pp 68, 123, 136.

charges, and were fined for this apparently false accusation; however, there was evidently no smoke without fire, because one of the co-defendants, Roger Smalrys, pledged a portion of the fine, and in an out-of-court settlement he agreed to ensure full access for Hugh and Alianora to their rights in the future, all of which suggests that ultimately he realised that Hugh and Alianora had a case.[43] Importantly, this court case provides evidence that the park at Lucan was being used to produce underwood, and specifically 'hoops, rods and hafts'. Hoops and rods are clear examples of the products of coppicing or pollarding, while hafts for tools would have been produced from branch-wood from mature trees such as ash or elm, or from the trunks of young trees and shrubs.

In some cases there is clear evidence that land incorporating substantial areas of trees and woodland was deliberately selected for emparkment. As we have seen, in 1299 at Nenagh, Co. Tipperary, Theobald Walter (Butler) applied for royal permission to divert a road around an area that he wanted to enclose for a park, which was specifically stated to be a wood up to that time.[44] In addition to wood-related place-names within the park itself, the townland names to the immediate east of the park also suggest that there were extensive woodlands stretching northwards to the site of the later-medieval manorial grange. The grange was situated two miles north of the town, in the modern townlands of Wellington, Grange Upper and Grange Lower, where Nenagh Mill is located on the first-edition OS map.[45] The townland to the south of the grange is Garraunanearla, the 'shrubbery' or 'coppice of the earl'. Moving further south, into the townland of Lisbunny, the northern extent of this is called Kyleeragh or 'the western wood' and further south in the townland is the minor place-name Garrannakill, the 'shrubbery' or 'coppice of the wood' or of the 'church'. All the evidence therefore suggests that at Nenagh the area to the east and north-east of the town, including the area believed to have been the high-medieval park, was managed woodland throughout the medieval period (fig. 27).

At Maynooth, Co. Kildare, there is also place-name evidence linking the park with pre-existing woodland. As well as a small part of the townland of Maynooth, the park boundary encompasses the townlands of Mariavilla and Crewhill. In Chapter 6 we will see that these names suggest an association with trees and woodland, in particular the sacred *bile* and *craobh* associated with kingship and community, and that the position of the park may be of symbolic significance. In addition, the adjoining townland of Timard has woodland associations, being

43 *CJRI*, i, p. 222; Murphy and O'Conor, 'Castles and deer parks in Anglo-Norman Ireland'. **44** *CJRI*, i, p. 234; Gwynn and Gleeson, *A history of the diocese of Killaloe*, p. 88; Murphy and O'Conor, 'Castles and deer parks in Anglo-Norman Ireland'. **45** Gleeson, 'The castle and manor of Nenagh', 261; Gleeson, 'The priory of St John at Nenagh' (1938), 201; Gwynn and Gleeson, *A history of the diocese of Killaloe*, p. 178.

27 The demesne of the post-medieval Brook-Watson estate north of Nenagh is an example of open wood-pasture. Note how the lower branches of the trees have been cropped by browsing animals.

translated by O'Donovan as *Tuim arda*, 'high bushes'.[46] These place-names in and immediately around the park show a preponderance of woodland/tree names, suggesting that in the early medieval period the land was well-wooded and not used for agricultural purposes and this may have been one of the practical reasons that this area was selected for emparkment.

OTHER USES OF PARKS

In 1378 John Piers and John Boudram received custody of the sixty-acre park at Wexford Castle to include 'all lands which by ancient custom were cultivated and now are cultivated within the park of Wexford, with moors and pastures within the bounds of that park'.[47] This suggests that in addition to the pasture and woodland contained in the park there was some arable land being cultivated and

46 Bunachar loghinmneacha na hÉireann, *Placenames database of Ireland.*   47 *CIRCLE*, PR 1 Rich. II, no. 11.

there may have been some turbary or turf-cutting on the 'moors'. Interestingly, this is the only example from the period in which arable agriculture within the park is specifically mentioned, and the only possible mention of turbary.

In this particular case the source directly connects the park and the functions within it; however, in some records manorial features such as warrens and dovecotes may be documented in conjunction with the park, without it being obvious whether these are necessarily inside the park or are elsewhere within the manor. For example, at Balydonegan in 1333 there was a ruined dovecote formerly worth 3s. 4d. 'beneath this park' (outside but adjacent to it), but 'the warren there, however, is worth 12d.' This suggests that the warren, park and dovecote were in proximity, but while the dovecote was certainly outside the park the warren could well have been within the bounds.[48] Similarly, in 1350 and 1373–4 when the lands of the archbishopric of Dublin were plundered,[49] the calendars are unclear whether features such as the rabbit warrens were situated within the parks:

> touching evildoers who broke the closes, houses, parks and stone walls of the manors at Swerdes, Tallagh, Balymore, Dublin, Baliboght, Clondolk, Ardnoth, Coloigne and Fynglas, Co. Dublin … while they were in the king's hand in the last voidance of the archbishopric, and entered the free warrens of the archbishopric and hunted in these and the said parks, felled trees and underwood there, tore out the lead from the gutters of some of the houses, vessels of lead and brass in the kitchens, brew-houses and other houses of the manors and places aforesaid in the furnaces, iron bars in windows and iron fastenings (*ligamina*) and locks in the doors of the houses, carried away the locks, fastenings, bars, vessels, lead, trees and underwood, the timber from some of the houses, stones from the walls and other goods of the temporalities, deer from the parks, and hares, conies, pheasants and partridges from the warrens …[50]

At Dunamase, Co. Laois, there is relatively scant evidence for herds of fallow deer, with only two out of eighty-nine deer bones being from fallow deer. Furthermore, there is no mention of deer in the inquisition post-mortem.[51] This may indicate that these were from a carcass brought into the site rather than from herds kept in the adjacent park, but the extent of the excavation was limited and further investigations within the castle bounds could reveal more fallow deer remains. Given the impenetrable, craggy nature of the rock upon which the castle

---

48 *CIPM*, no. 251; Murphy and O'Conor, 'Castles and deer parks in Anglo-Norman Ireland'. **49** *CPR*, viii, Edw. III, no. 590; xv, no. 309. **50** Ibid., xv, no. 309. **51** *CDI*, ii, no. 2028; *IEMI*, no. 54.

stands, the park would have been a suitable nearby place to retain horses and so may have also included stables and stud farms. In addition, there is a pond adjacent to a series of earthworks in the centre of the park, in an ideal location for a fishpond to supply the castle.[52] The inquisition also mentions a warren worth 2s. per year, but this seems to be associated with the New Town of Leys, rather than being within the park. The documentary evidence refers to emparked pasture land, and in addition the park could have been used for timber and underwood production. Tall stands of trees planted on the rocky outcrops in the park during the late eighteenth century and in the 1950s show that this ground is eminently suitable for the production of good-quality wood.[53]

MANAGING THE PARKS

Many of the parks described have a number of functions in the various documents, depending on the circumstances in which they were recorded. Regardless of whether one or several functions were performed within individual parks, it was essential to ensure that they were correctly managed in order to optimise their use. These uses could vary over time, and one park could also perform a number of functions simultaneously. Where they were single, non-compartmentalised spaces, a number of authors have argued that it was difficult to maintain a range of uses since grazing animals are incompatible with the economic management of woodland and meadow and, furthermore, deer would be in direct competition with cattle or sheep for pasturage.[54] However, Vera argued that wood pasture can be a sustainable way of both producing timber and grazing deer or cattle, as the trees can be separated from the open ground by groves of spiny shrubs, such as the blackthorn or sloe (*Prunus spinosa*) (fig. 28).[55] He argued that these will develop and regenerate in a natural cycle of non-linear succession. In this model, open, grassy areas gradually become overgrown by shrubs, which provide cover in which trees can regenerate. Eventually the trees shade out the shrubs from the centre of the growth, resulting in a stand of trees surrounded by shrubs. In turn, the trees die, leaving an open grassy grove in the centre once again. This model takes a very long-term view of a large landscape, and on a more immediate basis small parks especially would have had to be managed very carefully if multiple functions were to be carried out within them. Pollarding rather than coppicing is an obvious example of a technique that could

52 RMP LA013-051. **53** Grose, *The antiquities of Ireland: the second volume* (1795), p. 13; Coote, *Statistical survey of the Queen's County* (1801), pp 116–17; M. Dowling, pers. comm. **54** Mileson, 'The importance of parks in fifteenth-century society', pp 27–8; Cantor and Hatherly, 'The medieval parks of England', 72. **55** Vera, 'The wood-pasture theory and the deer park: the grove – the origin of the deer

be employed. Hedges could be planted to separate the different zones of usage and blackthorn would have been ideal for this. Fences could also be constructed, and although these were more labour-intensive than hedges to put in place and to maintain, they could provide an immediate barrier to movement.

Wild deer, whether inside or outside forest bounds, lived lives that were primarily independent of human management. They were hunted both by humans and by predators such as wolves, but were not usually fed and were rarely deliberately moved around the landscape. By contrast, park deer lived in an unnatural, enclosed space that lacked non-human predators, so that unsustainable stocking densities could develop. Furthermore, the enclosed nature of parks meant that deer could be easily caught for hunting, gift-giving and venison production. This manipulation brought with it the requirement to control stock levels and to provide winter feed.[56]

This means that constructing a park was only one stage of the process and that ongoing management costs in terms of labour and materials were significant portions of the manorial budget. In bad winters, or in parks that were overstocked with deer, winter fodder could be provided either in the form of hay or as browse wood that had been freshly cut from evergreen trees or had been cut from deciduous trees and stored for the winter. Sometimes this came from elsewhere on the manor, but it could also be bought in, and there was inevitably a cost for the associated labour and transport. For example, in 1389 the sum of 3s. 6d. was spent on winter feed at Castle Donnington in England.[57] This practice reduced winter deaths and enabled higher stocking densities of deer within the park, an important consideration, since it has been estimated that a red deer will consume its own body weight in fodder in less than a fortnight.[58]

Parks were managed by parkers. Their status was below that of the senior officials of the manor but was nevertheless significant.[59] Below them was a further tier of assistants who could be responsible for particular aspects of park management, such as the gatekeepers or *clausatores* of the park and those responsible for the sale of wood or pasture. In addition to parkers, lords might employ professional huntsmen either on a permanent or on a seasonal basis, and larderers could be employed to process and salt the meat.[60]

Parkers are referred to in records from Trim and Kilmainham (Kilmaynan), Co. Dublin, while in Wexford a 'constable' was appointed to oversee the castle

park', 107–9. **56** Pluskowski, 'The social construction of medieval park ecosystems: an interdisciplinary perspective' (2007), pp 74–5; Richardson, *The forest, park and palace of Clarendon, c.1200–1650* (2005), p. 34; Birrell, 'Deer and deer farming in medieval England', 112–26. **57** Cantor, 'The medieval parks of Leicestershire' (1970–1), 14. **58** Birrell, 'Deer and deer farming in medieval England', 117–18. **59** Franklin, 'Thornbury woodlands and deer parks, pt 1: the earl of Gloucester's deer parks', 155. **60** Ibid., 157; Birrell, 'Deer and deer farming in medieval England', 122. **61** Cited by Hore, *History of*

28 Blackthorn bush showing the thorns and sloes. © Alexandre Dulaunoy Creative Commons Licence.

and park. The appointment of a constable for Wexford Castle is a good example of the difficulties encountered in trying to run manors in Ireland when the king and his senior officials were based in England. In 1331 the manor of Wexford was in the king's hand due to the minority of Laurence, son and heir of John de Hastynges. At that time William de Aldesheles was constable of Wexford Castle and park and the park fencing was to be repaired at a cost of 30s.[61] In June 1335 John de Ruggeleye was given custody of the castle of Wexford.[62] In January of the following year there was a 'grant to William de Aldsheles of the keeping of the castle and park of Weyseford and of the prises of Weysford and the mills there'.[63] Unfortunately, in March, due to an oversight, the king also granted Wexford to John de Ellerker.[64] In May there was a document granting de Ruggeleye a number of rights including custody of the park of Wexford.[65] By June the problem was compounded as the king also appointed de Ellerker as constable of Wexford Castle.[66] This evidently caused a problem, and in October the grant to de Ellerker was rescinded on the grounds that de Ruggeleye had already been appointed.[67]

the town and county of Wexford, v, p. 106.   **62** CPR, Edw. III, iii, 123.   **63** CFR, iv, 470.   **64** CPR, Edw. III, iii, 225–6.   **65** Ibid., 257.   **66** Ibid., 272.   **67** Ibid., 320.

There are three references to parkers for the manor of Kilmainham, which was held by the Hospitallers of St John of Jerusalem. In 1326 the park and waters of the manor were the responsibility of Robert Gutters but by 1335 Hamundo Lee had taken over the keeping of the park.[68] At Trim, the park first appears in the documentary record in 1388, so technically this is outside the scope of this volume. Nevertheless, although the park was first recorded at this time it had evidently been in existence for a considerable time. A number of parkers are listed for Trim in the late fourteenth and fifteenth centuries, all with English names and interestingly they also had the responsibility of sergeant of the betaghry, making them responsible for dealing with Irish tenants.[69]

THE FUNCTIONS OF PARKS IN IRELAND

In the documentary sources, production of timber and wood is the most commonly described function of Irish parks. Within a park, the trees could be carefully managed to produce timber, which would have been important both for the use of the owner and as an asset for sale or gift. Large timber trees would have been essential to the elite as raw materials for roofs, floors and walls in castles, halls and ecclesiastical buildings as well as for more mundane manorial structures such as mills, barns and stables.[70] When grown within a park, trees and shrubs could not easily be accessed by unauthorised individuals, whereas outside they were much more vulnerable to damage and theft by the local populace. As such, a substantial well-guarded area of trees either as woodland or as wood pasture was extremely valuable.

The next most frequently recorded park function is for pasture, pannage or the corralling animals such as cattle and horses. Surprisingly, given the semi-wooded nature of parks and the frequent mention of this function in England,[71] there is only one direct reference to pannage, at Kilkea (Kylka), Co. Kildare.[72] This may reflect the much greater levels of woodland cover in later-medieval Ireland compared to England, so that the local population may have had much easier access to suitable woodland in the surrounding area and therefore may not have needed to pay to access the park. Herbage of the park was evidently economically important, as this is mentioned on a considerable number of occasions, and even if the land was not let to tenants, the grazing could have been of considerable importance to the landholder. Being able to corral or impound animals within

68 *Registrum de Kilmainham*, pp 8, 69, 74.   **69** Potterton, *Medieval Trim: history and archaeology* (2005), pp 125–8.   **70** Blair and Ramsey, *English medieval industries* (2001), pp 389–94.   **71** For example, Mileson, *Parks in medieval England*, p. 68.   **72** *CDI*, ii, no. 2340.

the park was a symbolic and practical demonstration of the control of a lord over his tenantry. Similarly, to be able to retain his own herds in this way was also important, since if he became a victim of theft it would have implied weakness and lack of control on his part.

In an Irish context, these functions of an enclosed park generally appear to have been much more important than simply to retain fallow deer. As described in Chapter 3, fallow deer were relatively uncommon and were an aspiration that was not achievable except for the highest echelons of the Anglo-Norman elite. Overall, for all grades of society that held an Irish park, the ability to control access to the pasture, underwood and timber within the park and the ability to corral and protect herds of cattle seem to have been the most important functions. These were portable forms of wealth that needed to be maintained in a secure environment and, as the court documents show, even enclosure was not always sufficient to protect them. There are likely to have been many more unrecorded pasture parks in the Irish landscape. Few records exist for the liberties of Ireland and, even in the shired counties, the parks of the middling tier of society only become visible when a crime has been committed. No royal inquisitions post-mortem were conducted on these lands, and their parks have generally passed into obscurity, being too small and too short-lived to have become embedded into the cartographic landscape.

CONCLUSION

Parks in Ireland had a number of uses. While hunting and venison were certainly important in some large, high-status parks, the preservation of timber and woodland was also a key function of all sizes of park. On a day-to-day basis, the provision of pasture and the ability to keep domestic animals within a secure location seem also to have been important. Form and function are inextricably linked, since it is necessary to design landscape features to be practical in terms of construction, maintenance and use. Having examined the function of high-medieval parks over these two chapters, it is now possible to take this evidence and look at the form in which the parks were expressed in the landscape.

CHAPTER FIVE

Morphology and features

Park design in the high-medieval period was affected by the function of the park, the resources of its owner, the landscape in which it sat and a general concept of what constituted a park. As with function, in order to understand the nature of parks in Ireland it is first helpful to understand the features and morphology of the English parks on which they were originally modelled. In England, parks usually took the form of an enclosed area of ground surrounded by a high, wide bank, usually with an internal ditch. They were often lobe-shaped, circular or square but this could be modified depending on the local topography, land availability and the presence of natural features such as lakes and rivers, which often formed one or more boundaries. Aristocratic parks often abutted and extended outwards from the castle and so provided an enclosed area of land adjacent to it, but many parks were also situated at a distance from the castle or manor house. The top of the bank was generally surmounted by pales, which were vertical slats of wood, but sometimes a hedge or, rarely, a stone wall was used. Stone-walled parks without banks and ditches were less common than those surrounded by wooden palings and were generally confined either to areas where there was an abundance of stone or to high-status parks where the cost of transportation of building materials was not an issue. If possible, park boundaries ran just below the brow of a hill or slope so that a deer could jump in, but could not jump back out because of the presence of the internal ditch and the uphill direction of the slope. This meant that over time the number of deer within the park should increase. Deer numbers could be further increased by using a 'deer leap', which was a section of the boundary where the fencing was absent or very low, but where a deeper pit was placed inside the gap to prevent the deer escaping in the opposite direction.[1]

In later-medieval England, parks varied in size from 30 acres to 4,300 acres, with examples of one hundred to three hundred acres most typical. The evidence suggests that minor gentry held the smaller examples, with great magnates and royalty having parks of up to or exceeding one thousand acres.[2] The earliest

---

[1] Watts, 'Wiltshire deer parks: an introductory survey', 88–98; Cantor and Wilson, 'The medieval deer-parks of Dorset: I–XVII' (1962–80); Rackham, *The history of the countryside*, p. 125; Cantor, 'Forests, chases, parks and warrens', p. 73; Moorhouse, 'The medieval parks of Yorkshire: function, contents and chronology', pp 104–6; Creighton, *Castles and landscapes*, pp 188–9. **2** Cantor and Hatherly, 'The

English parks were created by the great magnates and royalty and these were often large and of regular shape.[3] One example is the pre-Conquest Ongar Great Park in Essex, which was a rectangle with rounded corners and had an area of 1,200 acres, while Barnsdale Park in Rutland was oval. Later parks were often created by individuals of lower social status and these were likely to be more irregularly shaped since they had to fit within existing land boundaries and avoid existing settlement features.[4] As a result, these were often located on the periphery of manors where the least agricultural development had occurred, and for both earlier and later parks their boundaries often partly follow modern parish boundaries.[5] Parks ideally contained a range of habitat types including woodland and open grazing and had a requirement for a stream or ponds to provide the stock with water. By 1616, Liebualt, in his *Maison Rustique or the Countrey Farme*, identified that the ideal park

> must consist of divers hills, divers plains and divers valleys; the hills which are commonly called the viewes or discoveries of parks, would be all goodly high woods of tall timber as well for the beauty and gracefulnesse of the parke, as also for the echoe and sound which will rebound from the same … the plains which are called in parkes the lawnds, would be very champion and fruitfull, as well for the breeding of great store of grasse and hay for the feeding and nourishing of the deere or other wild beastes, as also for the pleasure of coursing with greyhounds …[6]

Despite this, many parks were not heavily wooded, either due to the natural landscape of the area, such as in Egton, Yorkshire, where the park is situated in moorland, or, especially in the case of later parks, due to the emparkment of land that had previously been utilised for arable farming.[7]

Where parks were large, or were situated at a distance from the manorial centre, they could incorporate a lodge from which the activities were managed. These were often moated sites, and the moats could be stocked with fish.[8] Lodges were usually at the highest point of the park with commanding views over the landscape.[9] Over time many of these changed from purely functional farm-like buildings to incorporate accommodation and dining facilities for the elite.[10] In addition, lodges could be accompanied by a range of other buildings, which

medieval parks of England', 73–4. **3** Bond, 'Forests, chases, warrens and parks in medieval Wessex' (1994), passim. **4** Rackham, *The history of the countryside*, p. 125; Rackham, *Trees and woodland in the British landscape* (1976), p. 144. **5** Cantor and Hatherly, 'The medieval parks of England', 75. **6** Cited by Shirley, *Some account of English deer parks: with notes on the management of deer* (1867), p. 234. **7** Rackham, *The history of the countryside*, p. 126. **8** Watts, 'Wiltshire deer parks: an introductory survey', 90. **9** Rackham, *The history of the countryside*, p. 126. **10** Birrell, 'Deer and deer farming in medieval

might include living accommodation, kennels and stables, facilities for storage of hay, browse and timber, and structures for the storage and maintenance of tools and materials used in the repair of hedges, fences and ditches.[11]

In summary, due to their distinctive morphology, former parks can often be identified from cartographic sources. Based on this starting point and in combination with cartographic and place-name evidence, it was possible to identify a number of parks in the physical landscape of Ireland and to visit and survey these in detail.

SIZE OF PARKS

In Ireland the majority of documented parks were less than 100 acres (fig. 29), but this generalisation disguises a great variety in size. The largest known high-medieval park was at Loughrea, which was recorded as being seven carucates.[12] This is equivalent to *c.*840 statute acres, and fieldwork has shown that it consisted of the entire townland of Earlspark, Co. Galway, which has an area of 913 statute acres on the first-edition OS map. The smallest examples were two four-acre parks; the first of these was at Baliduwil, Co. Kerry, and was owned by Thomas de Clare, while a second example, at Shankill (Senekyll), Co. Dublin, was owned by the archbishop of Dublin.[13] It is clear that a park of 840 acres and one of 4 acres must have been perceived and used in different ways.

In the current study, a number of different approaches were taken in estimating park sizes in Ireland. In some cases, as at Loughrea, the original documents give the acreage, but it must be borne in mind that medieval acres and carucates could vary in size. Some documents give acreages that include a park among other lands, as, for example, in the inquisition following the death of John Fitz John Bisset, which found that his lands included '100 acres with a park in villa de Haket [Ballyhackett] worth 27*s.* 5*d.*'[14] In this case the park must have been less than 100 acres and so for the purposes of comparison it was assumed that the park made up half of the total area quantified, that is, fifty acres. Sometimes both acreage and value are stated for land in particular manors and these give land values of between 1*d.* and 4*d.* per acre. In other cases where the acreage is not stated but where potential income from the park is given, a nominal, but generous value of 4*d.* per acre for grazing was used so that, if

---

England', 119; Cantor and Wilson, 'The medieval deer-parks of Dorset: I' (1962), 110. **11** Moorhouse, 'The medieval parks of Yorkshire: function, contents and chronology', pp 107, 115–17. **12** Knox, 'Occupation of Connaught by the Anglo-Normans after AD 1237', 134; Murphy and O'Conor, 'Castles and deer parks in Anglo-Norman Ireland', 69. **13** *CAAR*, 195; *CDI*, iii, nos 459, 894. **14** *IEMI*, no. 36.

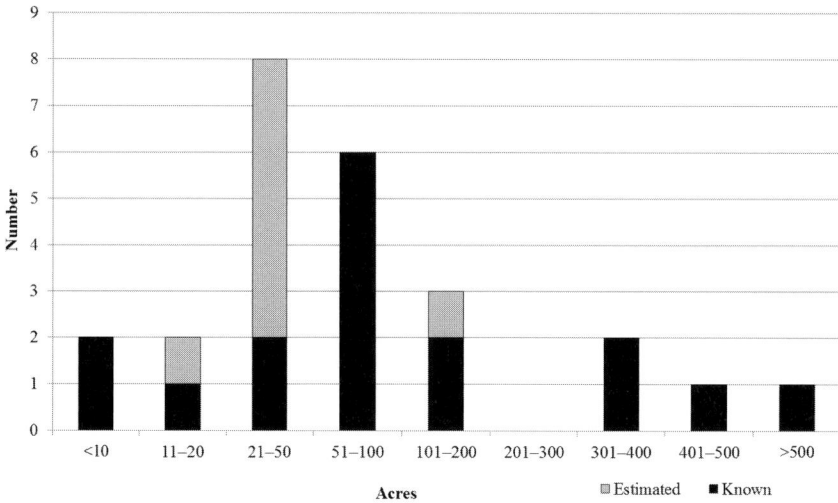

29 Size of Anglo-Norman parks based on documentary and physical evidence. Estimates inferred from the documents and on grazing values of 4*d*. per acre.

anything, this would underestimate the size of the parks. Finally, the most direct method was where it was possible to physically or cartographically identify the likely park boundaries.

Since large parks were significant features within the manor, they were more likely than small parks to be recorded in detail and an acreage given, whereas smaller examples are often only mentioned as an aside. Therefore, the smaller parks were more likely to require size estimates to be made, and depending on land values, some of those estimated at under fifty acres could belong in the fifty- to one-hundred-acre category. By contrast to Ireland, where the vast majority of parks seem to have been less than one hundred acres, in later-medieval England one hundred to three hundred acres was most typical, with a range from thirty to 4,300 acres. The evidence there suggests that minor gentry held the smaller parks and great magnates and royalty had parks of up to or exceeding a thousand acres.[15] This suggests a difference in the way that parks were used in Ireland, and indeed this was borne out when their function was considered. As Chapter 3 showed, only the largest, most prestigious parks had direct or indirect evidence for the keeping of fallow deer. While timber and wood were important in all sizes of park, the smaller, more modest parks were also associated with pasture and with keeping cattle, horses and other animals.

15 Cantor and Hatherly, 'The medieval parks of England', 73–4.

LAYOUT OF PARKS

Following on from the size to the shape and features of the parks, cartographic analysis and field survey was undertaken at a number of the larger documented examples and these are presented here as a series of case studies. At some of these parks it was possible to determine the boundaries with a degree of certainty while in other cases, such as at Nenagh, Co. Tipperary, there are a number of possibilities for one or more boundaries. Although all of the parks were different, there were important similarities in their layout, which were then brought together with documentary evidence from other sites. The smaller parks are more difficult to identify archaeologically, since there are less detailed records of these and since, in some cases, it is not clear exactly where they were situated. This is an unfortunate situation that creates an unavoidable research bias towards the more prestigious examples.

Earlspark, Co. Galway

Earlspark was the only one of the surveyed parks to have been surrounded by a mortared stone wall during the medieval period, and at 913 acres it was also the largest (fig. 30).[16] The park is essentially a square with rounded corners. The land within consists of a series of hills and valleys, with the mortared stone boundary wall constructed so that there is high ground outside much of the boundary. The exception is at the western side where the park abuts the lake of Lough Rea and is bounded by marsh and reeds, which would have prevented free movement by people or animals and provided a source of water for deer and other stock. The townland boundary wall, which is coterminous with the park boundary, extends over a length of 7.4km. Much of this currently exists only to a height of 1–1.6m, which is similar to the walls that define the surrounding fields, although in places sections of wall up to 2.6m high are present on the perimeter of the park. The wall is *c*.0.9m wide at the base, tapering to 0.8m at the top, and based on these dimensions it is calculated that 15,725m³ or 31,450 tonnes of limestone would have been needed to construct it.

Access and security would have been important for any park and even today there are only three roads through Earlspark. The most obvious feature was a gateway in the north-east corner of the park. At 3.04m or exactly 10ft wide, this was of a sufficient size to easily allow access for carts.[17] The gateway would have been fitted with a wooden gate and the form of the extant stonework shows that it was designed to be secured from the outside (fig. 31), while geophysics

---

16 Beglane, 'Theatre of power: the Anglo-Norman park at Earlspark, Co. Galway, Ireland', *passim*.
17 Verdon, *Travel in the Middle Ages* (2003), p. 25; Nugent, 'Pilgrimage in medieval Ireland' (2009), pp 198–210.

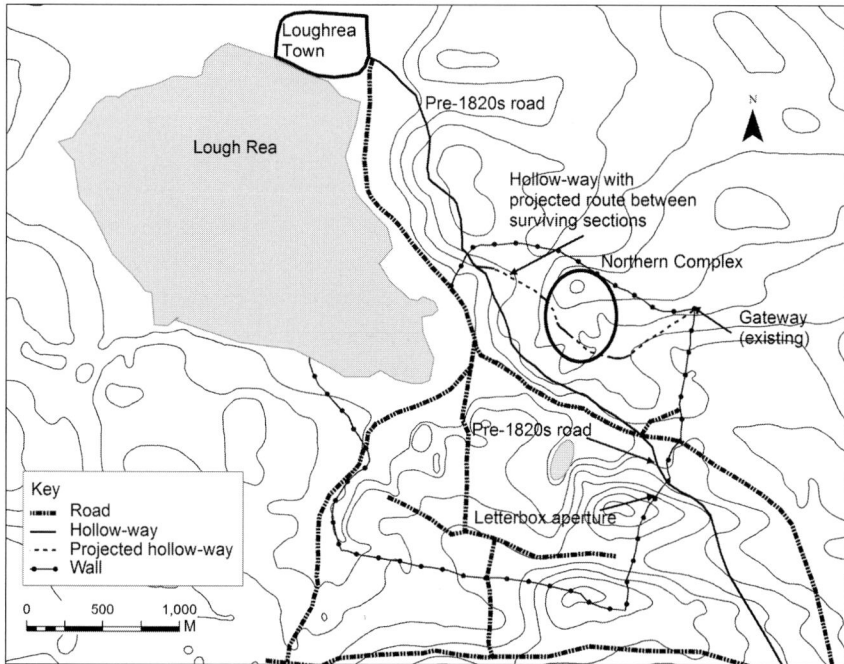

30 Key features of Earlspark, Loughrea, Co. Galway.

immediately outside shows evidence for a possible cobbled area and roadway, which may be associated with the management of the park.[18] At the north-western corner of the townland, a track from Loughrea enters the townland and then splits in two. One leg of this forms the line of the old Loughrea to Dalystown road, while the remains of a second relict road or hollow-way heads eastwards through the park (fig. 32) at least as far as an area termed the 'Northern Complex'. It is likely that this hollow-way contoured around to the gate at the north-eastern corner of the park; however, due to land improvements surface features beyond this point have been obscured. In addition to these gateways, there is a sub-rectangular aperture through the wall that was part of the original construction. This measures 0.2 x 0.2m and is situated 0.8m above ground level (fig. 33). It is found at the top of a hill on the east side of the townland, and lies close to a monument recorded as a univallate hillfort.[19] It may have been a 'delivery slot' similar to a modern letter-box that allowed small items to be passed into and out of the enclosed park and allowed people to communicate by speaking through the gap.

18 McCarthy, 'Earlspark and Moanmore East townlands, Loughrea, Co. Galway: report on an archaeological geophysical survey' (2010), p. 18. **19** RMP GA105-086.

31 The north-eastern gateway at Earlspark was designed to be secured from outside the park.

At Earlspark, the most likely location for the lodge or administrative centre of the park is a large enclosure that is recorded as a ringfort and is located at the northern edge of the townland in the zone referred to as the Northern Complex (fig. 30).[20] From this area there are extensive views over the townland, lake and

20 RMP GA105-080.

32 The relict road from Loughrea as it passes through the park.

town, with almost all of the townland visible. The Northern Complex has the densest concentration of archaeological monuments in the townland, including an unrecorded standing stone, known locally as the 'Lady Stone' or 'Earl's Chair', a possible hillfort with two associated structures, two monuments listed as ringforts, a rectangular structure and a pond. The park wall passes immediately to the north of this area, ensuring that the monuments of the Northern Complex are incorporated within the park. From a practical perspective, the monuments of the Northern Complex lie on the route of the hollow-way, midway between the gateways in the north-western and north-eastern corners of the park. The possible lodge enclosure has an external ditch that appears to have been re-cut at some point so that it is now *c*.3.5m wide at the base and *c*.7m at the top, with a flat bottom (fig. 34). In addition to what may be a number of buildings in the interior, geophysics has shown the remains of a second, internal ditch, suggesting that it was originally bivallate, and hence it may be a reused prehistoric or early medieval monument.[21]

21 McCarthy, 'Earlspark and Moanmore East townlands'.

a

b

33 A section of well-preserved wall meets a poorer section, from outside Earlspark. Note the rectangular hole on the left of the image (above). Close-up of the letterbox aperture from inside the park (below).

34 The flat-bottomed ditch of the large enclosure RMP GA105–080 at Earlspark.

Maynooth, Co. Kildare

The park of Maynooth has an area of 495 acres with a circumference of 6.3km. Overall, it has a sub-rectangular shape with a rounded corner at the north-western edge. The land is flat, with a single, round-topped hill called Crewhill in the interior of the park (fig. 35). Working anti-clockwise it is bounded on the south-western side by a substantial ditch, with a depth of 2–2.5m. For part of its length this ditch has an external hedge, which is probably the original boundary referred to in 1540–1, as well as an extremely low-lying internal bank that is likely to be up-cast from re-cutting the ditch and from ploughing (fig. 36).[22] On the south-eastern side, the park is bounded by the road now known as the Dunboyne Road, which is up a relatively steep incline from the Lyreen River below. On the north-east, the boundary is likely to be the river known as the Rye Water, but the area close to the river is marshy, wet flood plain that would have acted as a strip of watermeadow and would have been difficult to traverse. This low-lying area also contains a previously unrecorded decoy pond, which is probably of post-medieval date (fig. 62). On the north-western side, the park boundary is absent, but is likely to have been marked by the line of a now-defunct field boundary shown on the first-edition OS map within the townland of Timard.

22 *CSL*, 132–3.

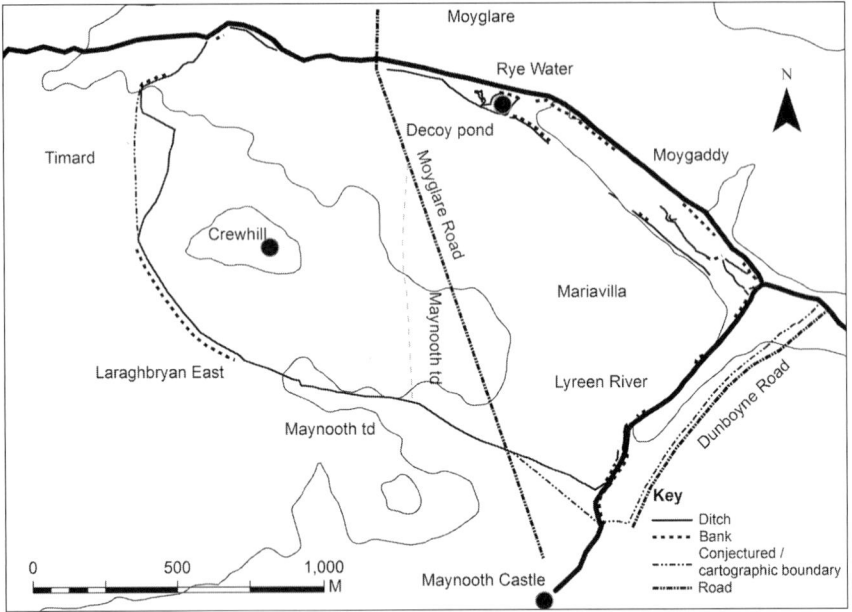

35 Key features of the park of Maynooth, Co. Kildare.

36 The boundary of the park at Maynooth, showing the hedgerow, ditch and slight internal bank.

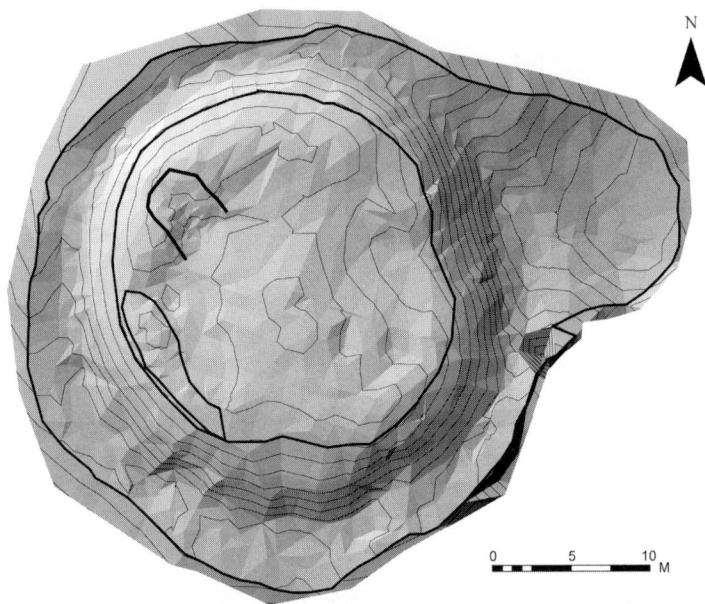

37 Previously unrecorded enclosure at Crewhill, Maynooth: a. from the south-east; b. total station survey.

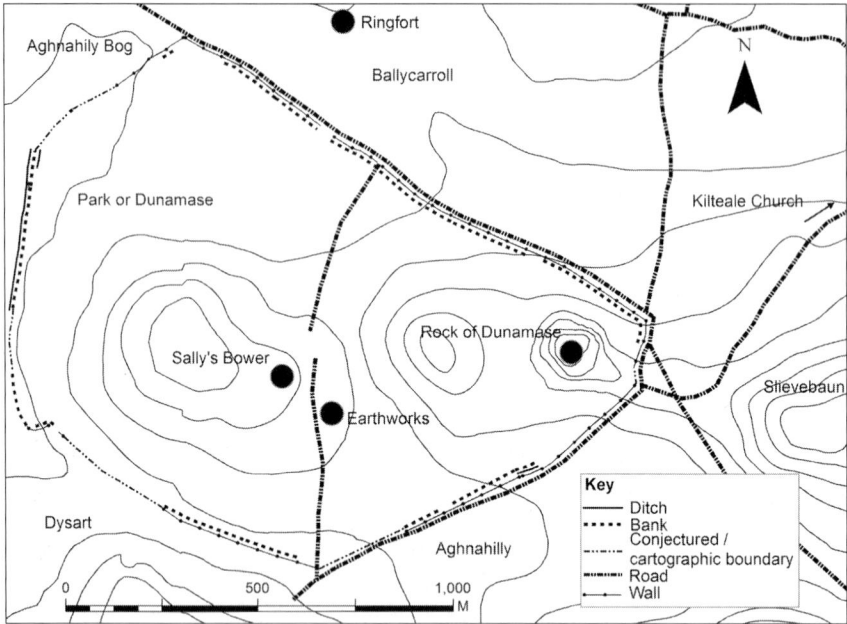

38 Key features of the park at Dunamase, Co. Laois.

In the interior of the park is Crewhill, the only high point within the park, which provides extensive views over the area, and which would have been the ideal location for a viewing stand or a parker's lodge. The hill is topped by a previously unrecorded enclosure with a souterrain immediately down-slope, suggesting that this is the site of a ringfort, which could then have been re-used in the later-medieval period (fig. 37). Interestingly, there is a local tradition that during the rebellion of Silken Thomas in 1535 Maynooth Castle was bombarded by cannons positioned on Crewhill.[23]

Dunamase, Co. Laois

Dunamase Castle is one of the most dramatic later-medieval castles in Ireland, sitting high on a rocky crag overlooking the townland of Park or Dunamase (fig. 11). This townland has an area of 338 acres on the first-edition OS map, and appears to be the extent of the medieval park (fig. 38). The Rock of Dunamase is the highest and easternmost of three outcrops that form an east–west line within the park. The lands to the west towards Portlaoise, to the south-west and to the north are flat, including areas of bog and reclaimed bog land, while to the east and south a range of hills separates Dunamase from Stradbally.

23 John Geoghegan and Bill Mulhern, pers. comm.

39 1.3m mortared stone wall on 0.5m bank, Dunamase.

In 2002 Hodkinson suggested that the northern boundary of the documented high-medieval park was represented by a series of curving hedges to the north of the east–west road separating Park or Dunamase from the townland of Ballycarroll, however he did not carry out any cartographic analysis or fieldwork,[24] and this potential boundary was added to the SMR in August 2010.[25] Cartographic analysis and fieldwork does not support the suggestion that this was the boundary of the park, which instead appears to be represented by the existing townland boundary.

The majority of the townland is surrounded by a mortared stone wall, up to 1.8m in height. This was almost certainly constructed by the landowner, Sir John Parnell, at the end of the eighteenth century,[26] although there is a possibility that this represented the reconstruction of an older, high-medieval wall. In addition, however, intermittent stretches of bank are present on all sides of the townland, up to 1.5m high, but typically 0.5–0.8m. These stretches of bank ran either inside, or sometimes under the wall, demonstrating that they pre-date it (fig. 39). This means that, at least initially, the high-medieval park boundary consisted of a

24 Brian Hodkinson, pers. comm.   **25** RMP LA013-121.   **26** Coote, *Statistical survey of the Queen's County*, pp 116–17.

bank with either a hedge or palings, although it is possible that a wall was constructed at a later date in the medieval period. The wall was absent, on the western side of the townland, and there a ditch ran parallel to the bank. There is, however, some evidence that a wall was present, or that an attempt to build one may have been abandoned as the bank is extremely stony in this area. Overall it is likely that the original high-medieval boundary of the park consisted of the bank, topped by palings or a tightly grown hedge.

From the castle, access to the park was possible via the postern gate on the south-western side of the rock. There would also have had to be a second gate into the park from the outside, to allow access for heavy carts. Regardless of whether the park was used for deer or for pasture of domestic animals, deliveries of hay and browse would have been needed in the winter months and it would have been necessary to remove cut timber and underwood for use elsewhere. Based on the lie of the land it is most likely that this gate was on the northern side.

A series of earthworks are located inside the park,[27] and conventional wisdom over the last 180 years has interpreted these as the remains of a medieval village, with some writers suggesting that this was the site of the New Town of Leys.[28] The previous surveys have interpreted these as an essentially rectangular main enclosure with rectangular features extending from this and aligned along a north–south hollow-way. However, a total station survey shows that the earth-works are more likely to date to the early medieval period (fig. 40). The form of the main enclosure in the south-eastern quadrant was previously identified as essentially rectangular, but this more detailed survey has demonstrated that it is in fact circular, with rectangular features abutting it. Coupled with the evidence for an external ditch to the south and south-west of this circular enclosure, this suggests that it is a ringfort, and so calls into question the dating of this monument to the high-medieval period. Ringforts with upstanding associated field systems are not common, and certainly fieldwork was in its infancy when this monument was originally surveyed for the first-edition OS map. Over the past decade, a number of early medieval settlements with associated field systems have been excavated, sometimes with fields extending in rectangular patterns from a central, circular enclosure.[29] It is therefore most likely that the earthworks at Dunamase represent early medieval habitation that was either already deserted or was vacated as a result of the construction of the park.

What had been interpreted as a later-medieval hollow-way running north–south through the site may have been constructed at an early date, but this is still

27 RMP LA013-051.   28 Bradley, 'Urban archaeological survey, pt vi: County Laois' (1986), p. 34; Bradley, 'Early urban development in County Laois' (1999), pp 262–3; O'Conor, 'The Anglo-Norman period in County Laois' (1986), pp 240–3.   29 For example, Wallace, 'Excavation of an early medieval

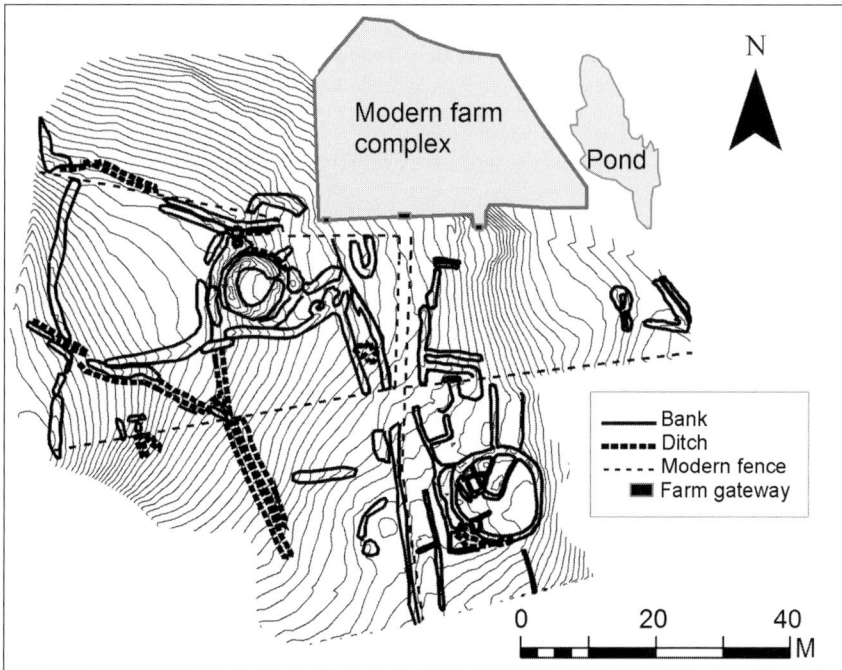

40 Topographical survey of earthworks at Dunamase (RMP LA013-051).

in use to access the central gateway into the modern farm complex and seems to have been in use as an access to the westernmost gateway, so that it may have continued in use or may have been a later feature. The circular feature known as Sally's Bower in the north-western quadrant of the site has been interpreted both as a ringfort and as a late eighteenth-century tree ring, with Bradley supporting the latter, and suggesting a construction date of *c*.1795, when landscaping works were carried out by Sir John Parnell.[30] It is bounded by a bank and external ditch and has an apparent entrance on the east side, as well as a suitable diameter and location for a ringfort. However, while the remainder of the site is made up of relatively low-level earthworks, the bank of Sally's Bower is much more substantial with a clear ditch feature surrounding it. One interpretation of this is that this is a more recent construction. It is likely that the better levels of preservation suggested this interpretation to Bradley, especially as the remaining earthworks were deemed to be later-medieval and hence post-date a ringfort. However, close examination of the previously unrecorded banks in the vicinity of Sally's Bower shows that these features respect the monument, suggesting that

cemetary at Ratoath, Co. Meath' (2010), passim.   **30** Bradley, 'Urban archaeological survey: Laois', p. 34.

they either post-date it or were part of the field systems associated with this feature. With the exception of the northern boundary banks, these banks do not appear on any of the OS maps, and were therefore obsolete by the 1830s. If Sally's Bower were constructed *c.*1795 this would provide only a small window of time for the banks to be constructed, used and fall out of use sufficiently that they were not recorded by the Ordnance Survey in the 1830s. It is therefore most likely that Sally's Bower is a genuine ringfort that has been preserved to a greater extent than the surrounding monuments by virtue of being surrounded by trees. A series of ditches in the south-west of the site are present on the first-edition OS map, but disappear from maps thereafter, so that these could date to any time prior to the 1830s but were likely to be in use at this time.

This series of earthworks was classified as a 'deserted medieval village' at the time of the survey carried out for the first-edition OS map, and this inter-pretation has not been thoroughly questioned since. Only excavation is likely to be able to conclusively prove the age and function of the earthworks described. Meanwhile, the interpretation of the site as a later-medieval deserted village becomes increasingly tenuous given the circular form of the main enclosure and its location inside the high-medieval demesne park. By definition, parks were enclosed spaces to which access was restricted and they would not have been constructed to surround a village that continued in use. It is more likely that this was an early medieval settlement and it is possible that use of the site continued into the later-medieval period, for a non-domestic purpose. Given its location inside the bounds of the park, and immediately adjacent to the pond – which is the only water source in the area – one possibility is that it functioned as the site of the parker's lodge. In England, especially in the twelfth and thirteenth centuries, lodges were usually functional rather than elite structures, often constructed at moated sites.[31] Being a high crag, the Rock of Dunamase is relatively inaccessible so that it would have been essential to have storage facilities that were more easily accessed by ox carts or on foot, making this the perfect location for the administrative centre of the park.

Carrick, Co. Wexford

At Carrick, the 308-acre park was laid out on a promontory that extends northwards into the estuary of the River Slaney. The majority of the park is within the modern townland of Park, but it also extends southwards into the townland of Ballyboggan, up an east–west ridge. As well as the Slaney to the north, the western boundary is demarcated by the Carrick River, and part of the southern and eastern boundaries by an unnamed stream, which greatly

---

31 Moorhouse, 'The medieval parks of Yorkshire: function, contents and chronology', pp 107, 115–17.

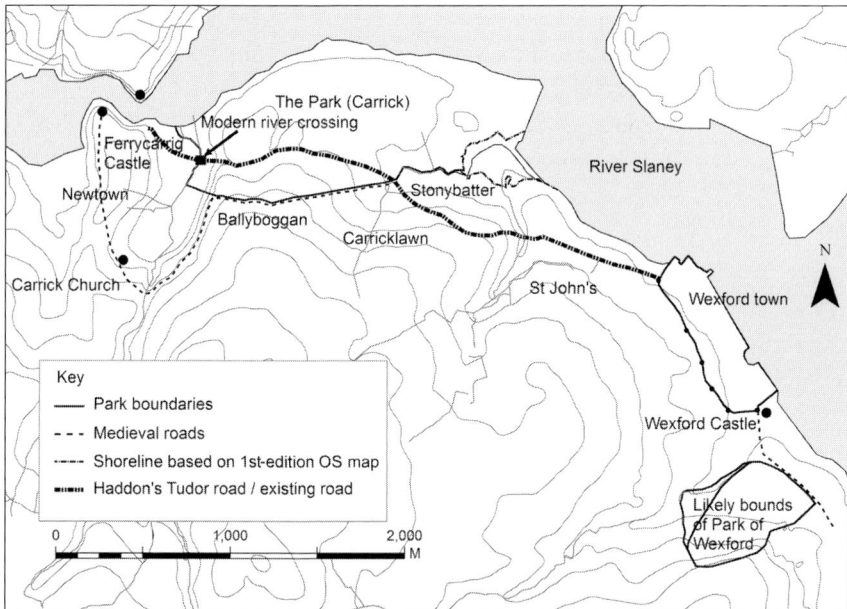

41 Key features of the park at Carrick, Co. Wexford.

minimised the work needed to construct the park. The remainder of the probable southern limit of the park survives as a set of curving field boundaries and an associated ditch up to 1.8m deep and 3m wide, with a relict road following this line, which can be followed for over a kilometre. It ran through the townland of Ballyboggan, close to a break of slope on the east–west ridge at a distance of up to *c*.300m south of the current townland boundary and road separating Park from Ballyboggan (fig. 41). Today the cartographic evidence clearly demonstrates a constructed southern boundary of the park and is more convincing than the physical remains at the site. The boundary is ephemeral and has been partially disrupted by the construction of a series of substantial eighteenth- and nineteenth-century suburban houses at the eastern end, and by a now-abandoned modern housing development at the western end. While the remaining section of the ditch is relatively deep and steep, it is not immediately obvious that it is of archaeological significance (fig. 42).

The park seems to have had only a relatively short lifespan in its primary function: it is mentioned in 1231x4 but not in inquisitions taken in 1307 and 1323–4,[32] and if the park fell out of its primary use then the pale would soon have become obsolete. It is likely that an outer, southern bank would have

---

32 *CERM*, 56; *IEMI*, nos 156, 228.

42 The boundary ditch of the park at Carrick is not particularly substantial.

formed the main barrier to retain the deer, probably with wooden palings, or possibly a tightly maintained hedge. At the Carrick River, it is likely that the river itself, in conjunction with substantial reed beds, would have been sufficient to retain the deer (fig. 43). At the eastern end, there is some aerial photographic

43 View south (upstream) from the modern bridge over the Carrick River, showing the treacherous nature of the reedbeds forming the park boundary.

evidence to suggest that prior to recent disruption there was a bank external to the unnamed stream that formed the boundary at this point.

Ferrycarrig Castle is situated on the south bank of the River Slaney in Newtown townland and should not be confused with the townland of Ferrycarrig, and the associated late-medieval tower house that lie directly opposite the ringwork on the northern bank of the Slaney. The initial construction was a ringwork, which was later rebuilt with stone.[33] The park lay immediately adjacent to the castle and so may not have had a lodge within it, instead being administered from the castle itself. If, however, a lodge was required, then the site of Slaneyhill House, a Georgian residence that is adjacent to the extant remains of the boundary, is the most likely location since it is at the highest point and commands good views over the park lands to the north.

In order to access the park from the Anglo-Norman ringwork and subsequent stone castle at Ferrycarrig, it would have been necessary to cross the Carrick River. At the probable river crossing point to the south of the park, a wooden or

33 *CDI*, i, no. 1872; Bennett, 'Preliminary archaeological excavations at Ferrycarrig ringwork, Newtown td, Co. Wexford', 25–43, passim.

stone bridge could easily have spanned the river (fig. 41). The modern crossing point, to the north-east of Carrick Church, is more direct but is much wider and is flanked by reed beds, and so would have presented a treacherous prospect. It is possible that there was a ford or a causeway there for use on foot and horseback, but heavy carts – for example to transport timber – would have been more likely to circumvent the reed beds and access the park using the relict road, so that it is likely that there was a gate into the park at the south-western corner.

It is also likely that there was a gate on the Wexford side of the park, since the two manors were so closely linked, both physically and as part of a single lordship. This would probably have been sited at the modern townland boundary intersection of Park, Ballyboggan, Stonybatter and Carricklawn, where the modern road crosses an unnamed stream and enters the park. While the evidence from the field boundaries suggests that the present road through the park is a later feature, believed by Haddon to be of Tudor origin,[34] it is quite likely that a path or track wound through this east–west valley bottom essentially following the same line, providing access to the park from Wexford and easy removal of timber to Wexford.

Nenagh, Co. Tipperary

The park at Nenagh probably had an area of *c.*130 statute acres and enclosed the highest point around Nenagh, which is now occupied by a water reservoir. To the east the land slopes gently down to the Nenagh River, which forms the eastern boundary of the park, while to the west it slopes down to the castle and town (fig. 44). The park is bounded on the west by existing roads, on the north-west by a relict road that was already redundant by the time of the first-edition OS map, and by a series of property boundaries that were present at the time of this map, but some of which have subsequently been removed. On the north side, it was bounded by Birr Road/Bulfin Road, and on the east by the Nenagh River (fig. 45). On the southern side of the park there are two main possibilities that need to be considered. One is that the park was bounded for its entire length by the current line of the Dublin Road/Thomas MacDonagh Street, passing through an archway at Ayres in Castle Street/Pearse Street and abutting Nenagh Castle.[35] In this case it is likely that the millstream running alongside the road for part of its length originated as a park boundary and was re-used for the corn mill shown on the first-edition OS map. Another, more likely option is that the park continued to the south of the current road, being bounded by the Nenagh River, which turns to come from the east. This would be logical for a number of

---

34 Hadden, 'The origin and development of Wexford town, pt 3: the Norman period' (1969), 3–12, map.
35 RMP TN020-037001.

44 Nenagh Castle and the remains of the main gatehouse.

reasons. Firstly, more of the boundary of the park would be defined by natural waterways, so reducing the cost and complexity of construction. Secondly, the line of the river and the ditch feeding into it from the west form part of the townland boundary of Nenagh North, and the river section also forms the barony and parish boundary. From there, the boundary could have extended due westwards, rejoining the Dublin Road/Thomas MacDonagh Street at a point where the first-edition OS map shows a kink in the line of the road at the 'Spout' well.

Due to post-medieval and modern development in Nenagh and its suburbs, it is difficult to determine what form of boundary was originally constructed around the park. The banks of the Nenagh River have been heavily modified in the last two hundred years, so that any features there have been destroyed. In addition to modern sections of stone wall that front twentieth-century housing estates, there are stretches of older mortared stone wall that run along the northern boundary and along the Dublin Road/Thomas MacDonagh Street. It is possible that some of these were originally later medieval, suggesting a walled park. It is most likely, however, that these are post-medieval, originating in the eighteenth century, when these lands were developed as part of the demesnes of

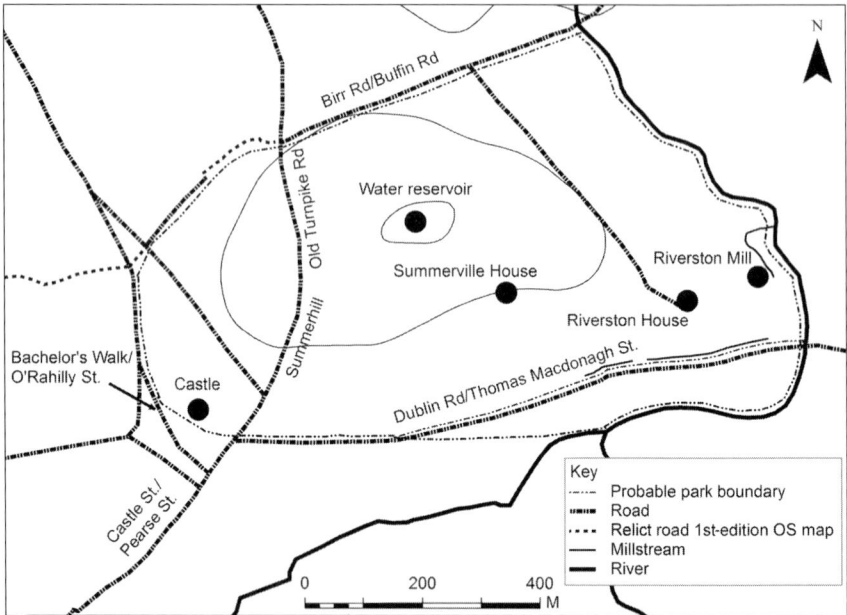

45 Key features of the park of Nenagh, Co. Tipperary.

Riverston House and Summerville House. The wall on the north side of the park is in the poorest condition, and so is likely to have had the least interference in its structure. There was evidence of a low bank underlying it and of occasional bricks close to the base (fig. 46). This suggests that the original boundary was a bank and palings, with a wall of stone and brick constructed in the post-medieval period.

The main access to the park was probably directly from the sallyport of Nenagh Castle, or there may have been a gate to access the park close to this. It is possible that a second entrance was located either close to Kyleeragh Bridge on the Birr Road/Bulfin Road or along the Dublin Road/Thomas MacDonagh Street to facilitate movement of materials into and out of the park, but no trace of any features remains. Since it abutted the castle, no administrative park lodge would have been needed, but if the Butlers wanted a viewing platform or a lodge for entertaining then the obvious site for this would be at the high point in the park, under the current water reservoir tower.

Glencree, Co. Wicklow

Westropp identified a curving ditch in the townland of Curtlestown Lower, Co. Wicklow, which he believed was part of the boundary of the park at

46 Bricks visible in the base of the boundary wall at Nenagh demonstrate that it is likely to be of post-medieval origin.

Glencree,[36] and which has subsequently been recorded as such.[37] Fieldwork shows that beyond the present recorded monument this ditch can be connected to a series of other extant and relict ditches, banks and roads/tracks to form an egg-shaped enclosure (fig. 47). This is approximately one hundred acres, and is situated within the bowl of a valley, encompassing parts of the townlands of Curtlestown Lower, Curtlestown Upper and Barnamire. On both the northern and the southern sides, the enclosure traverses steep ground, so that the outside is higher than the inside. On the western side the enclosure runs up to the pass at Barnamire between the base of the hill of Raven's Rock/Prince William's Seat to the north and the hill of Knockree to the south. Accordingly, it is only on the eastern side that the boundary traverses the valley so that the ground outside the enclosure is slightly lower than that within. This Curtlestown valley is good-quality grazing land and the enclosure is visible on aerial photographs as a notably green area, whereas the land beyond the pass, in the Glencree valley proper, is much wilder, rougher ground. Around the Curtlestown and Glencree valleys are steep hills that feature poor-quality land now given over mainly to plantations of forestry, with open ground on the higher hilltops.

36 Westropp, 'Earthwork near Curtlestown, Co. Wicklow', 185–6. **37** RMP WI007-008.

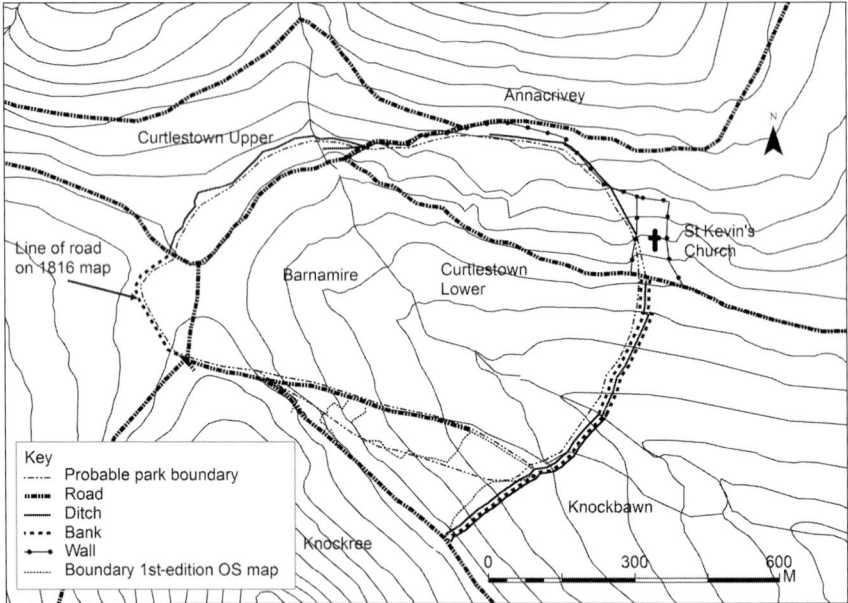

47 Key features of the enclosure at Glencree, Co. Wicklow.

At one hundred acres, this enclosure seems small for a royal park, but it is likely that the park at Glencree functioned only as a store for fallow deer to be provided as live gifts and venison to chosen recipients rather than as a hunting venue. Given the almost complete absence of the king from Ireland and the position of the park within a royal forest where hunting could easily take place in the wider landscape, its size would have been adequate for its purpose.

Place-name evidence is less secure than at the other park sites, but the pass at the west of the enclosure lies within the townland of Barnamire, the 'pass of the steward' or 'keeper' (*maor*),[38] and a lodge positioned there would directly overlook the entire enclosure to the east as well as much of the Glencree valley to the west. As such, a park at this site would have been well protected and ideal for confining valuable stock. The presence of a relict enclosure of a suitable size, and at a suitable site within the Glencree valley, coupled with the associated place-name, is good circumstantial evidence for this being the location of the park, although this cannot be confirmed, and as such it will be referred to as an enclosure rather than the actual site of the park.

The north-western quadrant of the enclosure is defined by a more recent wall that forms an arc, essentially following the line of the earlier monument. A

---

38 Price, *The place-names of Co. Wicklow* (1980), p. 285.

footpath in a steep-sided hollow-way follows the line of this wall north-east forming the western portion of this arc, before meeting a wider track. This wider track is an old roadway that comes from the Glencree valley and along the northern portion of the enclosure, before moving further north, away from the wall and continuing eastwards away from the enclosure. Much of the hollow-way on the western side appears to be part of the enclosure boundary, so that the walker is within the ditch itself, with walls to both sides. Where the ditch/footpath meets the wider track at the north-west, the ditch and the original route of the wider track pass into the area bounded by the more recent wall, but due to the presence of a quarry the land has been stripped of all features in this area and the exact location is not visible. They then run due east, inside the wall, and form the Curtlestown–Annacrivey townland boundary. The ditch is 0.5m deep and is bounded by a low bank with occasional hawthorn bushes on the south side and by a raised bank 4m wide on the northern, outer side, which appears to be the original route of the wider track. They cross back outside the more recent wall at a dogleg in the wall and continue south-east, immediately outside the wall, where the ditch has a depth of *c.*1.5m. The ditch then re-emerges on the south side of the wall and continues south-east, disappearing into the grounds of St Kevin's Catholic church, just to the north of the Enniskerry to Glencree road. This is marked as 'old road' on the Annacrivey section of the 1816 Powerscourt estate map, suggesting that the low bank is the original route of the wider track extending from the north-west of the enclosure.[39]

To the south of the Enniskerry to Glencree road the boundary runs south-west as a substantial ditch with a bank to both sides. This is much larger than surrounding field boundaries and runs down to an unnamed tributary of the River Dargle that flows to the south-east through the enclosure. On the south side of the river, the boundary consists of two deep ditches separated by a substantial bank that is topped by a stone wall, and in this case forms the townland boundary between Barnamire and Knockbawn. This runs uphill to two kinks in the boundary that turn westward to form two possibilities for the southern boundary of the enclosure. The first of these follows a field boundary that is present on both the first-edition OS map and the 1816 map and then an extant track that continues westward to meet the modern road. The second kink has been partially straightened since the first-edition OS map; again the potential boundary follows the line of a field boundary that is present on the 1816 map and partially present on the first-edition OS map, but is absent from later editions and not visible on the ground today, meeting the extant track at a point

39 Armstrong, 'Maps of the estates of the Right Honourable Richard, lord viscount Powerscourt, in the County of Wicklow and Dublin' (1816).

further to the west. From here the boundary crosses the road, becoming a curved, stony bank that makes up the western extent of the enclosure before meeting the east–west Enniskerry to Glencree road. This stony bank follows the line of a road shown on the 1816 map but which was superseded by the present north–south road by the time of the first-edition OS map. On the north side of the Enniskerry to Glencree road the boundary is a ditch running along the back of modern bungalow plots, and then a series of relict ditches/hollow-ways that run to the north-east through forestry plantation and eventually meet up with the ditch/footpath at a junction shown on the first-edition OS map at the start of the circuit.

THE MORPHOLOGY OF PARKS

In surveying the Irish parks, a number of common elements were found and, in many cases, these features are also commonly found in English parks. Documentary sources were important in identifying the general location of parks but they rarely gave much detail on their form. Some records indicated the size of the park, while in other cases a general size could be inferred from the pasturage values. Occasionally, the form of the park boundary was described; however, this was generally the limit of the information that could be gleaned from the primary sources. Physical survey of identifiable examples was therefore crucial in examining the form of the parks, although a survey bias towards the largest, best documented parks was noted since those examples are the most easily found within the landscape and so are more likely to have been surveyed than lesser sites. Small parks, such as the four-acre example at Shankill (Senekyll),[40] are unlikely ever to be located within a manor that in the thirteenth century encompassed modern Shankill, Dalkey, Rathmichael, Powerscourt and Kilmacberne.[41]

The size of the documented Irish parks varied between four medieval acres at Shankill and Baliduwil and 913 statute acres at Earlspark. Within this span, most of the parks were less than one hundred acres, suggesting that they were generally smaller than those in England, where between one hundred and three hundred acres was typical.[42] Size and function are inextricably linked, and the largest examples are those for which there is documentary or zooarchaeological evidence for fallow deer. By contrast, where the functions of smaller parks have been noted in the documentary sources, it is timber and pasturage that are mentioned. This

40 *CAAR*, 195; *CDI*, iii, nos 459, 894.   41 Murphy and Potterton, *The Dublin region in the Middle Ages*, p. 77.   42 Cantor and Hatherly, 'The medieval parks of England', 73–4.

highlights the differences between the small parks belonging to all of the higher social classes and the very large, high-status parks of the magnates.

Following from the size of a park is its shape and the form of its boundary. Of the sites surveyed, Earlspark is approximately square, Maynooth is a rounded rectangle, Dunamase and Nenagh are lobe-shaped, extending out from the castle, Glencree is egg-shaped and Carrick is a promontory defined by a sinuous boundary. All of these were designed to minimise the length of constructed boundaries, with rivers and lakes often being utilised as natural boundaries in an effort to minimise construction costs. In this, the parks are similar to examples from England, where the same types of shapes are common in early parks created in the first wave of park-making. No evidence was found for parks in Ireland being extended or created over a number of phases.

Watts suggests that in England few park banks and ditches survive as most have been ploughed out, mainly surviving as 'slight swellings in the ground or old field boundaries which have adopted the line of the park pale'.[43] The same is again true of the Irish parks. The park at Maynooth survived in its primary usage until *c*.1647 and was still recognised as a landscape entity into the nineteenth century,[44] and yet the south-western boundary consists of a hedge and bank with a large, but not exceptional, internal ditch, and this cannot be directly interpreted as related to a park. This does appear to be the original form of the boundary, since in 1540–1 the park was described as containing wild animals and being enclosed by hedges and ditches.[45] These ephemeral remains are typical of those found at the other surveyed sites, where boundary ditches and banks tended to be slightly sinuous, but the ditches were not excessively deep and no particularly large external banks were identified. If the cartographic and place-name evidence had not led to them, they would not have stood out in the landscape as potential park boundaries. Even where documentary evidence gives the form of the boundary, this is not always sufficient to readily identify the feature in the landscape. For example, at Bray, Co. Wicklow, an extent of the manor in 1311 states that the park is sixty acres and surrounded by a ditch, but this is not sufficiently detailed to track down the feature without more detailed research.[46] The exception to this is at Earlspark, Co. Galway, where a substantial and obvious wall has survived. This is known locally as Nora Novar's wall and is a striking feature, but even this had not previously been archaeologically recorded, despite 2m-high sections passing within *c*.20m of the 'Northern Complex' group of recorded monuments. This all demonstrates the importance of using a multidisciplinary approach to the identification of medieval landscape features.

43 Watts, 'Wiltshire deer parks: an introductory survey', 92. **44** Fitzgerald, 'Maynooth Castle' (1895), 223–39; *Leinster deeds*, p. 47. **45** *CSL*, pp 132–3. **46** *RBO*, no. 10 (trans. present author).

Although Watts noted that in England, many park boundaries did not survive, some did. At Tarrant Rushton in Dorset, much of the boundary exists as a bank 5m wide and 0.6–1.2m in height above a shallow ditch, while at Rye Hill in the same county there are banks up to 6m wide and 1.2m high.[47] The lack of evidence for substantial surviving banks, and the modest size of the surviving ditches in Ireland are in contrast to this, especially considering that the parks surveyed were among those of the highest status. Nevertheless, as Maynooth demonstrates, the boundaries were sufficient to prevent animals escaping. Form and function are inextricably linked and so another significant factor is the function of parks in Ireland compared to England. The Irish parks have a greater emphasis on cattle pasture and less emphasis on herds of fallow deer. Cattle are much easier to retain than deer and a well-maintained, tightly laid hedge is adequate since, unlike deer, cattle cannot jump over substantial fences or hedges. Furthermore, in England, royal forests were extensive so that many parks were close to areas of royal forest. If deer escaped from parks it would have been difficult for the owners to reclaim these as the foresters would have claimed them for the king. By contrast, in Ireland many of the high-status parks were in liberties, and as such the owner would have had rights over deer both inside and outside his parks. An escape was therefore of less significance since his parkers could round up the animals and return them to the park without any danger of them being claimed by the king or another lord. It is therefore probable that Irish parks commonly used hedges rather than palings for their boundaries. Although still requiring maintenance, these would have been cost-effective compared to palings since the raw material is produced *in situ* and does not need to be harvested, prepared and then fixed in place, and once it is laid a hedge can last up to fifty years as a stock-proof barrier (fig. 48).[48] Unlike palings, stone walls had the advantage that they did not rot; they were also less easily breached by poachers than palings or hedges and could be visually impressive. The major disadvantage of these was the cost of construction, especially in areas where stone had to be imported to the site, and this is probably the reason why the only known high-medieval stone-walled park is at Earlspark, which is situated firmly in 'stone wall country'.

In common with parks in England, many of the surveyed examples were situated on the parish, barony and even county boundary, but in the case of Earlspark this park spanned portions of two parishes. In all the parks, relict or existing roads and tracks defined parts of the boundaries, although the function of the roads themselves was to allow traffic to bypass the park rather than to

---

47 Cantor and Wilson, 'The medieval deer-parks of Dorset: viii' (1968), 242–6. **48** Durham Hedgerow Partnership, *Hedge laying and coppicing: field boundaries technical advice sheet 1* (n.d.), p. 6.

48 A laid hedge provides a formidable barrier for stock. © Can Stock Photo Inc./Garya.

demarcate it per se. These were particularly important in the cases of Carrick and Nenagh, where they provided the main evidence for the park boundaries. Watery boundaries were useful from a practical perspective, limiting necessary construction, providing strips of meadow grazing such as at Maynooth and Nenagh and providing raw materials such as reeds at Carrick and Earlspark. As we will see in the next chapter, they were often also aesthetically pleasing.

The lie of the land was important in defining the shape of the parks. Where they were situated in generally flat or only slightly sloping countryside they had been designed to incorporate a hill as, for example, at both Nenagh and Maynooth. In the case of Carrick, the park was on a sloping hillside, while at Glencree the bowl of a valley had been used and at both Earlspark and Dunamase the land was undulating. At Maynooth, Earlspark and Dunamase, archaeological features were found at the top of the slope or hill, suggesting that these were potential lodge sites, while at Nenagh and Carrick more recent buildings obscured these locations so that it is possible that lodges were also positioned there. At Earlspark, Glencree and Carrick the park is very clearly designed to maximise the proportion of the boundary where there is higher ground outside than inside, so minimising the risk of stock escaping. However, this was less feasible at Maynooth, Dunamase and Nenagh, as they were surrounded by flat land.

The shape of the parks and their location was, to a certain extent, likely to be influenced by the earlier land-use. Early medieval Ireland was less dependent on arable agriculture than England, with more emphasis on a pastoral economy. However, the landscape would still have been a patchwork of arable land, pasture and woodland.[49] There were a number of forms of land tenure in early medieval Ireland.[50] Individual landowners could hold both personal land, over which they had a considerable degree of control, and kin-land, which could not usually be sold without the agreement of the group, and which was subject to periodic redistribution. In addition to his personal and kin lands, a king had lands associated with his office and some officials in the king's household had entitlements to mensal lands or *lucht tighe* from the king. The incoming Anglo-Normans are unlikely to have discontinued the use of existing arable land, as preparing and ploughing new fields would have been time-consuming and difficult. Instead, existing areas of arable probably continued in use, while any new areas of arable would have been created from the unenclosed pasture and woodland available. Since the practical functions of the park required grazing and woodland, this suggests that it was predominantly unenclosed areas that would have been targeted as sites for parks and, as Chapter 6 will demonstrate, the symbolic associations of these locations could also be important in choosing the site of the park.

The quality of the land in which the parks were located was notably good. In the cases of Maynooth, Dunamase and Carrick, part of the land is currently used for arable agriculture. Any land capable of being used for arable agriculture in today's global economy would have been considered to be of excellent quality in the medieval period. Furthermore, while at Earlspark and Nenagh the land is now used for good-quality grazing, it has been used for arable in the past.[51] This evidence contradicts that from England where marginal land was often selected for emparkment. In the case of the Irish parks that could be identified on the ground, these were being created by the top tier of society. Although they seem to have been enclosed and stocked with deer at a later date, it is likely that when the manors were originally laid out in the late twelfth and early thirteenth century, the areas for later emparkment were designated and set aside. As a result, the parks were positioned in carefully selected locations, incorporating good-quality land. By contrast, in England many of the recorded parks were owned by the gentry and minor aristocracy who constructed their parks in a second wave of park formation in the fourteenth century, when the means to do so moved down

49 *Topographia*, 34–5; Ó Corráin, 'Ireland, c.800: aspects of society' (2005), pp 555–6; Edwards, 'The archaeology of early medieval Ireland, c.400–1169: settlement and economy' (2005), pp 264–9. **50** Kelly, *Early Irish farming: a study based mainly on the law-texts of the 7th and 8th centuries AD*, pp 398–408; FitzPatrick, *Royal inauguration in Gaelic Ireland*, pp 196–8. **51** Claire Smyth, pers. comm.; Gleeson, 'The castle and manor of Nenagh', 250; Gwynn and Gleeson, *A history of the diocese of Killaloe*, p. 288.

the social scale.[52] These individuals would have used otherwise uneconomic, marginal land for their parks, which had to be shoehorned into existing manors. Since they were less economically confident than the great lords, they would have been unable to justify taking some of their best land out of production for the purpose of conspicuous consumption.

CONCLUSION

The size of a park, its shape and the form of its boundary were dependent on a number of factors including its function, its location in the landscape and the status of the owner. The incorporation of pre-existing landscapes and monuments within park boundaries is an important aspect that has been touched upon in the case studies in this chapter. These form a key part of the discussion within Chapter 6, where the symbolic significance of park location within the landscape is examined in more detail.

---

52 Crouch, *The image of aristocracy in Britain, 1000–1300* (1992), pp 112, 309.

CHAPTER SIX

Parks as symbolic landscapes

When a park was developed a number of factors would have been important in its design, including the form of the boundary, any internal features such as divisions within the park, the location and form of any lodges, kennels, barns, hay sheds and water sources. The inclusion of these and their form and location would all have depended on the use to which the park was to be put. Other aspects of the park were also significant, including the landscape setting and its suitability for the activities taking place, the convenience of the location in relation to nearby castles or settlements, any existing symbolic associations of the location and the demonstration of status, power and identity. The practical aspects of form and function have been examined in the preceding chapters; however, these interact with the symbolic and less tangible factors. Although these can conveniently be listed, in reality the interaction between them and their relative importance would have varied between parks, and cannot be discussed in isolation. They would have been complex and indivisible, and to the park owners some of the factors may not even have been consciously perceived, instead being cultural 'givens' that were not vocalised or defined.

BOUNDING THE PARK

The three main functions of Irish parks were as a source of timber and wood, for pasturing domestic animals and for keeping deer. All of these relied on the presence and design of the park boundary to prevent unauthorised access and egress. At Earlspark, Co. Galway, for example, there is documentary evidence that deer were kept in the park. This park therefore needed a high wall around it, which survives to a height of 2.6m in places, whereas if only cattle or timber were enclosed then a lower, less expensive, construction may have been sufficient as both a practical and a symbolic barrier to movement.

The views from within parks and the views of parks from external viewpoints were both important considerations in the layout of the manor. Externally, parks could be seen by tenants and travellers or by the lords from their associated castles. From a distance, the boundaries of a park would have remained visible, but depending on the topography and the vantage point, it would also have been

49 The Rock of Dunamase from the park boundary.

possible to see into the park. This would have allowed the viewer a glimpse of the 'paradise' within the park, but would also have maintained some element of privacy for the activities taking place. These glimpses would have been most effective where the park was at a height, such as at Nenagh, or in rolling country-side such as at Dunamase, where the approaches to the castle were carefully manipulated to maximise the fortress-like, impregnable impression of the castle on the rock.

The visual impact of a boundary would have been heightened during the high-medieval period, when it would have consisted of freshly quarried lime-stone, or freshly chopped wooden pales or a substantial hedge, especially as many of the parks are likely to have been surrounded by open field systems or open pasture. From the perspective of the outsider walking along immediately outside, the lack of a view into a park would have been significant. In both the later-medieval period and the nineteenth century, elite landscapes such as parks, and imposing stone buildings such as castles and mansions, served to deter would-be rebels by demonstrating the otherwise unimaginable power of the elite,[1]

1 Orser, 'Symbolic violence, resistance and the vectors of improvement in early nineteeth-century Ireland' (2005), 392–407; O'Conor, 'Castle studies in Ireland: the way forward', 335; O'Keeffe, 'Concepts of "castle" and the construction of identity in medieval and post-medieval Ireland', 69–88; O'Keeffe, 'Were

providing 'physical reinforcement of the societal power structure'.[2] In addition to the park itself, the walls, hedges and palings surrounding both high-medieval and post-medieval parks would have added to this feeling of inferiority by towering over the observer, and restricting vision and movement, but simultaneously providing occasional glimpses of the features within.

At Dunamase, visitors to the area would have passed alongside the emparked boundary when travelling from the west, from Borris, near modern Portlaoise, or from the south-west, from Abbeyleix, via Dysart to the Rock of Dunamase. As a result, the high boundary would have defined the route of a portion of their journey. Depending on its actual height, the castle would have been visible over the hedge or palings, providing a tantalising view of this most dramatic of fortresses. Coming from the north-west, the same would have been true travelling along the northern boundary of the emparked area. Visitors arriving from Stradbally and Grange in the east, or from further afield such as Carlow, Athy or Kilkenny, would not have seen the park; instead, their first close-up view of the castle would have been aligned directly with the main gatehouse, with the castle suddenly rising up, facing the traveller. By contrast, those coming from the medieval church at Kilteale, to the north-east, would have had their view dominated by the rock and the castle for most of the journey Thus, approaching the rock from all sides, the visitor would be struck by its domination of the landscape, and the park would reinforce this by fringing the base of the rock and providing a backdrop for the dramatic castle (fig. 49). The later-medieval peasant would have had little doubt about his place in society as he walked around, rather than through, the emparked demesne of his lord. On arrival at the park boundary, even visiting aristocrats, be they Anglo-Norman or Irish, would have had cause to reflect on their own status and economic and military resources relative to that of the owner.

In addition to the pedagogical role, high boundaries can be used to prevent people seeing activities taking place within them. The enclosed area of a park therefore provided privacy for those on the inside, allowing them to carry out activities without being observed. At Maynooth, there is a definite feeling of privacy and seclusion within the park, although from the top of Crewhill there is a partial view of the town and castle. Today, however, trees and the Georgian Crewhill House obscure much of this view, while from elsewhere the town is invisible, with only the tallest structure, the nineteenth-century spire of St Patrick's Church, being visible from many places in the park (fig. 50). As a result, the park would have been almost completely secluded in the high-medieval

there designed landscapes in medieval Ireland?', 52–68. **2** Orser, 'Symbolic violence and landscape pedagogy: an illustration from the Irish countryside' (2006), 28.

50 A secluded spot within the park at Maynooth. The spire of the nineteenth-century St Patrick's Church is the only evidence of the nearby town.

period. This was partly due to the local topography and partly that there may have been more trees and undergrowth within the park at that time, and the surrounding hedges would have been impenetrable masses of vegetation.

While high walls, palings and hedges restricted the view of any observer passing close to the boundary, this was not true when the park was viewed from a distance, either from the castle or from outside. In recent times there has been a developing interest in examining how landscapes, parks and gardens could be viewed from castles.[3] At Earlspark, Dunamase, Nenagh and Carrick, the park is clearly visible from the associated castle, and abuts it in the case of Dunamase and Nenagh. At Maynooth, heavy tree-cover and large buildings currently exist between the castle and the park, and restrict the view, but if these were absent then the park would be visible, especially from the upper storeys of the castle, which are currently inaccessible. Furthermore, there is a north-facing balcony on

3 For example, Creighton, 'Room with a view: framing castle landscapes', 37–49; McNeill, 'The view from the top', 122–7; Creighton, 'Castle studies and archaeology in England: towards a research framework for the future' (2008), 86.

51 Maynooth Castle from the north, showing the balcony facing the park.

the first floor of the main keep, and although relatively low in the building, if the intervening trees and modern buildings were removed then this would look out across the river in the direction of the medieval park, providing an attractive vista and taking in the location of the manorial mills (fig. 51).[4] Thus, despite lying up to 2km from their associated castles, the parks were certainly designed to be viewed from them.

At Dunamase and at Nenagh the parks abutted the castles and funnelled out from them. At Nenagh, third-floor windows faced east and north over the park, with the east window of the upper floor providing the best vantage point. However, none of these windows were directly aligned with the park, which lies to the north-east so that the best view is gained by looking out at an angle. In this particular case, it is known that the park was not created until 1299, while the castle was certainly constructed prior to 1220.[5] It is therefore likely that there had not been an initial plan to construct a park, or that the original plan was for it to be located elsewhere within the manor and so the windows had not been constructed to take the view of the park into account. By contrast, at Dunamase windows at the western end of the two-storey solar block would have provided views across the park, giving what, even today, is a spectacular vista (fig. 52). There is also a tower at the western extent of the upper ward which has a very small internal area of $c.2m^2–3m^2$, and it is possible that this tower served primarily as a viewing platform for the park,[6] in addition to being strategically placed to provide a militarily significant observation point for the wider landscape. The townland is exceptionally picturesque: the rock and the two adjacent outcrops form a central ridge for the park and the land drops down on all sides from these high points. Furthermore, since the park abuts the western side of the rock it would have been very convenient to visit and would have provided a scenic venue for elite activities.

There has also been considerable academic study on the role of water as a vehicle for showing off the design of architectural and landscape features.[7] This control over the view can apply both to viewers from castles and to those from outside looking in. The classic, oft-quoted example is Bodiam Castle in England, where the routeway to the castle was carefully designed and manipulated to lead the visitor past ornamental fish ponds and terraces and where the view of the castle is gradually revealed until it appears to float above a lake.[8] The reflections of

4 O'Keeffe, 'Trim's first cousin: the twelfth-century *donjon* of Maynooth Castle' (2013), 30–1. 5 *CJRI*, i, p. 234; Gleeson, 'The castle and manor of Nenagh', 248; Gwynn and Gleeson, *A history of the diocese of Killaloe*, p. 178; Hodkinson, 'Excavations in the gatehouse of Nenagh Castle, 1996 and 1997' (1999), 178; McNeill, *Castles in Ireland*, pp 50, 52. 6 Kieran O'Conor, pers. comm. 7 For example, Johnson, *Behind the castle gate: from medieval to Renaissance* (2002), pp 19–54; Liddiard, *Castles in context: power, symbolism and landscape*, pp 7–11. 8 Taylor et al., 'Bodiam Castle, Sussex' (1990), 155–7; Everson, 'Bodiam Castle,

52 View from the solar at Dunamase, extending west across the park.

the castle in the water make it look larger, and by appearing to float in this way, it can appear almost magical, calling Arthurian images to mind.[9]

At both Carrick, Co. Wexford, and at Loughrea, Co. Galway, a large body of water lay between the castle and the park, so that the park would have seemed inaccessible and very private, a peaceful location away from the hustle and bustle of everyday life. The castle at Loughrea was probably located in the south-west of the town, close to the northern shore of the lake,[10] and Earlspark, lying directly across the lake, can be seen clearly from the town and from the probable castle site. Even standing at ground level, Earlspark is clearly visible from the shore adjacent to this area, so that assuming that the main buildings within the castle would have had at least two storeys, the view of Earlspark from the upper rooms of the castle would have been even clearer. This visibility would have been enhanced if the land surrounding the park was unenclosed pasture or open-field arable, since the stone wall boundary would then have been even more noticeable

East Sussex: a fourteenth-century designed landscape' (1996), passim. **9** Ashe, *Mythology of the British Isles* (1990), p. 218. **10** Spellissy, *The history of Galway* (1999), p. 401; McKeon, 'Anglo-Norman frontier urban settlement in the Plantaganet realm' (2008), pp 60–4.

53 The town of Loughrea from the Northern Complex.

from a distance. The park has high ground on three sides, which slopes down to flat land adjacent to the lake, so that from a vantage point in the town the park appears to have been spread out and displayed on the hillside. Similarly, from high points in the park, the castle and town would have been laid out for the viewer to see, providing the earls of Ulster and their guests with an appearance of the castle and town rising up from the waters of the lake (fig. 53). By contrast with Earlspark, much of the land around Loughrea is relatively flat, with the Slieve Aughty Mountains 11km south of the town, the hill of Knockroe 5km south of the town and the hill at Knockbaron 5km to the east. Earlspark, only 2km from Loughrea, is therefore the most conveniently accessible of the hills around and can be reached on foot or by rowing boat in twenty-five minutes. Hence, unlike the other nearby hills, Earlspark was perfectly located to provide a visual statement to any visitor to the town or castle.

Similarly, at Carrick, Co. Wexford, the park can be clearly seen across the water from Ferrycarrig Castle (fig. 54), as well as from the River Slaney itself and from the northern shore of the river. The ringwork on its dramatic outcrop can also be seen across the water from the park, highlighted between the river and the sky (fig. 10). Any travellers moving up or down the Slaney between Wexford and Carrick would have had to pass the park, and portions of it are also visible from

54 The park at Carrick, viewed from Ferrycarrig ringwork. The line of the park boundary has been highlighted and arrowed.

Wexford town. Anyone travelling between Wexford and Carrick by land would have had to pass through the park, if they were permitted to do so, or skirt it using the relict road on the southern boundary, in which case the view north-wards would be dominated by the park pale. The park was therefore sited for maximum impact, placed as it was between two functioning Marshal castles in adjacent manors.

THE PARK WITHIN THE MANORIAL LANDSCAPE

Researchers place varying degrees of emphasis on the practical and aesthetic aspects of parks, though, by contrast with earlier writers, more recent studies have seen the entire landscape around many castles as being at least partially designed to enhance the aesthetic appeal of the area.[11] To modern eyes, this concept can easily be applied to features such as parks and fishponds, but Liddiard extends it to the placement of apparently mundane features such as settlements and mills, noting the importance of 'landscapes of production' in demonstrating the social status of the lord.[12] Close to the castle there would have been an inner core consisting of gardens, orchards and small ponds, with more extensive areas beyond, in which parks, mills, settlements and warrens were located. These economic activities were particularly important in creating and maintaining an elite lifestyle and in displaying aristocratic control over resources, highlighting the way in which the overall layout of the manor was also a demonstration of the power of the lord, and could be used to showcase the status and wealth of its owner.

By displaying the agricultural, industrial and aesthetic resources in his possession, a lord was making a powerful statement about his membership of an

---

11 Creighton, *Designs upon the land: elite landscapes of the Middle Ages*, pp 75–84, 218–24; Creighton, 'Room with a view: framing castle landscapes', 37–49.   12 Liddiard, *Castles in context: power symbolism*

55 An idealised manorial landscape, in which each member of society has his/her allotted role to perform, from *Les très riches heures du duc de Berry*. © RMN-Grand Palais (Domaine de Chantilly)/René-Gabriel Ojéda, MS 65, fo. 3v.

elite group. Giraldus Cambrensis made this point clearly when he described Manorbier Castle in Wales, commenting on the presence of mills, fishponds, orchards and vineyards and concluding that 'it is evident, therefore, that Maenor Pirr is the pleasantest spot in Wales'.[13] This is further exemplified by the idealised images in later-medieval books of hours such as *Les très riches heures du duc de Berry*, which stressed the 'natural order' of society (fig. 55). Medieval European society was often conceived of as being divided into three interlinked and interdependent orders: those who work; those who pray and those who fight –

and landscape, pp 100–4.   **13** *Itinerary through Wales*, p. 85.

that is, the peasants, the Church and the lordly class respectively. This model was first developed by Bishop Adalbero of Laon in the early eleventh century, and while other models using two or four orders also existed, they all served to place and to keep individuals firmly within their own particular order.[14] If the human, agricultural and industrial resources of the manor were ordered and successful, then this reflected well on the lord.

The Park of Maynooth lies just 450m to the north-east of the castle, so that it is only a few minutes' walk away. In addition to this park, a 'Little Park' is referred to in 1652,[15] and although it is unclear whether this was a high-medieval or later creation, based on the knowledge that many 'Little Parks' were extensive areas of garden adjacent to the castle or manor,[16] it can be suggested that it was located immediately to the west of the castle, in the area now occupied by the gardens of St Patrick's College. In terms of an arrangement of space within the manor, an area in an arc from the south-west round to the north-east was dominated by the castle and its demesne, which included mills, haggards, gardens and parks, while the eastern side was given over to the streets and houses of the town, and beyond this to the agricultural fields of the tenants. The two halves were effectively separated by the eastern portion of the Lyreen River and a tributary that comes from the south and joins this river immediately to the east of the castle. This would have showcased the manorial landscape for any visitors to the town or for those passing through Maynooth as they headed westwards, away from Dublin. From the west-bound Kilcock road, the traveller would have been surrounded by the demesne lands, with the park to the north. Furthermore, viewed from the castle roof, the viewer could choose to see the lordly demesne, or, by looking in the opposite direction, could see the lands of the tenants. Thus, the castle at Maynooth and its setting within the agricultural and seigniorial landscape emphasised the power and success of the FitzGeralds. It positioned them at the top of an ordered and successful scheme, demonstrating their ability to control the environment and the people around them.[17]

The manors of Carrick and Wexford were immediately adjacent to each other, with the castles *c*.6km apart as the crow flies. The park at Carrick was equally well situated for access from either castle, being sited to the north-west of Wexford, on a direct route between the two. Both were seigniorial castles of the earl marshal, lord of Leinster and his heirs. Based on documentary and cartographic evidence, the park in the manor of Wexford was probably situated immediately to the south of the castle, which lay on the southern edge of the town.[18] With an area of just sixty acres this may well have originally been conceived as a Little Park. At

14 Bouchard, *Strong of body, brave and noble: chivalry and society in medieval France* (1998), pp 28–9. **15** *Leinster deeds*, p. 13.   **16** Fletcher, *Gardens of earthly delight*, p. 94.   **17** Hansson, *Aristocratic landscape: the spatial ideology of the medieval aristocracy* (2006), p. 160.   **18** *CIRCLE*, PR 1 Richard II, no. 11.

Wexford, the absenteeism of the lords meant that, unlike the continuity seen at Maynooth and Loughrea, both parks soon became agricultural land. Nevertheless, the original concept by the Marshals was grandiose in its scope, with a park at the major castle in Wexford that could have been used for pleasure gardens and orchards, coupled with a more extensive park of 308 statute acres in the adjacent manor of Carrick where venison and timber production could be concentrated (fig. 41).

The control of the landscape was an integral part of the Anglo-Norman policy of settlement. At the largest scale, forests were the ultimate symbol of royal authority since they monopolised natural resources for the crown and within them a landholder could not cut timber or hunt deer even on land held by him.[19] These limitations were also true of parks, albeit on a smaller scale. A park took woodland and pasture, which in the early medieval period would have been held by the tuath and, by enclosing it, prevented access to these natural resources, and restricted hunting to the park owner. It divided the landscape and provided a visible sign of the status of the landowner and the lack of status of the lower orders.[20] Lands at Dunamase, Maynooth and Carrick are partly used for arable agriculture today, as was some of Earlspark and Nenagh in the past, attesting to the quality of the soil within the bounds of these parks. At Dunamase the land is of excellent, arable quality and much of it is used for crops today. By contrast, the land to the north and west is poorer, including low-lying bog and heath. In this regard, the demesne park was created on what was being considered as a blank canvas, regardless of the presence of earlier settlement forms represented by the earthworks in the centre of the park. This was not marginal land at the fringes of the manor, but was centrally and deliberately placed in a location that suited the elite owners of the rock, regardless of the fact that it removed prime agricultural land from potential cultivation. Park-making can, therefore, be interpreted as the conspicuous consumption of potentially arable land for an economically marginal purpose. Furthermore, with the exception of Glencree, all the high-medieval parks that have been identified in Ireland were located at focal points within the manor rather than at an excessive distance from the core.

CONTROLLING THE LANDSCAPE

Walls and fences can serve a number of functions: to demarcate property, to restrict movement and to prevent outsiders seeing in. Boundaries restrict movement through the landscape by providing a physical or symbolic barrier that

19 Serovayskaya, 'Royal forests in England and their income in the budget of the feudal monarchy from the mid-twelfth to the early thirteenth centuries' (1998), p. 37.   20 Mileson, 'The sociology of park

must be circumvented and, where walls and fences delineate properties, the height of the boundary is often of less significance than its presence. The presence of boundaries was as much a controversial issue in the later-medieval period as it is now.[21] In two of the documented parks, at Nenagh, Co. Tipperary, and Garnenan (at Kilkea), Co. Kildare, these came to modern attention as a result of roads being diverted around the parks in the past,[22] and it was notable that all of the physically identified parks were bounded by roads or relict roads for at least part of the boundary. This lack of access to the land had practical implications for supplies of timber and firewood, pasturage and pannage, but also had symbolic implications by restricting access to pre-existing places. For the Gaelic population, many of the parks contained places that would have been imbued with memory, an issue that will be dealt with more fully below.

One important aspect of controlling the landscape was control within the park. This could be purely practical, as a security measure to monitor happenings within the park, but could also be symbolic. We have seen that the view from the roof or window of a castle was symbolic of control of the landscape, and in the same way the view from the parker's lodge would have expressed the power of the owner. In England, lodges were usually situated at the high point of the landscape, and were often moated sites.[23] No moated sites have been identified within the surveyed Irish parks, although at Loughrea, Maynooth and Dunamase archaeological features have been found at potential parkers' lodges. The likely locations for lodges at the high points of the parks at Nenagh and at Carrick have been subject to more recent building work so that no remains of any previous structures were visible at these points. At Loughrea, the suggested site for control of the park is in the Northern Complex, which contains a number of monuments including a large, bivallate, circular, earthen enclosure recorded as a ringfort.[24] At Maynooth, a previously unrecorded univallate, circular, earthen enclosure, with a nearby unenclosed souterrain is positioned at the top of the only hill in the park. Again, morphologically, this would be classified as a ringfort, especially in light of the presence of the souterrain.[25] Finally, at Dunamase there are a series of earthen enclosures that have previously been recorded as a later-medieval deserted village with a second, smaller, univallate earthen enclosure that has been interpreted either as an eighteenth-century tree ring or as a ringfort, but is most probably the latter.[26] A detailed survey of this site showed that the main enclosure, rather than being rectangular, as previously thought, appears to be circular, with an external

creation in medieval England' (2007), passim.   **21** Mileson, 'The importance of parks in fifteenth-century society', pp 33–7; *CJRI*, i, p. 234.   **22** *CDI*, i, no. 1642; *CJRI*, i, p. 234; Murphy and O'Conor, 'Castles and deer parks in Anglo-Norman Ireland'.   **23** Watts, 'Wiltshire deer parks: an introductory survey', 90; Rackham, *The history of the countryside*, p. 126.   **24** RMP no. GA105-080.   **25** Clinton, *The souterrains of Ireland* (2001), pp 207–10.   **26** RMP nos LA013-051001/002.

ditch, and again is morphologically similar to what would traditionally be interpreted as a ringfort.

There are, therefore, circular earthen enclosures at the likely sites of parkers' lodges in three of the four parks where the proposed location could be examined. This raises a number of issues regarding the dating of monuments traditionally classified as ringforts since these are generally deemed to date to the early medieval period.[27] There are a number of possibilities:

1 It is pure coincidence that early medieval ringforts are present at these locations, and lodges were either located elsewhere or were absent;
2 Early medieval ringforts at these locations were taken over and reused by the Anglo-Normans as the sites for parkers' lodges;
3 In Ireland, circular enclosures in the ringfort tradition were constructed as parker's lodges, in place of the rectangular moated sites more usually found in England.

The issue of ringfort dating is a thorny one, and has been the subject of a recent paper by FitzPatrick,[28] having previously been reviewed by O'Conor.[29] Both see evidence for the continuation of circular enclosed settlement in Gaelic areas into the later-medieval period, and FitzPatrick notes that the term is over-reductive, conflating a wide variety of morphologically and chronologically different site types.[30] Option 1 is unlikely, since three of the sites where the most likely location for a lodge could be examined had a circular enclosure at this location. Option 3 would be most likely if there was evidence for parkers being of Gaelic origin, but at Trim, Kilmainham and Wexford, where the names of several parkers are known, these are of Anglo-Norman origin. This leaves option 2 as the most likely: it can be suggested that early medieval ringforts were taken over and reused by the Anglo-Normans as the sites for parkers' lodges. This is not unreasonable, since there is considerable evidence for ringforts being converted to mottes.[31] Furthermore, they are similar in size and construction to moated sites, so that they would have been eminently suitable for the purpose. Only excavation at one or more of these sites could definitively show that they continued to be used in the later-medieval period; however, this would be a worthwhile exercise in understanding Anglo-Norman attitudes to the pre-existing landscape features.

Controlling access to the park and the activities within were important aspects of park management. A lack of control over the park was a lack of control over

---

27 For example, Stout, *The Irish ringfort* (2000), pp 22–3. **28** FitzPatrick, 'Native enclosed settlement and the problem of the Irish "ring-fort"'. **29** O'Conor, *The archaeology of medieval rural settlement in Ireland*, pp 89–94. **30** FitzPatrick, 'Native enclosed settlement and the problem of the Irish "ring-fort"', 274. **31** O'Conor, *The archaeology of medieval rural settlement in Ireland*, p. 90.

the manor and hence reflected poorly on the owner. If this control broke down, for example through poaching or park-breaking, then there were serious implications for the honour and status of the landholder.

POACHING, POUNDS AND PARK-BREAKING

While most people may generally respect a symbolic barrier, a relatively high and robust wall or fence may be necessary in order to prevent animals from straying and to keep ill-intentioned people outside the property. In the case of parks surrounding or abutting castles, the boundaries were also the outermost of the defences that needed to be at least symbolically breached in order to gain access to the castle.

The Irish documentary evidence yielded a number of examples of poaching in forests and parks. Public perception is often that later-medieval poachers were starving peasants looking for a meal, but the truth is more complex, and often park-breaking and poaching were inherently political or social acts. Hunting was an important and exciting elite activity, to which further spice would be added if the hunting was illicit.[32]

In 1291 the abbot and monks of St Mary's Abbey in Dublin were accused of poaching in the royal forest at Glencree using greyhounds, nets and 'engines', meaning ingenious devices. The abbot was acquitted when he successfully argued that he had regularly taken deer with the full knowledge and consent of the forester and this form of poaching can probably be seen as an illicit pleasure on the part of the monks and probably a source of extra revenue for the forester.[33]

A more political motive could be behind the case from 1305 when William Waspayl was found guilty of poaching, theft and breaking the park of Richard de Burgh, earl of Ulster, at Balydonegan, near Carlow.[34] William was a knight and had acted as a juror; furthermore, in 1306 he married Margery, widow of Geoffrey le Poer, who held her lands directly from the king.[35] As such, he was a man of means and his poaching of deer and theft of timber was not due to an empty stomach, or a desperate need for firewood. Instead, it may have been aimed as a personal attack on Richard as part of some ongoing dispute between them. He may even have considered this to be a noble act in the style of Robin Hood, battling against oppression. Park-breaking as a political act was certainly not without precedent, and was common practice in England.[36] To attack a lord's

32 Birrell, 'Deer and deer farming in medieval England', 112–26. 33 *CSMA*, nos 1, 118a; Murphy and O'Conor, 'Castles and deer parks in Anglo-Norman Ireland'. 34 *CJRI*, ii, p. 136; Murphy and O'Conor, 'Castles and deer parks in Anglo-Norman Ireland'. 35 *CDI*, ii, nos 1645, 2361. 36 Mileson, *Parks in*

park or to slaughter his deer was an affront to his dignity and honour, striking at the heart of his ordered manorial landscape.

A later and very public example of this took place during the siege of Maynooth at the time of Silken Thomas' rebellion in 1535, when Holinshed described how the king's forces first took the park and then attacked the castle from there. 'The lord deputie forewarned of his drift, marched with the Englishe army, and the power of the pale to Maynoth, and layde siege to the castell on the north side, towards the parke'.[37] Local tradition has it that during the siege the castle was bombarded with guns stationed on Crewhill, *c*.1.5km to the north-west of the castle and within the park.[38] This would appear to be too far away from the castle to have actually caused much damage, although use of such a weapon would have provided an impressive demonstration of military might.[39] In support of this legend, the present owner, John Geoghegan, found what he described as a cannonball that was about the size of a tennis ball (diameter *c*.8cm) on the land, but unfortunately this can no longer be located. It is most likely that a command post was set up on the hill, reusing what appears to be a previously unrecorded ringfort on the site (fig. 37). This would have been practical, given the excellent views from this high point in an otherwise flat landscape and would also have been a symbolic assault on the honour of the FitzGeralds. Conversely, repairing park boundaries was seen as representing the strengthening of authority and order. In the case of the English royal park of Clarendon, on a number of occasions the pale was repaired immediately after the accession of a new monarch.[40] Similarly, at Maynooth, after the forfeit of the lands as a result of Silken Thomas' rebellion, Leonard Grey offered to rent the manor, and specifically 'also to enclose the parke agayne at his awne chargis'.[41] This re-establishment of order would have been highly significant in demonstrating the power and authority of the king over Kildare and his removal of the FitzGeralds from their role as earls.

Another important function of a park was as a secure place for holding animals, and we have already seen that there are a number of references to domestic livestock being forfeited by tenants and retained in parks, as, for example, at Ballykene, Swords, Co. Dublin, in 1306.[42] References also exist to parks being broken and livestock removed, either by thieves or by the original owners from whom they had been confiscated, as, for example, at Kildare in 1298.[43] This use of a park as an allegedly secure location within the manor again demonstrates the role of the lord in administering justice and maintaining order

medieval England, p. 155. **37** *Chronicles*, iii, p. 97. **38** John Geoghegan and Bill Mulhern, Maynooth, pers. comm. **39** Damien Shiels, pers. comm. **40** Richardson, *The forest, park and palace of Clarendon*, *c.1200–1650*, p. 116. **41** *SPH8*, ii, 299–300. **42** *CJRI*, ii, p. 326. **43** Ibid., i, p. 200.

within his manor. It also emphasises again the importance of the high boundary, such as that found at Earlspark, where the high wall and the position of a field still called the 'pound field' well within the interior of the park served on a practical level to prevent unauthorised access and egress and on a symbolic level to highlight the authority and power of the elite.

ROYAL LICENCES AND ANGLO-NORMAN IDENTITY

Possession of a park was a status symbol, and as we have seen, relatively few Irish parks contained deer. Instead, parks with fallow deer were an elite possession to which only the highest magnates could aspire. While high status was demonstrated by access to a park, elite status was demonstrated by access to fallow deer venison from a park. In England, many regional surveys of historical documents have been based on the availability of 'licences to empark'. However, these can be unreliable in identifying parks since they were only necessary where a park was in or close to a royal forest, in which cases parks could reduce the availability of deer in the forest and so required permission.[44] Additionally, the erection of any boundaries within forests, even to prevent damage to crops, required royal permission.[45] Thus, licences to empark can only reliably provide evidence of those parks in or near forests and cannot identify parks outside these areas. Furthermore, a licence to empark does not necessarily mean that a park was ever constructed. Since these were akin to 'planning permission', even if the park was never built, having a licence could be considered as a form of royal favour and hence a status symbol in itself, and for this reason licences exist in England in areas far from royal forests.[46] Another form of documentary evidence can be found in licences to construct deer-leaps. A licence was necessary, since providing a leap meant that extra deer would enter the park, again to the potential detriment of the stocks in nearby royal forests.[47] While both of these licence types could be considered as a mark of royal favour, they were also a lucrative source of revenue for the crown.[48] Since the majority of parks in Ireland for which there is documentary evidence were constructed within liberties or palatine lordships, there would not have been a requirement for any form of royal permission because the lord of the liberty had control over almost all aspects of local administration.[49] As a result there is only one known example of a licence to

---

44 Cantor, 'Forests, chases, parks and warrens', p. 75; James, *A history of English forestry*, p. 6. **45** James, *A history of English forestry*, pp 14–15. **46** Cantor and Hatherly, 'The medieval parks of England', 73; Cantor, 'Forests, chases, parks and warrens', p. 75; James, *A history of English forestry*, p. 6. **47** Cantor and Hatherly, 'The medieval parks of England', 73. **48** Ibid. **49** Otway-Ruthven, *A history of medieval Ireland*, p. 181.

empark in Ireland and this also included a licence to construct a deer-leap. This was the permission sought by John, archbishop of Dublin, for his manor at Kilmasantan (Kicopsentan), Co. Dublin, in 1207.[50]

As we have already noted, two other parks received a form of royal permission. In 1228 Walter de Ridelisford sought permission to divert the road around his existing park at Garnenan, in Kilkea, Co. Kildare.[51] Similarly, in 1299 Theobald Walter (Butler) petitioned the court for permission to divert the existing road around his proposed park at Nenagh.[52] This is an interesting example because the date of the construction of the park is very late by comparison with many of the other documented sites. It is likely that the peak of park-building in Ireland was in the period up to *c*.1260. For Theobald Walter (Butler) to have created a park between eighty and one hundred years after the stone castle was built at Nenagh would seem to be somewhat belated. There are a number of possible explanations for this. The first is that woodland was beginning to come under significant pressure in the manor so that he wished to ensure a sufficient supply for the future by enclosing it. Another option is that he had secured a herd of fallow deer and needed an enclosed park in which to maintain them. The final option is more political than practical, and hinges on the notion that there was sufficient woodland around Nenagh to provide for the Butlers' needs and that sufficient wild red deer were available to provide venison and sport, so that a park was unnecessary for purely practical reasons.

As well as being a status symbol, possession of a park was very much a symbol of Anglo-Norman identity. In 1295 John Wogan was appointed justiciar of Ireland and charged with raising taxes and reducing corruption. As a result, in 1297 he summoned what can be regarded as the first true Irish parliament.[53] Legislation passed by this parliament included measures designed to minimise absenteeism, restrict private armies, improve bridges and clear roads that passed through woodland, in order to reduce the danger of 'forestall', or highway robbery. The parliament also passed the first in a series of laws that aimed to prevent those of Anglo-Norman origin from taking on Irish dress and hairstyles.[54] It therefore had a clear agenda of reasserting Anglo-Norman, and specifically royal control over Ireland, at a time when Anglo-Norman lords were increasingly taking on Gaelic customs. The final possibility for why the park at Nenagh was constructed *c*.1299 was that Theobald Walter (Butler) might have wished to provide a clear demonstration of his Anglo-Norman identity and loyalty to the crown by being in possession of this most Anglo-Norman of status symbols. The

---

50 *CDI*, i, no. 47; Murphy and O'Conor, 'Castles and deer parks in Anglo-Norman Ireland'. **51** *CDI*, i, no. 1641; Murphy and O'Conor, 'Castles and deer parks in Anglo-Norman Ireland'. **52** *CJRI*, i, p. 234. **53** Orpen, *Ireland under the Normans, 1169–1333*, iv, pp 39–40. **54** Ibid., p. 43; *1297 parliament*.

petition to divert the road would therefore have served two roles. Firstly, it was a vehicle for advertising this statement of Anglo-Norman identity to the king, stressing his loyalty to the king and the parliament. Secondly, by seeking permission to reroute the road, rather than going ahead with it and disregarding his tenants, Theobald Walter (Butler) was also very publically demonstrating his high regard for the law and being seen to follow proper procedure. To have gone ahead with park construction and rerouting the road without approval could have left him open to both royal disfavour and criticism from John Wogan.

PARKS IN THE PRE-EXISTING LANDSCAPE

Allsen has argued that in the ancient world parks and paradises had a number of purposes and meanings.[55] In addition to being venues for hunting, he showed that they had symbolic associations as places of 'material abundance and spiritual bliss' as well as political and ideological symbolism. Material abundance was demonstrated by the inclusion of orchards and timber stands within parks and, on a less tangible level, the park could symbolise the pristine natural world, of which probably the most familiar exemplar in a European context is the Garden of Eden. He notes Briant's analysis of the paradise as an 'outpost of central authority', a 'model of agricultural prosperity' and an 'ideological statement' of the link between the ruler and the prosperity and fertility of the land.[56]

Parks were therefore intrinsically linked to ideas of order and civilisation. By contrast, at the time of the Anglo-Norman invasion, Ireland was perceived by the newcomers to be a relatively under-populated land with large areas of woodland, open countryside and pasture, inhabited by a supposedly wild and uncivilised people.[57] As with much of Europe, the population density in Ireland was lower than that of England, which was relatively crowded, and in Ireland there was therefore less pressure on agricultural land, with more woodland available.[58] Giraldus must have seen these open spaces as an excellent opportunity for his Geraldine relatives. In terms of perceptions of 'civilisation', there were two factors at play. Firstly, a belief that a strange or different way of life is less civilised than the culture of the viewer, so that Giraldus would have seen a more pastoral economy as being of a lower standard of civilisation than an economy based primarily on arable agriculture.[59] Secondly, and following on from this, an argument that the native population was uncivilised has often been used as

---

55 Allsen, *The royal hunt in Eurasian history*, p. 47.   56 Ibid., p. 49.   57 *Topographia*, 34–5, 101–2.
58 Campbell, *English seigniorial agriculture, 1250–1450*, p. 388; Gardiner, 'The quantification of assarted land in mid- and late twelfth-century England', 165–86.   59 *Topographia*, 101.

justification for colonialism to 'bring civilisation' to the people.[60] From Giraldus' perspective, therefore, these landscapes and their people needed to be tamed and civilised by being brought into the arena of arable agriculture.[61] Wild landscapes were considered to be empty of anything of value, and the word 'waste' was used to describe uncultivated land, despite its importance for pasture, pannage and gathering wild foods.[62] Waste land was therefore meaningless 'space' between areas of productive land that was perceived as needing to be re-formed and recreated as Anglo-Norman 'places'. In doing so this would allow the Anglo-Normans to become rooted in their new country and to take on an identity built around their new homes. 'Space' is devoid of meaning, but becomes 'place' by being imbued with memories, meanings and symbols.[63] This happened when the landscape began to contain such features as the graves of ancestral settlers, new buildings and monuments and tilled fields. A part of this 'civilising' effect was the re-creation of a familiar landscape, creating a 'piece of home' in the new land.[64] In the context of the parks examined, all of them were designed landscape features that had been put in place for a reason. They created an idea of 'England in Ireland', bringing familiar landscapes to the settlers and embedding the settlers into the landscape. At Earlspark, for example, the park was probably constructed in the 1250s, less than a generation after the erection of the castle. It is likely that having completed work on the castle and town, the masons moved directly on to the park boundary wall, so demonstrating the importance of this symbol of lordship in creating the idea of the manor.

Enclosing a park or ploughing ground for arable agriculture tamed that land. This pushed out the limits of 'civilisation' and, in turn, brought previously unused land into use for pasture or for managed woodland.[65] History, cartography and pollen analysis show that this policy was only partly successful. It was hampered by the contraction of the Anglo-Norman colony and the fourteenth-century fall in population due to warfare and disease. As a result, even as late as the seventeenth century, Ireland was a generally well-wooded country, with timber trees as well as shrubby underwood in plentiful supply.[66] In 1612, Sir John

---

60 Kohn (2011), 'Colonialism' in Zalta (ed.), *The Stanford encyclopedia of philosophy* (fall 2011) (2011). http://plato.stanford.edu/archives/fall2011/entries/colonialism/, passim; O'Conor et al., 'The Rock of Lough Cé, Co. Roscommon', p. 36. 61 Leerssen, 'Wildness, wilderness and Ireland: medieval and early modern patterns in the demarcation of civility' (1995), 25–39; *Topographia*, 101–2. 62 Luscombe and Riley-Smith, *The new Cambridge medieval history, c.1024–c.1198, pt 1* (2004), pp 36–7. 63 Tilley, *A phenomenology of landscape: places, paths and monuments* (1994), p. 15. 64 Ashcroft et al., *Post-colonial studies: the key concepts* (1998), pp 93, 177–80; Tuan, *Space and place: the perspective of experience* (1977), pp 149–60; Kealhofer, 'Creating social identity in the landscape: Tidewater, Virginia, 1600–1750' (1999), passim; Knapp and Ashmore, 'Archaeological landscapes: constructed, conceptualised, ideational' (1999), passim. 65 Beglane, 'Deer and identity in medieval Ireland', passim. 66 Nicholls, 'Woodland cover in pre-modern Ireland' (2001), pp 209–10; Hall and Bunting, 'Tephra-dated pollen studies of medieval

Davies, attorney-general for James I, recognised the taming effect of agriculture, suggesting that if

> those English lords, among whom the whole kingdom was divided had been good hunters, and had reduced the mountains, bogs and woods, within the limits of forests, chaces and parks then Ireland would have been long since subdued.[67]

Davies, in the early seventeenth century, therefore saw parks as a specifically English phenomenon, being rare in Ireland, and his evidence supports that of Moryson, who, when writing a decade earlier, noted that there were very few parks in Ireland at that time.[68] It therefore supports the idea that after the initial creation of parks for fallow deer during the thirteenth century, they fell away in popularity, before a new wave of park creation by both English and Gaelic lords and gentry during the seventeenth century.[69]

The corollary of parks being created as a version of England in Ireland is that they were inevitably placed into a pre-existing Irish landscape. In two cases there is clear evidence of the importance of the symbolic incorporation of pre-existing landscape features into the park. These are at the two largest and best documented Irish parks at Earlspark, Co. Galway, and Maynooth, Co. Kildare, and are worth examining in detail.

THE SYMBOLISM OF EARLSPARK, CO. GALWAY

As well as being the most impressive and well-preserved of the parks surveyed, Earlspark, Co. Galway, has a very rich symbolism and mythology associated with it. It provides an excellent example of the way in which the associations between parks and lordship developed as Irish society changed through the medieval period. In order to understand how the park came to be viewed it is first necessary to examine the historical background of Loughrea before conducting a detailed survey of the monuments and mythology associated with the park.

Historical background

In early medieval times the area around Loughrea had been part of Máenmaige, an area that was under the control of the Uí Fhiachrach Aidni, part of the Uí Maine, and whose leaders styled themselves *rí Locha Riach*, or 'King of Lough Rea', in the ninth century.[70] In 1236, following his successful conquest of

landscapes in the north of Ireland' (2001), passim; Glasscock, 'Land and people, *c*.1300', passim. **67** *Discovery*, p. 132. **68** *Itinerary*, iv, pp 193–4. **69** Reeves-Smyth, 'Demesnes', p. 198. **70** Orpen,

Connacht, Richard de Burgh, lord of Connacht, built a castle at Loughrea and founded the associated town, so that from this time Loughrea was the caput of the de Burgh family.[71] He was succeeded by his son Richard, and subsequently by his younger son Walter, who received the title of earl of Ulster in 1263 or 1264.[72] In 1310–11, Richard III de Burgh, the 'Red Earl', unsuccessfully petitioned the king for a liberty in Connacht similar to that which he held in Ulster.[73] He was a close confidant of the king, but he was also able to defy him and act independently, with little royal control over his actions, and by declining his request for a liberty the king probably sought to limit the power of the earl, which was already at semi-regal levels.[74] After the death of the 'Red Earl' in 1326 and the subsequent murder of William, the 'Brown Earl' in 1333, the Connacht lands of the de Burghs became split into two gaelicised factions, the Clann Uilliam Íochtair, the Lower, or Mayo de Burghs, and Clann Uilliam Uachtair, the Upper de Burghs, or Clanrickards.[75] The Clann Uilliam Uachtair, or Clanrickards continued to be based at Loughrea until the caput was moved to Portumna by the fourth earl of Clanricarde, Richard Burke, early in the seventeenth century.[76]

Mythology

The mortared stone wall around Earlspark is known locally as Nora Novar's Wall. The story of Nora Novar was recounted at various times by local residents Fergal Nevin, Seamus O'Grady and Michael (Micky) Murphy. A literature search did not reveal any information about Nora Novar, but the outline of the same story has been documented by MacWeeney and Conniff. Their version, as told by one Willie Leahy from the Loughrea area, is reproduced below:

> 'There was this woman had no place to sow potatoes', he began. 'No place at all, at all. And she had family. And she went to the big estate and she said "Will you ever give me a plot of land to sow potatoes?" And they said "No, no, we have no time for that." And she kept begging – "the family is starving" – and they said "No, no." So she said "Won't you even give me the ground I can build a wall around in a night?" and they said "Yes", just to be rid of her. So she communicated this to friends and neighbours and

Ireland under the Normans, 1169–1333, ii, p. 183; iii, p. 191; MacCotter, *Medieval Ireland*, pp 140–1. **71** Spellissy, *The history of Galway*, p. 401; Knox, 'Occupation of the county of Galway by the Anglo-Normans after AD1237' (1901), 366; Orpen, *Ireland under the Normans, 1169–1333*, iii, p. 191; McKeon, 'Anglo-Norman frontier urban settlement in the Plantaganet realm', pp 41–99; Otway-Ruthven, *A history of medieval Ireland*, pp 98–9. **72** Lydon, *The lordship of Ireland in the Middle Ages* (2003), p. 86; Orpen, *Ireland under the Normans, 1169–1333*, iii, pp 266, 280. **73** *DAIKC*, no. 86. **74** Lydon, *The lordship of Ireland in the Middle Ages*, pp 86, 112. **75** FitzPatrick, 'Assembly and inauguration places of the Burkes in late-medieval Connacht' (2001), pp 364–5; *FJC*, 1333; *AFM*, iii, 550n–551n. **76** Spellissy, *The history of Galway*, p. 380; Cunningham, 'From warlords to landlords: political and social change in Galway, 1540–

they all turned out with horses and carts and gathered stones from all over the area. And whether it was 300 or 400 acres that the wall enclosed, I can't say, and what the Man Above was doing'.[77]

The version told to the present writer by both Nevin and O'Grady was fundamentally the same but attributed the wall being built in a single night to the use of magic rather than the labour of her neighbours and Nora was described as a witch as well as an old woman, so that their versions had a more supernatural connotation. Similarly, in a version told by Murphy, Nora was offered as much land as could be bounded by the contents of her ball of golden thread, which was of a miraculous length. In its various forms, this story is related to the tales told about St Brigid who claimed the land she could cover with her cloak from the king of Leinster and the cloak then miraculously spread to encompass a vast area. This story is based on a common motif, and probably originates with Dido, who founded the city of Carthage. Dido was given as much land for her city as her ox-hide cloak could encompass, but she cut it into thin strips and enclosed a vast area with the cloth.[78]

The name Novar does not appear to be a typical Irish surname, which implies that it has been corrupted or that it is not a surname in the usual sense of the word Nóilín Ní Iarnáin, a professional translator and native speaker, has suggested that Nora Novar could be a form of *Nora na fomhair* relating to harvest or autumn or could be *Nora na fobhar* relating to a well,[79] while the origin of the name of the Novar estate in Scotland is believed to be *Tigh 'n fhuamhair* or the 'house of the giant'.[80] Notably, another local tale told by Joe Dunne explains that the lake of Lough Rea was created when a woman drawing water from a well accidentally left the cover off, resulting in the water rising up to create the lake. As a result, the 'old town' of Loughrea became engulfed by water and the present town was built to replace it. The many recorded crannogs and the presence of submerged features in the lake are said to be the remains of the old town.[81] Again, probably connected with this is that Nora Novar was said to have died by drowning and to have been buried within Earlspark in the Northern Complex at the 'Lady Stone' or 'Earl's Chair'.[82]

The importance of this local legend of Nora Novar is that it emphasises that local people identify the wall as being different from other boundaries in the area.

1640' (1996), p. 97.   **77** MacWeeney and Conniff, *Ireland: stone walls and fabled landscapes* (1998), p. 85. **78** Bourke, 'Irish stories of weather, time and gender: Saint Brigid' (1999), pp 13, 23; Rollin, *The ancient history of the Egyptians, Carthaginians, Assyrians, Babylonians, Medes and Persians, Macedonians and Grecians* (1832), p. 156; Ó hÓgáin, *Myth, legend and romance: an encyclopedia of the Irish folk tradition* (1991), pp 63, 257; Ó hÓgáin, *The lore of Ireland: an encyclopedia of myth, legend and romance* (2006), p. 54. **79** Noilín ní Iarnían, translator, pers. comm.   **80** Ainmean-Àite na h-Alba, *Gaelic place-names of Scotland*. **81** Joe Dunne, Loughrea, pers. comm.; NMS, *National Monuments Service*.   **82** Fergal Nevin, Loughrea,

As a mortared stone wall *c*.2.5m high and 1m thick it is up to four times the size of the surrounding field boundaries and is known locally as the 'double wall'.[83] This myth is particularly relevant since Loughrea is in 'stone wall country', where dry stone walls make up the majority of the field boundaries. It is likely that the legend originates from local people trying to make sense of the reasons a mortared stone wall of this magnitude should be present in the area, but the symbolism also runs much more deeply than this.

The Northern Complex

In the centre of the northern part of the park is an area termed the 'Northern Complex', which seems to be important in understanding the significance of the siting of the park (fig. 56). This area has the densest concentration of archaeological monuments in the townland, including the previously unrecorded standing stone called the 'Lady Stone' or 'Earl's Chair', at which Nora Novar was buried, an extremely large enclosure of 70m external diameter that is recorded as a ringfort with a field system extending to the south of it,[84] a smaller ringfort,[85] a pond and a rectangular structure that seems to be associated with this pond,[86] as well as a hilltop enclosure that may be a hillfort and which contains the remains of at least two buildings.[87] The relict roadway coming from Loughrea is visible as far as this area and then seems to head towards the gateway at the north-east of the townland. The boundary wall of the park passes immediately to the north of the 70m-enclosure and the hilltop enclosure ensuring that all of these monuments are incorporated into the park. This part of the park had evidently been an important location in the early medieval period, with a dense cluster of monuments, and so would have been imbued with meaning and memory for local people. This suggests that closing off access to this area was important to the builders of the park, being symbolic of taking control of the region.

The 70m-enclosure was surveyed extensively.[88] The ditch, which holds water, appears to have been re-cut at some point so that it is now *c*.3.5m wide at the base and *c*.7m at the top, with a flat bottom. Geophysical survey of the interior identified a number of features and anomalies including possible buildings. The most important of the features identified were arcs of high and low resistance that followed the line of the inner bank of the enclosure; flag iris growth also follows this line and in combination this seems to be evidence for an additional, internal, ditch (fig. 57).[89] Since an internal ditch would not be typical for a ringfort, there are a number of possibilities. An additional internal bank originally may have been present inside the inner ditch, and in this case the external ditch may be a

pers. comm. **83** Michael (Micky) Murphy, Loughrea, pers. comm. **84** RMP no. GA105-080. **85** RMP no. GA105-081. **86** RMP no. GA105-208. **87** RMP no. GA105-205. **88** RMP no. GA105-080. **89** McCarthy, 'Earlspark and Moanmore East', p. 17.

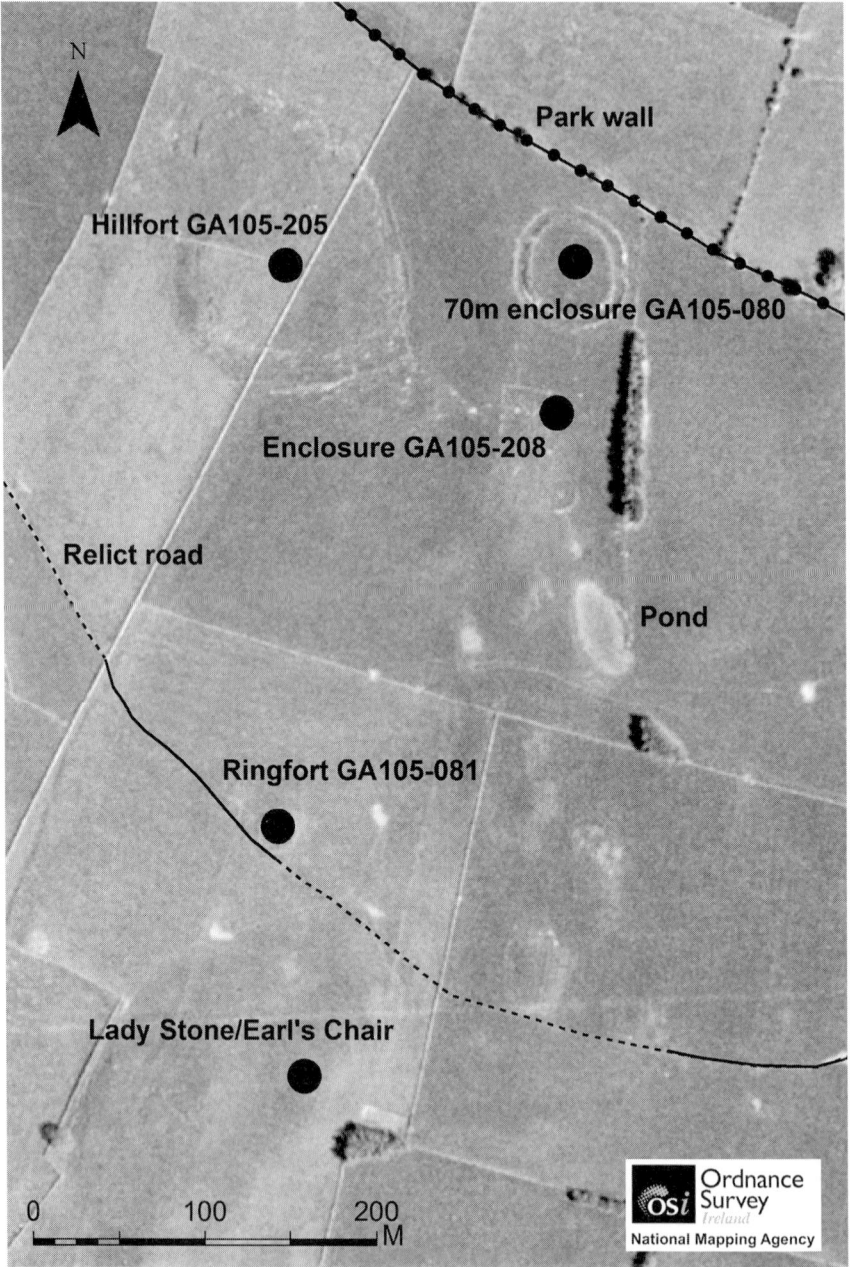

56 Aerial photograph of the Northern Complex at Earlspark. Ordnance Survey Ireland
Permit no. 8959 © Ordnance Survey Ireland/Government of Ireland.

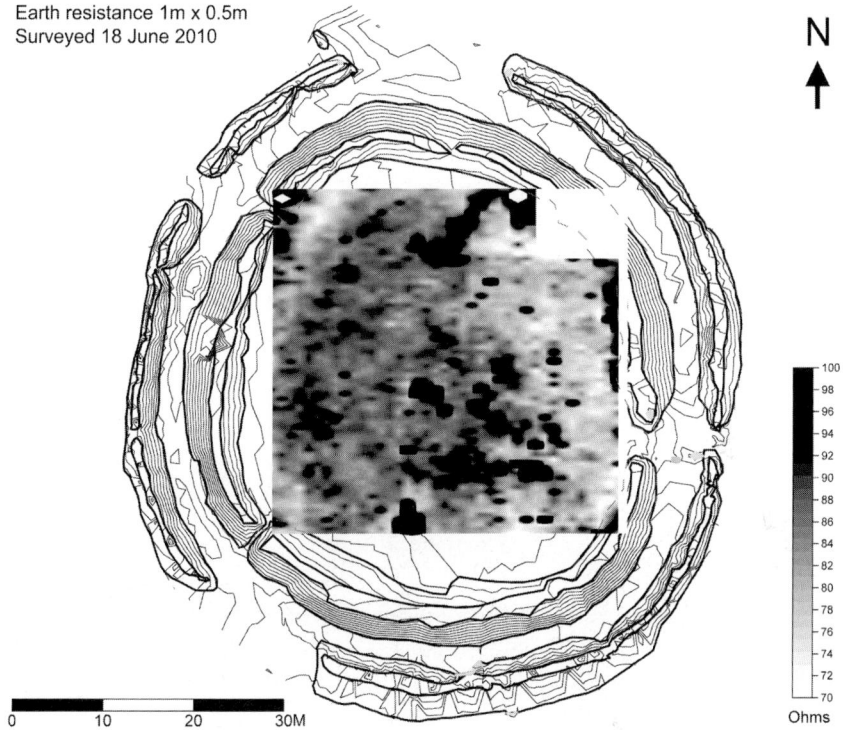

Earth resistance 1m x 0.5m
Surveyed 18 June 2010

N

0   10   20   30M

Ohms

57 Topographical survey and earth resistance data at Earlspark (RMP GA105-080). © Fiona
Beglane and Martina McCarthy.

later addition. Another possibility is that the monument was not originally
constructed as a ringfort, but instead either pre-dated the early medieval period or
post-dated it. If the monument was originally prehistoric, it could be a modified
bivallate barrow, or a henge monument.[90] Finally, if the monument was
constructed in the later-medieval period, it could have been designed as a circular
moated site, a site-type that has occasionally been identified elsewhere.[91] If this is
the case, then it is likely that the monument was deliberately constructed as part
of the development of the park. If, as seems more probable, the monument pre-
dates the later-medieval period, then it is likely to have been reused and modified
during this period. Regardless of when it was constructed, it is highly likely that
in the later-medieval period this was the location of the park lodge. It has
extensive views over the townland, lake and town and the only part of the park
that cannot be seen is the extreme south-east portion of the park. Many park

90 For example, RMP no. RO022-057001; Newman, *Tara: an archaeological survey* (1997), pp 77–83;
Danagher, *Monumental beginnings: the archaeology of the N4 Sligo Inner Relief Road* (2007), pp 50–5.
91 O'Conor, 'The ethnicity of Irish moated sites' (1999), 92–102; English heritage, *List entry: Littywood*

lodges in England were constructed as moated sites and it is tempting to see this as a prehistoric or early medieval monument that was modified into something resembling a circular moated site.[92] It was important to provide water for deer and therefore parks could include lakes, ponds or rivers within them. In addition, ponds could be constructed in parks, which could double as a source of wild fowl, so that the presence of a pond nearby is potentially relevant.[93] From a practical perspective, the monuments of the Northern Complex lie on the route of the relict road and are midway between the gateways at the north-east corner and the west of the park so that anyone travelling along the relict road between the two gates would pass directly in front of this 70m enclosure.

The 'Lady Stone' or 'Earl's Chair' and the chair at St Dima's Well

Some 450m south of the 70m-enclosure,[94] and 170m south-south-east of the small ringfort, is a north-east–south-west ridge upon which lies a small, but prominent, steeply sided hillock.[95] The hillock rises some 7m above the surrounding land and on the summit there is an upright standing stone, aligned north–south and known locally as the 'Lady Stone' or the 'Earl's Chair' (figs 58, 59). The hillock appears to be a natural topographic feature but its sides may have been scarped to enhance the steepness of the slope. Local folklore holds that Nora Novar, the builder of the park wall, is buried at this location.[96] The stone is not marked on the Record of Monuments and Places or on the Sites and Monuments Record or on any of the editions of the OS maps. It stands *c.*80cm tall and measures *c.*55cm north–south by *c.*24cm east–west. The northern end is higher than the southern end so that looking along the stone one's eye is directed to the probable hillfort.[97] This upright stone is bedded into a stony base that forms a small knoll on top of the hillock and it is likely that this stone was set on the hill in antiquity, either as a prehistoric standing stone or, as we will see, in the later-medieval period as an inauguration or assembly stone.

In the nearby grounds of St Dima's or St Dymphna's Well in Killeenadeema,[98] some 250m to the south-west of the limit of the park, is a highly unusual stone chair (fig. 60) that bears a remarkable resemblance to the Clandeboye or *Clann Aodha Buidhe* inauguration chair of the O'Neill's, which has been tentatively dated to the fifteenth century.[99] The National Monuments Service recorded the chair at St Dima's as having a base 0.84m long with a maximum height of 1.14m and with a seat height of 0.49m above ground level. The chair is not mentioned

moated site, 1017856 (1992). **92** Rahtz, *Excavations at King John's hunting lodge, Writtle, Essex, 1955–7* (1969), passim; Pluskowski, 'The social construction of medieval park ecosystems: an interdisciplinary perspective', p. 65. **93** Pluskowski, 'The social construction of medieval park ecosystems: an interdisciplinary perspective', p. 65. **94** RMP no. GA105-080. **95** RMP no. GA105-081. **96** Fergal Nevin, Loughrea, pers. comm. **97** RMP no. GA105-205. **98** RMP no. GA105-124. **99** FitzPatrick,

58 Location of the Lady Stone or Earl's Chair at Earlspark shown with an arrow, with the small ringfort (RMP no. GA105-081) in the middle distance, from the north.

by O'Donovan in the Ordnance Survey letters of 1 November 1838,[100] but it is understood locally that early in the twentieth century a Mrs Hawkins, who was the mother of a local priest, developed the holy well into a grotto, and that at that time she arranged for the chair and other stones to be moved to the site.[101] These were previously located on a small hillock immediately to the east of the well, on the opposite side of the road to Loughrea. The road is shown on the first-edition OS map, but not on Larkin's map of 1819, and on the OS map the field boundaries suggest a sub-circular enclosure of *c.*150m diameter surrounding the well and the reputed earlier location of the chair. It is possible that O'Donovan missed, or failed to mention, the chair, or that it was brought to the site from another location during the nineteenth century. Nevertheless, its presence so near to the park and to the 'Earl's Chair' or 'Lady Stone' is highly likely to be significant.

Royal inauguration in Gaelic Ireland, p. 172. **100** O'Donovan, *Ordnance Survey letters: Co. Galway* (1838). **101** Hawkins, 'Killeenadeema' (2009), 45; Maura Hawkins, Killeenadeema, pers. comm.

a

b

59 The Lady Stone or Earl's Chair at Earlspark from the west (above) and the south (below).

Sovereignty and gaelicisation

An incoming group must seek to establish the legitimacy of the new rulers. While practical measures are important, symbolism is also key to creating this image of legitimacy, so that constructing new markers of authority and taking over existing

60 The stone chair at St Dima's Well, Killeenadeema, Co. Galway.

symbols both have a role to play.[102] Enclosing an area of land with a high wall is a very visible sign of control since land that was once accessible becomes inaccessible and locations within the wall become the exclusive preserve of the owners,

102 McNeill, *Castles in Ireland*, p. 1.

who control access to the monuments and resources within. In this case it can be argued that the wall constructs a new marker of authority and at the same time appropriates existing symbols in the landscape.

The folklore tale of Nora Novar may be integral to this. The version recounted by MacWeeney and Conniff stated that the woman sought land to feed her family,[103] while the versions told to the current author included details of the name, Nora Novar, that she was an 'old widow' and a witch with supernatural abilities to construct the wall, and that she drowned and was buried at the 'Lady Stone' or 'Earl's Chair'. MacWeeney's and Conniff's version in particular places the events in a post-medieval context, stating that she went to the 'big estate' and that she planned to grow potatoes. Since radiocarbon dating has already established that the wall is of thirteenth-century origin, either the story is medieval and has become corrupted with more recent details due to the oral nature of its transmission or the story is much more recent.

It has been suggested that 'Novar' is a corruption of *na fomhair*, relating to harvest or autumn, or *na fobhar*, relating to a well, or *n Fhuamhair*, relating to a giant. One possibility, which is in keeping with all these potential origins for the name is that Nora Novar is an embodiment of the sovereignty goddess. In connection with this, it is possible that the stone monument known as the 'Lady Stone' or 'Earl's Chair' was an inauguration or assembly site. At the time of the creation of the park, prior to 1333, inauguration would not have been practised by the de Burghs, but the act of enclosing earlier landmarks including the stone and the large enclosure,[104] and placing them within a landscape that was designed to demonstrate the status and authority of the de Burghs would have provided a powerful statement of lordship. This would explain the association of both the earl and Nora Novar with the stone monument. It is possible that the Lady Stone was used for inauguration later in the medieval period, as the de Burghs became gaelicised and took on Gaelic customs.

The concept of the sacred marriage, in which the king symbolically married the goddess of the land, is well known and has been studied widely. In an Irish context, the first written sources date to the Christian writers of the seventh century, however, similar concepts were described by classical writers in Gaul and the Rhineland at much earlier dates. For an agricultural society, ideas of fertility, fecundity, harvest, the changing of the seasons and protection of the people, crops and animals from disease all contributed to this concept of sovereignty, where the female land was balanced by the male king.[105] In Ireland the best known example of this is Medb, the queen of Connacht, who is a central figure in the story of the

---

103 MacWeeney and Conniff, *Ireland: stone walls and fabled landscapes*, p. 85. **104** RMP no. GA105-080. **105** Herbert, 'Goddess and king: the sacred marriage in early Ireland' (1992), p. 265; Enright, *Lady*

Táin Bó Cuailgne.[106] Medb can be translated as 'she who intoxicates', a name that is probably an allusion to the ritual of the bride offering a drink to her betrothed during the wedding ceremony.[107] In the tale of Niall of the Nine Hostages, Niall kisses an old woman, who immediately becomes young and beautiful and declares that she is Sovereignty.[108] In this way, Sovereignty is regenerated from an old woman into a young girl by the marriage of the land to the rightful king and the land itself maintains its fruitfulness. The Irish word *caillech* can be translated as old woman, hag, crone and witch, but Ní Dhonnchadha has shown that the original meaning was probably 'veiled woman', meaning a woman who is married or promised in marriage.[109] Thus, Nora Novar, rather than being an 'old widow' or 'witch', becomes Sovereignty, who is betrothed and then married to the rightful lord, rejuvenating the land.

Inauguration ceremonies in early medieval Ireland seem to have taken a number of forms, including the famous story told by Giraldus in which the king of Cenél Conaill was inaugurated by having intercourse with a white mare, bathing in the water in which the meat of the slaughtered mare was cooked and then eating the meat and drinking the water.[110] A number of common elements are associated with the ritual of inauguration, which Clancy considered to be part of a 'package' in which one or more of the elements could be selected in individual cases and which could change over time.[111] Inauguration ceremonies recorded during the early medieval period included less controversial roles for horses and the bestowing of wands or rods of hazel on the king. The ceremonies took place at a traditional site and incorporated a ritual of processing around the new king and proclaiming his kingship.[112] Many inauguration and assembly sites were associated with a mound on which the ceremonies took place and from which proclamations could be made, so providing the audience with an unfettered view of the proceedings. Documentary sources demonstrate the use of mounds in this way during the early medieval period both in Ireland and Britain, and this was also the case in late-medieval Ireland. Some mounds were entirely artificial, and in some cases reused earlier prehistoric monuments, a practice that lent an air of antiquity to the proceedings and legitimised the king. In other cases, hillocks and eskers could be used in their natural state or could be modified

with a mead cup; ritual prophesy and lordship in the European warband from La Tène to the Viking Age (1996), p. 260; Simms, *From kings to warlords: the changing political structure of Gaelic Ireland in the later Middle Ages* (1987), pp 21–2, 24; Frazer, *The golden bough: a study in magic and religion* (1922), pp 2–4, 140. **106** Kinsella, *The Táin* (1969), passim. **107** Enright, *Lady with a mead cup; ritual prophesy and lordship in the European warband from La Tène to the Viking Age*, p. 264; Jaski, *Early Irish kingship and succession* (2000), 66–9; Bhreathnach, *Tara: a select bibliography* (1995), 5–6. **108** De Paor, *Landscapes with figures: people, culture and art in Ireland and the modern world* (1998), p. 81. **109** Ní Dhonnchadha, 'Caillech and other terms for veiled women in medieval Irish texts' (1994–5), 71, 96. **110** *Topographia*, 110. **111** Clancy, 'Kingmaking and images of kingship in medieval Gaelic literature' (2003), p. 90. **112** Simms, *From kings to*

for use.[113] Another important feature of inauguration and assembly sites is the presence of recumbent stones or chairs. Recumbent stones or *leaca* appear to pre-date chairs or thrones, being mentioned in the Irish sagas and saints' *Lives*, and *leaca* is the term used in Irish sources throughout the medieval period.[114] By contrast, chairs and seats are first associated with inauguration in English docu-ments in the sixteenth century, although the Clann Aodha Buidhe inauguration chair of the O'Neills has been tentatively dated to the fifteenth century, and there is evidence to suggest that some *leaca* were provided with backs and arms to convert them into chairs. Stones containing a single 'footprint' could also be part of the ritual, with the new king stepping into the footprint in order to take on the royal role.[115]

Significantly, as early as the early thirteenth century some Anglo-Norman families such as the de Burghs began to take on some Gaelic customs and by the fourteenth century they may also have begun to undertake inauguration ceremonies.[116] It has already been noted that after the death of Richard the 'Red Earl' in 1326 and the murder of William, the 'Brown Earl' in 1333 the de Burghs split into two factions, the Clann Uilliam Íochtair and the Clann Uilliam Uachtair. The inauguration site of the Clann Uilliam Íochtair was recorded as being at 'Ratsecer', which has been identified as the ringfort of Raheenagooagh in Rausakeera North, Co. Mayo. This is first mentioned in 1333 as the location for the proclamation of the king's peace.[117] The evidence for inauguration being practised by the Clann Uilliam Uachtair is more slender, as there are no docu-mentary references to this.[118] Nevertheless, two potential inauguration/ assembly sites have been identified by FitzPatrick, both called *Caher na Iarla*, or the 'Fort of the Earl'.[119] The first of these is in Coppanagh townland on the slopes of the Slieve Aughty mountains, 11km south of Loughrea. At this site a number of flat slabs are set up in the approximate form of a chair, although it has been suggested that the original chair was dismantled and that it has been roughly reconstructed from these slabs.[120] The second chair was in Castlegar townland, Dunkellin, *c*.15km east of Loughrea, and originally consisted of a 'throne mound' and a 'stone chair' inside an enclosure. The position of the chair was recorded by O'Donovan during the Ordnance Survey in 1838 and by Redington in 1911, although by that time no chair was present, and the entire site has now been destroyed.[121]

warlords: the changing political structure of Gaelic Ireland in the later Middle Ages, pp 21–6.   **113** FitzPatrick, *Royal inauguration in Gaelic Ireland*, pp 41–9, 166–72; FitzPatrick, 'An Tulach Tinóil' (2001), 23. **114** FitzPatrick, '*Leaca* and Gaelic inauguration ritual in medieval Ireland' (2003), pp 107–8. **115** Doherty, 'Kingship in early Ireland' (2005), 9–11; FitzPatrick, '*Leaca* and Gaelic inauguration ritual in medieval Ireland', pp 110–17, 172.   **116** FitzPatrick, 'Assembly and inauguration places of the Burkes in late-medieval Connacht', p. 357.   **117** Ibid., pp 358–65.   **118** Ibid., p. 365.   **119** Ibid., pp 365–6. **120** Roy, 'Caher na Earle (The Earl's Chair)' (2000), 144–6; FitzPatrick, *Royal inauguration in Gaelic Ireland*, p. 167.   **121** FitzPatrick, *Royal inauguration in Gaelic Ireland*, pp 166–8; Roy, 'Caher na Earle (The

The addition of a new Earl's Chair, at Earlspark, 2km south of Loughrea town, as well as what appears to be a late-medieval-style inauguration chair 250m south of Earlspark at St Dima's well, adds a level of complexity to the picture. Inauguration, whether of a king or of a lord, is likely to have taken place at a single location, but it would be logical to have a number of locations where meetings and assemblies could be held, and this would suggest that several assembly sites would be needed within a single large territory. It is possible that all three were assembly sites, so that each of these would then serve different localities, with only one being the primary inauguration site, but all being associated with the exercise of power by the ruling dynasty.

In later-medieval Ulster, inauguration sites were often on the *lucht tighe* lands held by the vassal responsible for inaugurating the chief, or were on the demesne lands held directly by the chief.[122] Furthermore, FitzPatrick recently demonstrated place-name evidence linking hunting grounds and assembly places in later-medieval Gaelic Ireland.[123] Earlspark can be considered central to the demesne lands of the de Burghs. At some time between 1333 and 1585 the park probably ceased to hold deer and, although much of the land was retained in demesne, some may have been tenanted by vassals of the Clann Uilliam Uachtair. Initially at least, the walls are likely to have been essentially complete, but over time the wall would have deteriorated and stone would have been robbed for other uses. If the site of the Earl's Chair or Lady Stone in Earlspark were used for assembly or inauguration during the time of the Clann Uilliam Uachtair, then access would have been through a limited number of points. This combination of a mound with a stone, adjacent to the large enclosure of early medieval or prehistoric origin, the smaller ringfort, the hillfort and the probable high-medieval buildings that formed the lodge, coupled with the still impressive walls of the park, could have been used to highlight the important nature of the assembly for the lower orders. Furthermore, since the access points were restricted, attendance could be tightly monitored so that absences could be easily noted and outsiders excluded where necessary. The old road from Loughrea leads directly to the park and then a relict road continues, running immediately to the south of the large enclosure,[124] and the possible hillfort.[125] This route would also lead the traveller immediately to the north of the Earl's Chair or Lady Stone, providing direct access to this monument. Similarly, on Bartlett's map of Tulach Óg, the ancient inauguration site of the O'Neills in Ulster, a road runs directly between the castle and the inauguration site and FitzPatrick has highlighted the

Earl's Chair)', 150–1. **122** FitzPatrick, *Royal inauguration in Gaelic Ireland*, pp 196–7. **123** FitzPatrick, '*Formaoil na Fiann*: hunting preserves and assembly places in Gaelic Ireland', 95–118. **124** RMP no. GA105-080. **125** Ibid., GA105-205.

importance of good infrastructural links to inauguration sites.[126] The presence of
an upright rather than recumbent stone at Earlspark suggests that this may not
have been an inauguration stone in the early medieval period, although if it was a
leaca it could have been placed on its end during the later-medieval period. It
may also have been a prehistoric standing stone or been newly created in the
later-medieval period. If newly created by the Clann Uilliam Uachtair, it is likely
to have been deliberately located in the focal area of the Northern Complex.
Inauguration would probably have come to an end in 1543 when Ulick na
gCeann became the first earl of Clanrickard.[127] By this time, the Tudor government was trying to eliminate Gaelic practices,[128] providing a possible end-date for
the use of the Northern Complex as a symbolically significant area within the
park.

Earlspark as a symbol of lordship

Taking the evidence for the myth of Nora Novar, the Northern Complex of
monuments and the construction of the wall to surround this complex, in
conjunction with the later creation or re-invention of the 'Lady Stone' or 'Earl's
Chair', the folklore tale could then be re-interpreted as follows: the sovereignty
goddess took a new husband, Richard de Burgh, lord of Connacht, who held the
land of Connacht by right of his marriage to her. She flooded the older
settlements under the lake and the later-medieval town of Loughrea was
constructed. In recognition of the rights of de Burgh to control Loughrea, a wall
was built surrounding and enclosing the monuments that were symbolic of the
kingship of the area. Possession of this land ensured the prosperity of the de
Burghs and symbolised their legitimacy since they were now, in essence, the
family of the goddess. To the local population, the building of the wall was a
sudden and abrupt change in the landscape. Land that was previously accessible
was 'overnight' private and enclosed, limiting access for grazing, pannage and
collecting wood. The park was an Anglo-Norman symbol of lordship, associated
with manorial settlement and with the 'civilising' of the landscape, but this was
overlaid on an older landscape, appropriating earlier symbols of authority at the
Northern Complex.

   The lineage of the de Burghs was illustrious, being related to the kings of
France, England and Scotland and to the Irish king Brian Borumha,[129] and their

126 FitzPatrick, *Royal inauguration in Gaelic Ireland*, p. 209.   127 FitzPatrick, 'Assembly and inauguration
places of the Burkes in late-medieval Connacht', p. 373.   128 FitzPatrick, '*Leaca* and Gaelic inauguration
ritual in medieval Ireland', p. 111.   129 Webb, *A compendium of Irish biography: comprising sketches of
distinguished Irishmen, and of eminent persons connected with Ireland by office or by their writings*, pp 126–7;
Lodge, *The genealogy of the existing British peerage* (1838), p. 77; Orpen, *Ireland under the Normans, 1169–
1333*, iv, pp 149–50.

level of control in Ireland was extensive, both through their estates and through royal offices. A park of this size and of such an impressive design demonstrated their status in a European context, it placed them firmly in the upper echelons of the European aristocracy and imbued them with an almost-royal status. By siting the park so that it was visible from the castle and so that it surrounded the historically important symbols of local kingship and lineage, the de Burghs aimed to legitimise their status and demonstrate their overlordship of the Connacht region.

Over time, the nature of the lordship changed from one that was focused on the English court to a gaelicised lordship. Richard, the 'Red Earl', died in 1326 and subsequently William, the 'Brown' Earl, was murdered in 1333. The Connacht lands of the de Burghs then became split into two factions and the Clann Uilliam Uachtair, or Clanrickards, held the lands in Galway and around Loughrea. Nominally these had been inherited by Elizabeth, the baby daughter of William, but she was unable to enter or derive benefit from these.[130] The de Burghs moved away from using Anglo-Norman symbols of status as these no longer had meaning in a Connacht that was becoming increasingly independent of the English crown, instead adopting Gaelic customs such as inauguration and the use of Irish names.[131] As a result, the park was undoubtedly allowed to fall out of its primary use of retaining deer. Nevertheless, Earlspark remained an important demesne property, as the Northern Complex became a site associated with assembly and with the lordship of the region. The southern portion remained at least partially wooded as late as 1685,[132] and the memory of the original function of the townland has been retained in the place-name to the present day.

THE SYMBOLISM OF MAYNOOTH, CO. KILDARE

The name 'Maynooth' comes from *Mag Nuadat* or the 'Plain of Nuadu', the grandfather of Fionn Mac Cumhaill.[133] We have already seen that from a practical perspective the Park of Maynooth is convenient to the castle, lying only 450m north of the castle and that in terms of a practical and symbolic arrangement of space within the manor, an area in an arc from the south-west round to the north-east was dominated by the castle and its demesne, while the town and

---

130 FitzPatrick, *Royal inauguration in Gaelic Ireland*, pp 166–8; FitzPatrick, 'Assembly and inauguration places of the Burkes in late-medieval Connacht', pp 357–8; FitzPatrick, 'Assembly and inauguration places of the Burkes in late-medieval Connacht', pp 364–5; *FJC*, 1333; Otway-Ruthven, *A history of medieval Ireland*, p. 273; Lydon, *The lordship of Ireland in the Middle Ages*, p. 124. **131** FitzPatrick, *Royal inauguration in Gaelic Ireland*, pp 166–8; FitzPatrick, 'Assembly and inauguration places of the Burkes in late-medieval Connacht', pp 357–74. **132** Petty, '*Hiberniae delineatio*: atlas of Ireland' (1685). **133** Fitzgerald, 'Maynooth Castle', 223.

the agricultural land of the tenants were restricted to the eastern side. Towards the end of the period of use of the park, during and after the rebellion of Silken Thomas, its breaking, control and repair were symbolically important in controlling the lands of Kildare.

Whereas Loughrea is in the west of Ireland and became gaelicised from the fourteenth century, Maynooth is in the east of the country, within the bounds of the Pale. There have been a number of other demographic changes to Maynooth. By the twentieth century the Land Commission had moved farmers from the west of the country to this area,[134] some of the land in and around the park was and still is owned by St Patrick's College/Maynooth University and, furthermore, as a modern commuter town there have been many incomers to the area. As a result of these population changes, much of the local folklore and history has been forgotten. Nevertheless, there is evidence that when the park of Maynooth was created, it was placed at a symbolically important location within the existing landscape. The park incorporates the modern townlands of Crewhill and Mariavilla, as well as a small portion of the townland of Maynooth. There is a previously unrecorded ringfort on the top of Crewhill, with a souterrain further down the slope. The presence of the ringfort shows that this area was not devoid of meaning and memory. On the contrary, it is likely that the area that became the park was extremely important prior to the arrival of the FitzGeralds, and that, as at Earlspark, the incomers may have deliberately enclosed an area of ancestral significance to the pre-existing populace.

The Place-names Commission has documented research into the origin of various townland names.[135] On the surface, Mariavilla might be considered as an eighteenth-century house name given in recognition of a wife or daughter, but it appears in the inquisitions of Elizabeth as 'Merywall' so that it is documented back at least to Tudor times, and O'Donovan considered it to have originated as *Machaire bhile*, 'plain of the ancient tree'. In early medieval Ireland the *bile* was the ancient or sacred tree of a *tuath* and was associated with kingship.[136] Crewhill is a steep-sided rounded hill and the name was translated by John O'Donovan as *Creamh-choill*, 'wood of the wild garlic'.[137] There is, however, another alternative, which is that the first part may have originated as *craobh*, either in the form *Craobh*-hill or as *Craobh-choill*. *Craobh* means 'tree' or 'branch' and Flanagan and Flanagan have noted this at Crew Hill, Co. Tyrone, where the name is given to a 'steeply rounded hill with an associated standing stone'.[138] It is also found at Crew Hill in Glenavy, Co. Antrim, which is recorded as an assembly place of the

134 Duffy, 'The territorial identity of Kildare's landscapes' (2006), p. 10.   **135** Bunachar loghinmneacha na hÉireann, *Placenames database of Ireland*.   **136** Mac Coitir, *Irish trees: myths, legends and folklore* (2003), pp 5–6; Lucas, 'The sacred trees of Ireland' (1963), 16–54.   **137** Bunachar loghinmneacha na hÉireann, *Placenames database of Ireland*.   **138** Flanagan and Flanagan, *Irish place-names* (2002), pp 63–4.

Ulaid and the site of a sacred tree.[139] At Maynooth in the medieval and Tudor periods, the name was recorded as 'Crenegele' or 'Cravile',[140] and later 'Creugele' or 'Crewile',[141] suggesting that in this case 'hill' is not the origin of the second syllable. As with *bile*, the word *craobh* is often associated with totemic properties and symbols of kingship and community,[142] and *bile* and *craobh* were often used interchangeably.[143]

The *Metrical Dindsenchas* includes a poem entitled *Bile Tortan*, which describes how the sacred Tree of Tortu fell. This was a sacred ash tree that stood near Ardbraccan, Navan, Co. Meath, and it is believed to have fallen in the period AD657–64.[144] It was described as having a height that, when converted from cubits, equated to 137m and a 'thickness', presumably a circumference, of 22m. The tree was a meeting place for the men of Tortu and on falling had crushed fifty victims who were attending the fair being held there. The height given is three times the maximum height of an ash tree, poetically highlighting the giant and hence sacred nature of the tree.[145] The poem says that 'The plain of Tortu is a plain without a ruler since it lost its noble tree' and that 'two parts of its prosperity are gone since the Tree fell', clearly showing the association between the tree, sovereignty and the land.

Therefore, if the sacred tree of the *tuath* was within the area enclosed by the park then the FitzGeralds would have been making a very powerful statement about their control of the Plain of Nuadu.[146] The park boundary would have restricted access to the *bile/craobh*, and would have defined it as a FitzGerald possession. By controlling this they had control over the land and thereby sought to legitimise their claim to the area and its people. The importance of this symbolic aspect should not be understated; there is no requirement in this for the FitzGeralds to have taken on Irish customs at this early stage, but there would have been an awareness of the importance of embedding the lineage into the land.

CONCLUSION

Despite the emphasis on the practical aspects of park ownership and the debate on their aesthetic qualities, there is universal agreement that parks were one of the ways to express lordship and status.[147] As in other countries, parks in Ireland were

---

139 MacDonald and McIlreavy, 'Data structure report: site evaluation and excavation at Crew Hill (Cráeb Telcha), near Glenavy, County Antrim 2007' (2007), p. 2. **140** *RBK*, no. 119. **141** *CSL*, pp 279–80. **142** Flanagan and Flanagan, *Irish place-names*, pp 30–1, 63–4. **143** Mac Coitir, *Irish Trees: myths, legends and folklore*, p. 6. **144** *Metrical Dindsenchas*, pp 440–1. **145** Eppinger, *Field guide to trees and shrubs of Britain and Europe* (2006), p. 74. **146** Mac Coitir, *Irish trees: myths, legends and folklore*, pp 5–6; Lucas, 'The sacred trees of Ireland', 16–54; FitzPatrick, 'Assembly and inauguration places of the Burkes in late-medieval Connacht', *passim*. **147** Mileson, 'The importance of parks in fifteenth-century society', pp

not designed to be regularly used for the lowly task of cultivation. Instead, they were designed to hold deer, cattle and timber that were for the exclusive use of the lords, highlighting their control over these precious resources. The ability to create and maintain a high-medieval park could be used to demonstrate the power of the owner in a form of symbolic violence, showing the unimaginable wealth of the owner and the insignificance of the viewer. Where parks were broken and the stock within was removed or poached this had a negative impact on the status of the owner, demonstrating that he was unable to maintain standards of 'civilisation' and order within his manor. The construction of a park pale reduced access to grazing, timber and underwood for the local inhabitants and could take in areas that had previously been arable or inhabited land. Emparking also prevented movement across the landscape, resulting in roads being blocked and necessitating their rerouting. Park boundaries could also restrict views into and out of the park, but conversely could also frame the park and any features within, providing a bounded view of 'paradise'.

Within the manorial system, parks were part of the ordered demesne lands of the lord and could be sited for the maximum dramatic impact. At Loughrea and at Carrick the parks were across a stretch of open water, accentuating the separate and distinct nature of a park as an area outside the mundane economic sphere. At Nenagh and Dunamase, the park fanned out from the castle, giving views over this elite and private space, and similarly at Maynooth the balcony on the north side of the castle provided views of the park, river and mills of the manor. Within the parks, the evidence suggests the presence of lodges at suitable vantage points. In at least some cases these potential lodges are monuments from earlier periods that appear to have been reused. Their location at vantage points made them a practical choice, but at Loughrea and Maynooth these also appear to have been places of great significance in the landscape, tied in to Gaelic concepts of rightful kingship and sovereignty. In both cases, a round-topped hill was used as a focal point for these activities, a landscape feature that has been linked to both hunting and assembly among the late-medieval Gaelic elite and with evidence to suggest that this association goes back to the early medieval period. By taking over and enclosing these places, the new elite were therefore claiming rights not only over the land itself, but also over the associated memories and history of the people and place.

20–1; Creighton, *Castles and landscapes*, p. 188; Liddiard, *Castles in context: power symbolism and landscape*, p. 97; Orser, 'Symbolic violence and landscape pedagogy', 28–44; Liddiard, *Landscapes of lordship*, p. 123.

CHAPTER SEVEN

Demise and reinvention

The focus of this work has been on the evidence for high-medieval parks and the examples presented have shown that it is possible to identify these in the modern landscape. With the exception of Earlspark, the remains are ephemeral, but a combination of cartographic, historical and field-based research has brought some of these to light. A similar situation is found in England, where many of the parks can only be recreated using maps.[1] This chapter examines what has happened to the parks in Ireland in the time since they were recorded in the high-medieval period and discusses the common themes identified.

The original Anglo-Norman colonists laid out and planned their manors, villages and towns and included some parks in their designs. A century and a half later, Ireland was no longer a land of opportunity and expansion. Instead, during the fourteenth century Ireland was a turbulent country, with wars, rebellions, famines and, of course, the Black Death.[2] All of these had an impact on the economy and on the lifestyle of the landholders, many of whom lost lands to the resurgent Gaelic lords, for whom a time of opportunity had come.[3] It has become clear that, even at the peak of Anglo-Norman control, Ireland had relatively few parks, and that few of these contained fallow deer, which were owned only by the first tier of the elite. Many parks are likely to have gradually reverted to ordinary pasture, arable and woodland, albeit in many cases still held in demesne. This would not necessarily have been a dramatic change; instead, the decline would be gradual, as rotten palings were not replaced, hedges were not repaired and ditches were allowed to silt up. For example, in 1321, Ardrahan, Co. Galway, was subject to an inquisition following the death of Thomas Fitz Richard de Clare. This stated that 'the wood there had previously been emparked, but it is now open and contains 100 acres of brush and thicket worth nothing in profits'.[4] Other parks are stated as having no value for grazing or wood, specifically 'on account of war', which could also reflect a lack of demand from tenants as much as any damage to the park itself.[5] It was important to manage woodland carefully in order to maximise the potential profit from timber and underwood, and any park

1 Watts, 'Wiltshire deer parks: an introductory survey', 92. 2 Otway-Ruthven, *A history of medieval Ireland*, pp 224–339. 3 Compare map 3, p. 174 with map 14, p. 592 in Cosgrove (ed.), *A new history of Ireland, II: medieval Ireland, 1169–1534* (1987). 4 *IEMI*, no. 204. 5 For example, *CAAR*, 19.

containing deer would certainly have needed to be secure. However, even in the absence of woodland management and a substantial boundary, scrub and pasture could have continued to be used for grazing, although this would have been much less valuable than an enclosed park. From the sixteenth century, the Tudor dissolution of the monasteries and the transfer of ecclesiastical lands, including their parks, to the laity, together with the later land redistributions of the Elizabethan, Stuart and Cromwellian periods, were major factors in the continued disappearance of high-medieval parks.[6]

Although outside the scope of this book, there were at least two further significant waves of park-building in Ireland. Ironically, as a result of the various redistributions of lands, many former ecclesiastical manors and large secular manors were granted to upwardly mobile English settlers, and this in itself fuelled the creation of a new generation of parks.[7] Another type of more recent park development is at Leamaneh, Co. Clare, where Reetz has identified and surveyed a probable seventeenth-century park close to the site of an O'Brien tower house and later fortified house, which was built in the 1640s.[8] Similarly, Cardinal Rinuccini noted the presence of a park with an incredible three thousand deer when he visited the O'Brien castle at Bunratty in 1646.[9] This may originally have been a high-medieval park, since in the thirteenth century the manor was held by de Muscegros and then by de Clare, or it may have been a post-medieval development.[10] Of interest with these two examples is that they were associated with the O'Briens, a family of Gaelic origin. It is significant, however, that the O'Brien, fourth earl of Thomond, who was probably responsible for the works at Bunratty, was noted for his English upbringing and loyalty to the crown,[11] suggesting that, as with Theobald Walter (Butler) some three and a half centuries previously, the creation of a park was a public sign of loyalty to the crown. A final wave of landscaped park construction came in the eighteenth and nineteenth centuries, when naturalistic landscapes became fashionable and many large deer parks were created in Ireland and Britain.[12]

Despite generally disappearing, some high-medieval parks did survive into the post-medieval period, either as formal entities that continued to be stocked with deer and managed for timber or as areas of pasture land that remained in demesne. For the smaller parks and those in minor manors the demise was probably the quickest and the remains are the most ephemeral. These parks were least likely to retain place-name evidence or to have a cartographically visible

6 Stout and Stout, 'Early landscapes: from prehistory to plantation' (1997), pp 60–3.   7 Reeves-Smyth, 'Demesnes', p. 198.   8 Reetz, 'The elite landscape of Leamaneh Castle, County Clare'.   9 Frost, *The history and topography of the county of Clare* (1843), p. 374.   10 Sherlock, 'An introduction to the history and architecture of Bunratty Castle' (2011), pp 204–6.   11 Ibid., p. 216.   12 Reeves-Smyth, 'Demesnes', p. 198; Finch and Giles (eds), *Estate landscapes* (2007), passim.

footprint by the time map-making became sufficiently detailed to note them in the eighteenth and nineteenth centuries. The larger, better-documented parks can give a flavour of the ways in which these landscapes were reused or even reinvented.

EARLSPARK: A CLEAR SURVIVOR

As the last chapter showed, after the fourteenth-century break-up of the de Burgh lordships in Connacht and Ulster, Earlspark seems to have continued to be associated with the de Burgh/Clanricarde lordship, but to have been reinvented as a gaelicised symbol of this lordship, becoming associated with assembly or possibly even inauguration. The park continued to be an important site within the landscape and has retained its name to the modern day.

The *Compossicion Booke of Conought* lists major landholdings in 1585, and in this the *Indenture of Clanrickard* stated that Ulick, earl of Clanrickard, held 'also the mannor of Loghreagh consisting of twelue quarters adioyning to the house and in the parke 4 quarters' with similar wording and the same quantities of land given in the *Office of Clanrickard*.[13] A quarter is given as 120 acres so that at this time the earl held approximately 480 plantation acres or *c.*772 statute acres in the park. This is somewhat less than the 913 statute acres recorded in modern times, suggesting either a surveying error or, more likely, that the documents only considered good-quality land and ignored the marshy ground abutting the lake at the west of the townland.

The park is shown on Petty's maps of Connacht and Galway,[14] which were based on information gathered in the 1650s for the Down Survey.[15] A particular feature of this map is the presence of trees in the area of 'The Parke' in Killeenadeema parish, suggesting that this was at least partly wooded or still emparked at the time of the survey. The portion in Loughrea parish is shown as 'Parkbeg' (Small park), but is not marked with trees. These place-names are also recorded in a number of earlier seventeenth-century documents, as well as Pairkavore/Payreckvore/Parkmore (Park-Mhór, the Great or Large Park) and Parkeyrkaragh/Parkegheragh/Park-Icharagh (Earl's Park).[16] Specifically in 1641 in Loughrea parish, 'Earle Clanrickard' held 'Great Parke and Parkbeg 1 qur', which was listed as containing 124 profitable acres. Overall, the place-name and cartographic evidence suggests that in the seventeenth century the park remained essentially intact.

---

13 *CBC*, 32, 49.   **14** Petty, '*Hiberniae delineatio*'.   **15** Prunty, *Maps and mapmaking in local history* (2004), pp 49–50, 57.   **16** *BSD*, 330, 334–5; Inquisitions of Galway, III.33, cited by Bunachar loghinmneacha na hÉireann, *Placenames database of Ireland; CPRI, Jas I*, p. 173.

By 1617 Richard Burke had built Portumna House and had moved the family caput to this new dwelling.[17] In 1625 he was also redeveloping Loughrea and planned to create a new park at 'Teniosty' near the town, as a result of which the tenants of this townland were to be offered leases in the town.[18] Cunningham has suggested that the 124 acres of Great Parke and Parkebeg recorded in 1641 were this new park, but these place-names are clearly shown on Petty's map within the bounds of the medieval park, while the modern townland of Tonaroasty, which can be equated to Teniosty, is shown in its correct position as 'Tonrosta'. This townland contains a deserted settlement,[19] and at some point since the departure of the tenants a 2m-high wall with a pedestrian access gate has been created along the Loughrea to Portumna road. This implies that at least part of Richard's plan was undertaken, although the park itself has not survived as a visible or mapped feature. Furthermore, it means that although the medieval park was still present and wooded on maps surveyed a generation later, in 1625 the earl considered it to be obsolete and evidently felt that a new park was needed, although this was either never fully completed or became obsolete itself by the time of the Down Survey.

The first map of the area with roads clearly marked is part of the 1778 series by George Taylor and Andrew Skinner, and shows the old Loughrea to Dalystown road running over Knockanima Hill and through the park, although the park itself is not mentioned.[20] This road still exists as a track from Loughrea and can be traced into the park. Shortly after entering the park, it splits in two at a recumbent stone known locally as the 'resting stone' (fig. 61),[21] with the more northerly portion becoming the relict road that leads to the Northern Complex of monuments and then on to the north-eastern gateway, while the more southerly portion tracks through the townland before exiting on the eastern side. By 1819 the line of the current Loughrea to Dalystown road is dotted as the proposed course of the 'New Road', while the track over Knockanima remained as the existing route.[22] The park contained at least three clusters of buildings along this older road: at the extreme west of the townland in the area of Seven Springs, in the centre of the townland in lands held by the Smith/Smyth family from the nineteenth century onwards and at the extreme east of the townland. The southern portion of Earlspark is shown on this map as 'Parkamerle', that is 'the park of the earl', partly anglicising the place-name.

In the 1830s when the first-edition OS map was being surveyed, the park had been subdivided into a patchwork of fields, many of which still exist, and a number of houses are shown on the map, so that at this stage the park was truly

---

17 Fenlon, 'Portumna: a great, many windowed and gabled house' (2012), p. 49. **18** NLI MS 3111, fo. 117 cited by Cunningham, 'Richard Burke (*c.*1572–1635) and the lordship of Clanricard' (2012). **19** RMP no. GA105-189. **20** Taylor and Skinner, 'Maps of the roads of Ireland' (1778). **21** Michael Linnane, Loughrea, pers. comm. **22** Larkin, 'A map of the county of Galway' (1819).

61 The 'resting stone', Earlspark, Co. Galway, at the junction of the old Loughrea to Dalystown road with the relict road to the Northern Complex.

obsolete. The field boundaries respect the line of the older road through the townland as well as the line of the relict road that leads to the Northern Complex, showing that they post-dated these routeways. By the time of Griffith's Valuation, the immediate lessor of almost all the lands of Earlspark in both Killeenadeema and Loughrea parishes was a Michael Nugent, who held Brick Lough in fee,[23] and in 1898 the landlord was the earl of Westmeath, Anthony Francis Nugent, so that the park had been sold by the Clanricardes.[24]

With the exception of the western portion of the possible hillfort, all of the monuments of the Northern Complex are within a single farm.[25] This has remained unchanged in size and has been tenanted and then owned by the Smyth family since the time of Griffith's Valuation. Notably, while the fields to the west of the Northern Complex are small, those on Smyth's lands and further east are much larger, and do not respect the probable line of the relict road to the gateway in the north-east of the townland. The Northern Complex was identified in Chapter 6 as having immense symbolic value within the park, in terms of both its creation and its possible reuse as an assembly site, and it may well be that when

23 Griffith's Valuation maps (1847–64). 24 *Judicial rents*, p. 86. 25 RMP no. GA105-205.

the land first became tenanted it was still considered important for this to remain as a single unit, so that it was not subdivided into fields until a much later date than the remainder of the townland.

The state of preservation of the enclosing wall is remarkable, given that it dates from the period 1251–97 and that for at least 180 years since the first-edition OS map was surveyed the land has been divided into agricultural fields. Remarkably, of 193 surveyed locations, there were only thirty-six points at which no original walling now exists, demonstrating the sturdy nature of this construction method. Nevertheless, in many places the wall has been at least partially destroyed and currently exists to a height of only 1–1.6m, of which typically 0.4m is original construction with the remainder being more recent drystone repairs of a sufficient height to provide a barrier to the movement of domestic animals.[26] Once a wall reaches 1.6m there is no increase in its efficiency in retaining cattle, so it is likely that as the wall deteriorated, any loose stone was used to divide the park into fields rather than to rebuild the wall to an unnecessary height. For example, the modern Holstein-Friesian breed has a withers height of 160cm for bulls and 144cm for cows.[27] This height is to the shoulders and means that walls above 1.6m would be higher than the cattle being retained and Holstein-Friesians are among the largest of modern breeds. Not surprisingly, the best-preserved areas of original walling are those protected by bushes and trees. This is true of many points in otherwise open land around the wall, but is particularly true in the south-western portion of the townland where the ground is wet almost to the point of being inaccessible. The bushes and trees at the margins of this ground are heavily overgrown and in many places the wall actually forms a revetment against a steep natural bank on the external side, factors that combine to result in the best levels of preservation in this part of the former park.

The history of Earlspark has been an interesting one. It is likely that it ceased to function as a park for deer during the fourteenth century, but this was not the end of its association with the de Burghs as a symbol of their lordship. Instead, it appears to have become a gaelicised landscape used as an assembly and possible inauguration site during the late-medieval period. The road from Loughrea to the Northern Complex and on to the north-eastern gateway is likely to be of high-medieval date, while the leg running through the townland and on to Dalystown could be of medieval or post-medieval origin. The field systems suggest that the north-eastern quadrant, containing the Northern Complex of monuments, remained as a single, uncompartmentalised area until much later than the

26 Beglane, 'Theatre of power: the Anglo-Norman park at Earlspark, Co. Galway, Ireland', passim. 27 DAD-IS (2014). Domestic animal diversity information system (DAD-IS), food and agriculture organization of the United Nations.

north-western part of the park, possibly because the Northern Complex of monuments was still considered to be significant when the north-eastern portion became occupied. The southern half remained as parkland until later than the northern half, as it was still shown to be wooded on the Down Survey maps, although a generation before this it was evidently no longer fit for purpose since the earl planned to replace it with a new park at Tonaroasty.

MAYNOOTH: LONG LIVED BUT LOW KEY

By comparison with Earlspark, the park at Maynooth seems to have survived as a functioning park until a later date, since it still contained deer in 1603,[28] and it continued to be acknowledged as a park into the nineteenth century. However, the less-substantial nature of the boundary and the much higher levels of urban development in Kildare compared to Galway mean that the park has become lost from local memory.

In the war of 1641, an Edward FitzGerald and his associates and followers took possession of the castle and park from the earl of Kildare. As a result of the turbulence of the early 1640s the castle was partly ruined and after this it was no longer occupied by the FitzGerald family.[29] It is therefore likely that the park fell out of use at this time, as by 1652 it was leased out to a tenant, John Rinnsford/ Raynsford/Rainsford, citizen of London, draper, who held

> those two parkes within the lordshipp of the mannor of Mynouth in the County of Kildare in the realms of Ireland being part of the demeane of the said lordshipp comonly called the great Parke, or further known by the name of Crew hill and the little Parke conteyning by estimation one thousand acres or there abouts be the land more or less to geather with all woods underwoods and comodities thereunto belonging for the terme and time of forty one years as by the said indenture may more at large appear.[30]

In 1674 and again in 1677 Thomas Emerson surveyed the lands and recorded that the park was 346 plantation acres, or 557 statute acres.[31] Over the next few decades the park was rented to a number of individuals,[32] but in 1683 a new lease was enacted for the park, assigning it to James Swanton for a rent of £70 per half year and again giving its size as 346 plantation acres, all of which suggests that Rainsford's lease had been terminated early.[33] By 1719 and again in 1725 the area of 346 plantation acres that had previously been leased to Swanton was leased to

28 *Itinerary*, iv, pp 193–4. **29** Fitzgerald, 'Maynooth Castle', 232. **30** *Leinster deeds*, p. 13. **31** *Kildare estates*, 415. **32** Rent roll 1684. **33** Ibid.

James McManus Senior. In this case, more details of the boundaries of the landholding emerge that show that this was the bounds of the park as surveyed.[34]

The manor of Maynooth was mapped by John Rocque in 1757, providing a superb insight into eighteenth-century landholdings.[35] At this time, Councillor McManus, who was presumably a direct descendant of the James McManus Senior referred to in 1719, held 579 plantation or 933 statute acres, part of which is shown on the map as 'Maynooth Park'. The boundaries of this landholding include those held by James McManus, as well as the castle area and additional lands lying to the west of the castle, in what is now the townland of Collegeland, as well as land between the town and the park itself, in what is now Maynooth townland. It is highly likely that this 933 statute acres was essentially the same area as the one thousand acres leased to John Rainsford in 1652 since, being an Englishman, he may well have contracted the lease in statute rather than plantation acres.

A second estate map was created in 1821,[36] which was similar to that produced by Rocque some sixty-five years previously, and this is the first of the more detailed maps not to make a reference to the Park of Maynooth.[37] By the time the first-edition OS map was surveyed in 1837, the park had disappeared from the cartographic record, having been effectively divided into the townlands of Crewhill, Mariavilla and part of Maynooth itself, but this was not the last record of the park. On 16 February 1843 an indenture between Augustus Frederick, duke of Leinster, and Charles William, marquis of Kildare, listed lands of Maynooth that again included the 'park of Maynooth', so that while the park was no longer relevant on a day-to-day basis, it was remembered within the FitzGerald family and was still considered to be a legal entity.[38]

Rocque's map shows a decoy pond adjoining the Rye Water at the north-east of the park (fig. 62), and there is a further example on the separate map of Laraghbryan West.[39] However, the pond is absent on Sherrard, Brassington and Green's map of 1821, suggesting that it was no longer in use at that time.[40] It is still present in the landscape and when surveyed it was found to be sub-rectangular, measuring 65–90m south-east–north-west by *c*.70m south-west–north-east and it had a depth of *c*.0.5m,[41] although due to drainage and straightening of the riverbed it no longer contains water. The north-eastern edge of the pond is bounded by a nineteenth-century bank running alongside the river, which partly covers the original northern extent of the pond. The south-western extent is bounded by a slope of rising ground that runs parallel to the

---

34 Cited by Horner, *Irish historic towns atlas, 7: Maynooth*, pp 2–3.   **35** Rocque, 'The manor of Maynooth' (1757).   **36** Sherrard et al., 'Survey of the manor of Maynooth, Co. Kildare' (1821).   **37** Rocque, 'The manor of Maynooth'.   **38** *Leinster deeds*, p. 47.   **39** Rocque, 'The manor of Maynooth'.   **40** Sherrard et al., 'Survey of the manor of Maynooth'.   **41** NGR 293443 239368.

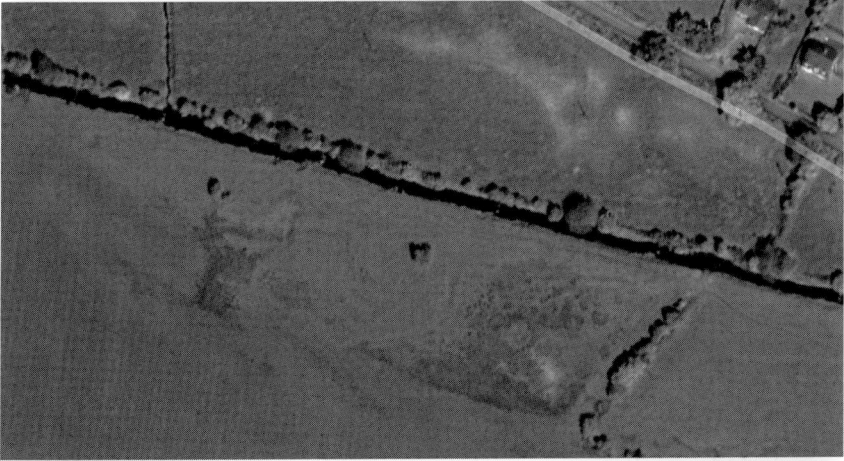

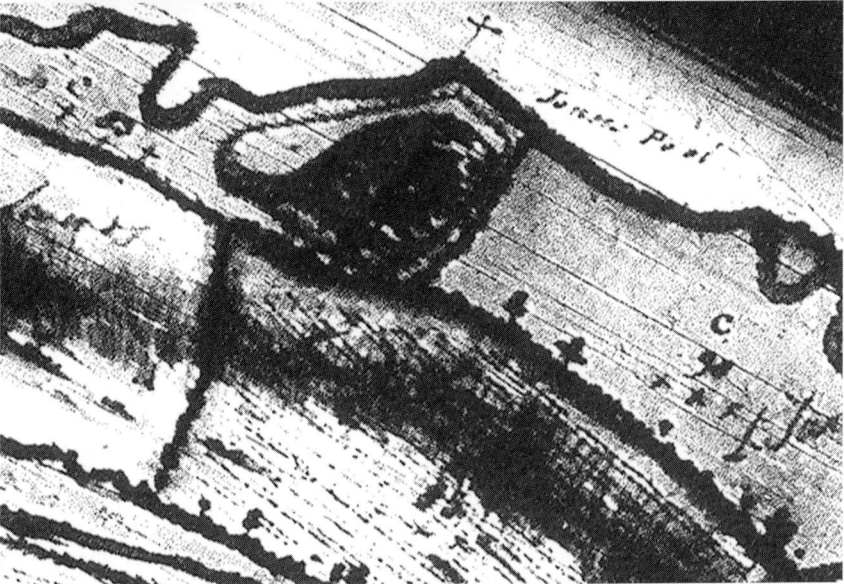

62 The decoy pond at Maynooth. Top: from the north-east; middle: GoogleEarth. Map data © Google, DigitalGlobe; Google and the Google logo are registered trademarks of Google Inc., used with permission. Below: John Rocque, 'The manor of Maynooth' (1757). Courtesy of the National Library of Ireland.

river and separates the flood plain from dry land. At the extreme north-east there is a gap in the riverside bank to allow a narrow channel to run from the pond to the river, while at the south-western corner a palaeo-channel enters the pond, curving in a sinuous fashion.

'Decoy' comes from the Dutch for a duck cage, *eendenkooi*. It has been suggested that some decoy ponds may date to the later-medieval period; however, the majority were constructed from the 1660s onwards. In their post-medieval form they originated in Holland and Reeves-Smyth has argued that in Ireland they were most common in the period 1680–1780,[42] while Alexander considers that in England they were mainly constructed in the eighteenth and nineteenth centuries.[43] They are relatively unusual in Ireland, with only sixty-two recorded by Reeves-Smyth.[44] In this case, the cartographic evidence suggests that it falls into the earlier chronological category. Although it is possible that the pond dates to the later stages of the FitzGerald occupation of Maynooth, it may also have been constructed by one of the tenants prior to 1757. With the exception of smaller, short-term tenants, who seem to have been in arrears and therefore of limited means, the creator of the decoy pond is likely to have been one of John Rainsford, James Swanton, James McManus Senior and Councillor McManus. Rainsford, a diaper from London, may be the strongest contender, since he was evidently a person of substantial means. At some point in or after 1652 he may well have chosen to import the latest idea of fashionable landscape design and create a decoy pond within his new holding as a symbol of his wealth and increasing status in the world. Unfortunately, his pleasure was short-lived, as his forty-one-year lease was terminated early, sometime prior to 1683.

One notable aspect of the park at Maynooth is that there is surprisingly little to distinguish it from the surrounding land, despite being in use for up to four hundred years. It had been constructed before 1328, probably by the mid-thirteenth century, and existed until c.1647, with deer still present in the early seventeenth century. Even after this, the area was still recognised as the 'Park of Maynooth' up to the nineteenth century. The main surviving features are the decoy pond, which is likely to be post-medieval, and the steep-sided boundary ditch, which is notably large, but is no larger than the east–west ditch that runs off westward from the boundary ditch on the western side. Even the main boundary ditch has had its route modified at its southern extent in the last two hundred years. Today, arable agriculture is carried out on only the best lands in the country, but substantial areas of the former park and its immediate surroundings are under crops. This attests to the excellent quality of the land

42 Reeves-Smyth, 'Natural history of demesnes', pp 566–7.   **43** Alexander, *Introductions to heritage assets: animal management* (2011), p. 5.   **44** Reeves-Smyth, 'Demesnes', p. 198.

incorporated into the park, and it is likely that ploughing has removed many features within the park. One example is the boundary at the extreme north-west in Timard, which is not visible today, but can be traced cartographically.

Of all the parks identified in this book, the park at Maynooth seems to have been the longest surviving in its primary function as a park for deer and, even so, this has not resulted in substantial remains being present. This demonstrates clearly the ephemeral nature of these designed landscapes and highlights one of the main reasons that these monuments have lain unidentified in the landscape for so long. The FitzGeralds were among the least gaelicised of the former Anglo-Norman families and their Leinster lands lay on the edge of the Pale. As a result, they retained close ties with England and with English culture, so that these are probably the reasons for the long survival of the park at Maynooth and its subsequent direct replacement by the grounds of Carton demesne.

DUNAMASE: RECREATING AN IMAGINED MEDIEVAL WORLD

The post-medieval history of the park at Dunamase is in many ways more interesting than the high-medieval park itself, because in the late eighteenth century the medieval park was recreated as part of an elaborate re-envisioning of the medieval heyday of the manor.

Following the death of the last earl marshal in 1245, the lands of Leinster were divided among a number of female heiresses. Dunamase became part of the de Mortimer lands until 1330, when Roger de Mortimer was executed for treason and his possessions confiscated by the crown. Around this time, but possibly slightly earlier, Lysaght O'More is recorded as having taken the castle and lordship from the de Mortimers.[45] Although the crown granted the forfeited de Mortimer lands to Fulke de la Freigne in 1334, Hodkinson contends that this was probably a speculative grant, as he notes that there is no mention of Dunamase in later-medieval records after this and, furthermore, his excavations revealed little evidence for activity at the castle after *c.*1330.[46]

There is, therefore, a gap in the documentary evidence until 1538 when Piaras Mac Maol-Lochlainn O'More submitted to the king, keeping much of his land by surrender and regrant, but renouncing title and lordship to the castle at Dunamase and acknowledging the king as his overlord.[47] The O'Mores retained

45 *Clyn's Annals*, 1264, 1342; Hodkinson, 'A summary of recent work at the Rock of Dunamase, Co. Laois', pp 46–9; Ó Cléirigh, 'The impact of the Anglo-Normans in Laois' (1999), p. 169; Delaney, *The Rock of Dunamase* (1996), p. 8; O'Leary, 'The Rock of Dunamase' (1909–11), 161–71; Orpen, *Ireland under the Normans, 1169–1333*, i, p. 375; iii, pp 103–4.   **46** Hodkinson, 'A summary of recent work at the Rock of Dunamase, Co. Laois', pp 43, 49.   **47** *SPH8*, iii, CCLI; Carey, 'The end of the Gaelic political

Dunamase until 1577 when Robert Piggott received extensive grants of lands from Queen Elizabeth.[48] Following his death in 1607, an inquisition noted that among other holdings Piggott was 'seised in fee of the ... townes and lands of Carrickneparke, al' Carryneparke', which translates as 'Rock of the Park'.[49]

The castle itself changed hands a number of times during the 1640s but may have finally been destroyed by the Cromwellian army in 1650, although during his excavations Hodkinson did not find any evidence for this in the form of, for example, cannonballs or musket balls.[50] By 1791 the ruined castle was in the possession of Sir John Parnell, whose descendants continued as the major landowners in the area until three Fitzpatrick brothers purchased the castle and associated townland through the Land Commission. Their nephews, the Kelly brothers, inherited the land and, in turn, the Dowling brothers, who were nephews of the latter, took possession of the agricultural land and still hold it today. Ownership of the castle and the rock itself was transferred into state care in the time of the Kellys.[51]

By the late eighteenth century, Sir John Parnell, ancestor of Charles Stewart Parnell, was the owner of Dunamase and had 'very much improved the aspect of this rock by clothing it with trees and on the eastern (*sic*) side he has built a banqueting-room'.[52] Although often regarded as having been carried out in 1795,[53] it would appear from Grose and Coote that the landscaping and building work described above was begun a few years prior to this, since Parnell had received Dublin Society grants in 1789 and 1793 to enclose areas of thirteen and fourteen acres of plantation and the banqueting room and tree planting is described by Grose in 1795.[54] Coote gives an extensive description of the history and ruins at Dunamase, before continuing with an eye-witness account of Parnell's work:

> Sir J. Parnell, who wishes to preserve the venerable appearance of this celebrated place, is rebuilding the castle on its ancient site, in the same style of gothic architecture. The apartments within are laid out with taste and comprise a complete banquetting room, ball room, dressing-room, kitchen

order: the O'More lordship of Laois, 1536–1603', pp 216–17; Fitzgerald, 'Historical notes on the O'Mores and their territory of Leix, to the end of the sixteenth century', 25, app. iv; Comerford, *Collections relating to the dioceses of Kildare and Leighlin*, 3 (1886), p. 362; *IRCH*, Eliz. (1). **48** Comerford, *Collections relating to the dioceses of Kildare and Leighlin*, 3, p. 276; *IRCH*, Eliz (5), Jac. I (1). **49** *IRCH*, Jac. I (1). **50** Bradley, 'Urban archaeological survey: Laois', p. 25; Ledwich, *Antiquities of Ireland* (1804), p. 296; Hodkinson, 'A summary of recent work at the Rock of Dunamase, Co. Laois', p. 44. **51** M. Dowling, Dunamase, pers. comm.; Grose, *The antiquities of Ireland: the second volume*, pp 12–13; O'Leary, 'The Rock of Dunamase', 168. **52** Grose, *The antiquities of Ireland: the second volume*, p. 13. **53** Bradley, 'Urban archaeological survey: Laois', p. 25; O'Leary, 'The Rock of Dunamase', 168, 170. **54** Grose, *The antiquities of Ireland: the second volume*, p. 13; Coote, *Statistical survey of the Queen's County*, p. 221.

and cellars: the well will again be opened. The land, on which stands the rock, is the property of Sir John Parnell, who has above two hundred acres here inclosed. Some fine timber is on this demesne, and the plantation, for which Sir John received the Dublin Society's premium, is admirably enclosed with high stone ditches, breasted with a double row of quicks, and the trees thriving in proper heart.[55]

The work carried out by Parnell included the renovation of part of the castle to provide lavish entertainment facilities. This allowed him to offer hospitality that would have been enjoyed as much in the thirteenth as in the eighteenth century. The reconstruction included new window- and doorframes and major rebuilding work, all of which is still visible today.[56] These banqueting facilities were situated at the northern end of the keep and looked out to the west over the park, as had the original solar, five hundred years previously. As a result, Parnell needed to ensure that the view from the castle fitted with his re-creation of a romantic past. He chose to create his interpretation of a medieval park as the backdrop for his medieval banqueting hall. As an educated man, he undoubtedly knew that hunting and parks were intimately associated with later-medieval castles, he may well have read some of the historical sources that referred to Dunamase, and it is likely that he recognised that the name of the townland signified the original location of the high-medieval park. One feature of note is the mention of 'above two hundred acres here inclosed', which is *c*.322 statute acres and is the approximate area of the modern townland.[57] This clearly suggests that the mortared stone wall currently surrounding the townland was constructed or rebuilt by Parnell as part of his redevelopment of the castle.

In rebuilding Dunamase, and in creating a sylvan landscape there, Parnell was at the forefront of late eighteenth-century fashion and improvement. This was the heyday of landscaped parks surrounding large country houses and, as such, Parnell had a wealth of models to choose from in his development, including his own home at nearby Rathleague, which was well stocked with exotic trees, a Grecian-style temple and picturesque gardens and water features.[58] A park that appeared to be natural was one much sought after in the period from the mid-eighteenth to the mid-nineteenth century, following on from, and reacting against, the formalised symmetrical gardens of the preceding century, and in addition, the Dublin Society provided improvement grants for landowners who were prepared to plant stands of particular species of trees on their lands and to

55 Ibid., pp 116–17. **56** Hodkinson, 'Excavations in the gatehouse of Nenagh Castle, 1996 and 1997', 162–82; Hodkinson, 'A summary of recent work at the Rock of Dunamase, Co. Laois', passim. **57** Coote, *Statistical survey of the Queen's County*, pp 116–17. **58** Ibid., p. 97.

63 Dunamase Castle, from Francis Grose, *The antiquities of Ireland· the second volume* (London, 1795). Courtesy of the National Library of Ireland.

retain them for a minimum of ten years.[59] The ideal was the supposedly 'natural' countryside of southern England, rather than an Irish 'midland-bog' naturalism that might today be considered more appropriate in such a setting. Furthermore, Parnell would have seen the castle as being English in origin, and hence would probably have considered an English landscape to be the most appropriate backdrop. These landscaped parks aimed to provide open expanses of grassland, interspersed with clumps of trees and real or re-created ruins. They were often surrounded by demesne walls, with trees planted on 'glens, rocky knolls and even archaeological sites'.[60] All of which can be seen at Dunamase, with the added advantage that the ruins were genuine and dramatic (fig. 63).

Sir John Parnell, second baronet, was an influential politician and major landowner. He was a long-standing member of the Irish parliament, served as chancellor of the exchequer of Ireland from 1785 to 1798 and was a member of the privy council of both Ireland and Britain. He was a loyal member of the government and a strong supporter of the Protestant interest, having opposed

59 Tomlinson, 'Forests and woodlands' (1997), p. 127; Coote, *Statistical survey of the Queen's County*, p. 221.
60 Tomlinson, 'Forests and woodlands', pp 127, 129; Reeves-Smyth, 'Demesnes', p. 201; McErlean, 'The archaeology of parks and gardens, 1600–1900: an introduction to Irish garden archaeology' (2007), p. 276; Orser, 'Estate landscapes and the Cult of the Ruin: a lesson in spatial transformation in rural Ireland'

Catholic relief bills in the 1770s and 1780s and voted against Catholic emancipation in 1795. In 1798, however, he was sacked from his position in the government as a result of his determined opposition to the Act of Union, which came into effect in 1801.[61] Both his opposition to religious reforms and his opposition to the Act of Union can be considered as forms of conservatism, a feeling that the status quo should continue to exist, and that the introduction of new forms of government should be resisted, and it is in this light that his redevelopment of the castle and lands at Dunamase can be interpreted.

At Dunamase, Parnell sought to recreate an imagined past, with picturesque ruins set amid a parkland landscape. By repairing the castle and enclosing the townland and the rock with a demesne wall, Parnell was reconstituting a mythical Golden Age in which the castle and its Anglo-Norman lord were central to society. This 'Cult of the Ruin'[62] could be used to convey 'the comforting notion that the social order was somehow natural, immutable and inevitable'[63] by promoting 'a sense of antiquity and continuity.'[64] For a conservative such as Sir John, the social and political changes of the late eighteenth century must have been threatening, with the Anglo-Irish ascendancy coming under pressure, both from their tenants and from the government of England. This was at a time when the French Revolution of 1789 had stoked calls for revolution and reform throughout Europe. Many of the penal laws against Catholics had been repealed, resulting in the rights of Catholics to purchase and lease land, found schools, practise their religion and vote, and, in addition, these reforms led to the removal of restrictions on employment.[65] The union of Scotland and England in 1707 had provided a potential template for a union of Ireland and England, and this was periodically suggested in the eighteenth century. After the rebellion of 1798, calls for union became stronger, as this was seen as one way in which trouble could be averted in the future and economic prosperity improved. Parnell was one of the MPs who opposed the plan, which would greatly reduce the political power of the Anglo-Irish, Church of Ireland, landowning class, diluting their influence within a Westminster parliament.[66]

In recreating a mythical past at Dunamase, it can be argued that Sir John sought to reassure himself of the extent of his power and control at a time of social and political change. Eighteenth- and nineteenth-century landscape parks provided privacy and a feeling of seclusion, where the outside world was not visible. They existed at a time of low tree-cover, in a period of intense agricultural

---

(2007), p. 78. **61** Johnston-Luik, 'Parnell, Sir John' (2009). **62** Orser, 'Estate landscapes and the Cult of the Ruin', p. 88. **63** Reeves-Smyth, 'Demesnes', p. 203. **64** Orser, 'Estate landscapes and the Cult of the Ruin', p. 88. **65** Kelly, 'The parliamentary reform movement of the 1780s and the Catholic question' (1988), 96; McDowell, 'The age of the United Irishmen: reform and reaction, 1789–94' (1986), pp 290, 307–13. **66** McDowell, 'The age of the United Irishmen: reform and reaction, 1789–94', pp 364–73.

usage of the land, yet within the parks, new trees were deliberately planted and existing trees maintained.[67] They were landscapes in which status was demonstrated by the ability to control access to land and to restrict agricultural use of the landscape,[68] and in which those 'inside' the walls considered themselves socially, ethnically and religiously superior to those 'outside' the walls.[69] It is notable that many of these were the same drivers that were present in the high-medieval period and that caused the original high-medieval parks to be created.

CARRICK, CO. WEXFORD: AN AGRICULTURAL PARK

The park at Carrick started well, being documented at the relatively early date of 1231x4,[70] and fallow deer bones were found during excavations at the associated Ferrycarrig Castle.[71] However, as with Dunamase, the castle and its lands were part of the lordship of Leinster, and as a result they were inherited by Joan Marshal's daughter, Joan de Munchensy, and her husband William de Valence. Subsequently, the lands passed into the hands of the Hastings and then the Talbot families, before being taken into the king's hands in 1537 as a result of the continued absence of the lord.[72] Probably due to the peripheral status of Carrick in the lands of the de Valences and their successors, the park at Carrick seems to have fallen out of its primary use by the time of Joan's death in 1307 and the death of her son Aymer in 1324.[73]

In the sixteenth century a number of documents record rights to sixty acres of land in the park at Carrick, which were usually mentioned in association with the right to operate the ferry across the Slaney. Many of these documents list William Synnott as the holder; however, Richard Devereux had a twenty-one-year lease from 1567 and Lancelot Allford held it for a time prior to 1575, with George Bourchier having the rights in 1582.[74] The Synnott family evidently favoured the name William since this name is associated with the park through to the 1650s. In 1635 Sir William Brereton noted that, travelling from Carrick to Wexford,

> about a mile hence lies a farm called the Park, which is now leased unto one Mr Hardye, an Englishman, who lives upon it and hath an estate in it [of]

67 McErlean, 'The archaeology of parks and gardens, 1600–1900: an introduction to Irish garden archaeology', pp 276, 279. 68 Ibid., p. 276. 69 Orser, 'Estate landscapes and the Cult of the Ruin', p. 78. 70 *CERM*, 56. 71 McCormick, 'The mammal bones from Ferrycarrig, Co. Wexford', passim. 72 Orpen, *Ireland under the Normans, 1169–1333*, iii, pp 79–107; Bennett, 'Preliminary archaeological excavations at Ferrycarrig ringwork, Newtown td, Co. Wexford', 27–31; Colfer, 'Medieval Wexford' (1990–1), 13–21; Hadden, 'The origin and development of Wexford town, pt 4', 5; Hore, *History of the town and county of Wexford*, v, pp 41–8; Lewis, *A topographical dictionary of Ireland*, pp 700–1. 73 *IEMI*, nos 156, 228. 74 *CPRI*, 49, 517; Hore, *History of the town and county of Wexford*, v, pp 34, 180, 182, 186;

about thirteen years. The landlord is one Mr William Synode of the Lough, a man that needs money. This land is [worth] about £16 per annum. He saith it contains about 300 acres, others say 200 ...[75]

Hardye, an Englishman, would be assessing land in English acres, and so reckoned his holding at three hundred acres, while 'others', being Irish, would reckon land in plantation acres and so would arrive at a figure of closer to two hundred. This confirms that the area of Park, and hence of the high-medieval park associated with Carrick, was of the order of three hundred statute acres.

The *Books of survey and distribution* show that in 1641 William Synnott was still the landowner, owning all of 'The Parke' and most of the modern townland of Ballyboggan.[76] The land areas in the *Civil Survey* of 1654–6 initially appear to contradict the *Books of survey and distribution*, but overall the figures for the two townlands give a similar total to that of the earlier survey. These lands are shown on Petty's map of the 'parrish of Carrigge' and can be compared to the townland and field boundaries of the first-edition OS map (fig. 64). This shows that Synnott's land included all of the modern townlands of Park and Ballyboggan, apart from fifty-three plantation acres called Fortumny. In addition, the modern townlands of Stonybatter and Carricklawn did not exist, with the land split between Park, Ballyboggan and Fortumny. Furthermore, the extreme western extent of the modern townland of Park was also part of Ballyboggan. What this clearly demonstrates is that while the townland names are essentially unchanged, their boundaries have moved quite considerably in the past four hundred years, and were much more fluid than they are today. In 1659 Pender lists three residents of Parke townland, of which two are English and one is Irish.[77] This suggests a small number of households, with the land not subdivided. Ballyboggan, by contrast, was occupied by a total of twenty-four people, of whom two were English and the remainder Irish. The townland of Park was essentially a single block of land rather than being subdivided into numerous small tenancies, suggesting that it had been held in demesne prior to being let out to a substantial tenant.

A century later, Vallancey's map of 1776 was principally military, and concentrated on features such as roads, maritime navigation and the location of big houses and demesnes.[78] This clearly shows the road running from Wexford to Ferrycarrig, which Haddon called the 'Tudor Engineered Road', but unfortunately he gave no evidence for the dating of this road.[79] The map does not name

CSPI, ii, 389. **75** Cited by Hore, *History of the town and county of Wexford*, v, p. 246. **76** *BSD*. **77** *Census 1659*, 542. **78** Vallancey, 'Military itinerary to the south of Ireland' (1776). **79** Hadden, 'The origin and development of Wexford town, pt 3: the Norman period', 3–12 map.

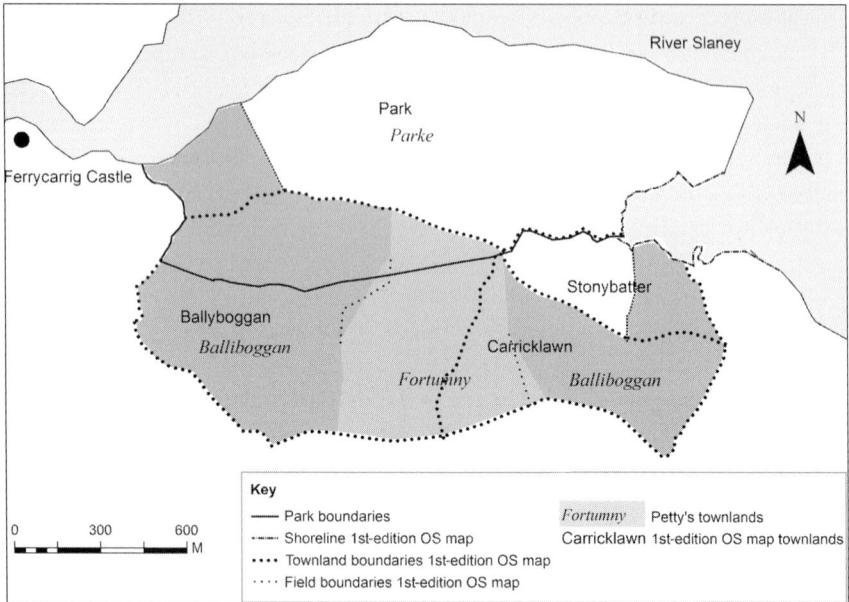

64 William Petty's parish map transposed onto townland and field boundaries from the
first-edition OS map with the proposed Carrick park boundary.

the Park area, but it does provide a view of what at first appear to be field boundaries, although close comparison of these with the first-edition OS map suggests
that they are *c.*30 acres each and are more likely to represent land-ownership
blocks, or the boundaries of former open-field systems. Interestingly, no
boundaries are shown within the bounds of the park; instead the boundary of the
final set of blocks is in the approximate location of the proposed park boundary.
It is therefore possible that even at this late date this area was undivided, but
caution must be expressed due to the schematic nature of the cartography.

By the time of the first-edition OS map, the park was well and truly obsolete,
the land having been divided into fields and the new Mail Coach Road having
been constructed through the townland to connect Wexford with Ferrycarrig.
The southern boundary and relict road skirting the park had also been forgotten,
and a number of gentry villas had been built at the eastern end of Ballyboggan,
with their rear garden walls reflecting but not respecting the curving boundary of
the medieval park.

The fate of the park at Carrick is probably typical of the fate of many of the
smaller parks and those at the minor manors of the elite. It very quickly became
agricultural land, being rented to tenants, but seems to have retained a distinct
character and to have been considered to be a single entity, at least until Brereton's

visit of 1635,[80] and possibly as late as the late eighteenth century.[81] This is a park that could only be found by cartographic means, showing how easily they can disappear from the physical landscape. The place-name evidence was key to identifying this park, but the only remaining physical feature of the park is the relict road bounding it to the south, and much of this has been destroyed by eighteenth-century suburban development and nineteenth-century agricultural improvements.

NENAGH, CO. TIPPERARY: AN URBAN PARK

The park at Nenagh was probably one of the latest of the high-medieval parks to be developed, and it is located within the fabric of an urban setting, so that it is ironic that it has actually retained the most park-like feel in the modern landscape.

It was created in 1299 but,[82] as was the case in much of Ireland, Nenagh was unstable in the fourteenth century, with the town being burnt during the Bruce Wars in 1316 and again by the local O'Kennedys in 1348.[83] Nevertheless, the castle was still held by the earls of Ormond and there was a series of peace accords between the Ormonds and the O'Kennedys in the fourteenth century.[84] By the late fourteenth century, the earls of Ormond had moved to Gowran, and later they moved again, this time to Kilkenny Castle, which they purchased in 1392 from the de Spensers.[85] At some point after this, Gleeson suggests that the castle and manor of Nenagh passed into the hands of the Mac Uí Brian sept, who held it until 1533, when it was regained by Sir Piers Butler.[86] Empey refutes this, however, arguing that Nenagh and its castle remained in Ormond hands.[87] Regardless, the earls of Ormond were still acknowledged as overlords of Nenagh, apparently receiving rents from the O'Kennedys for their lands until at least 1653.[88] In 1703 the Butlers sold the manor and town of Nenagh to Nehemiah Donnellan, and in 1733 the lands were sold again, this time to the Holmes family.[89]

The *Civil Survey* of 1654 lists the countess of Ormond as the owner of the majority of the land in the part of the parish of Nenagh that was in Lower Ormond, of which there were 130 plantation acres (210 statute acres) described as 'shrubby wood' and ten plantation acres (sixteen statute acres) of 'underwood'.

80 Cited by Hore, *History of the town and county of Wexford*, v, p. 246. **81** Vallancey, 'Military itinerary to the south of Ireland'. **82** *CJRI*, i, p. 234. **83** Gleeson, 'The castle and manor of Nenagh', 251–2. **84** Ibid., 250–3; Empey, 'The Norman period, 1185–1500' (1985), p. 89. **85** Gleeson, 'The castle and manor of Nenagh', 248–9, 251, 253. **86** Ibid., 254–5. **87** Empey, 'The Norman period, 1185–1500', p. 88. **88** Gleeson, 'The castle and manor of Nenagh', 252–3. **89** Ibid., 258–9; Gwynn and Gleeson, *A*

The description of the boundaries of the barony of Lower Ormond makes it clear that the area of the medieval park was known as Derryneana, the 'Oaks of Nenagh'.[90] The park is not mentioned anywhere except in 1299, although 'a wood called le Dirre' is recorded in 1339, so this seems to have been a long-standing name and it continued to be used up to the late eighteenth century,[91] when it was used in the Holmes leases.[92] In the eighteenth and nineteenth centuries, a number of leases were assigned that shed light on the development of the town and the area around the castle. These, which were collated and studied by Sheehan, show that at that stage the western part of the park, adjacent to the castle, consisted of small landholdings, individual fields and residential units.[93] Bradley suggested that much of the current street plan of the town may date to the sixteenth or seventeenth century, rather than the medieval period, so it is possible that this was when the western area may have been laid out.[94] By contrast, to the east of Summerhill/Ormond Street/The Old Turnpike Road, the land was still rural, with references to features such as the 'Wood-field' and to the value of the timber in this area.[95] The eastern area of the park has a somewhat complex history, having become the demesne lands of Riverston and Summerville, owned by the Donnellan family and Holmes family respectively, however, as a result of marriage and inheritance the two estates were brought back together late in the eighteenth century.[96]

In 1732, when Nehemiah Donnellan was constructing the house at Riverston, the well-known traveller, Mrs Delany, visited and recorded her impressions of the site:

> Nature has done everything for him he can desire – fine woods of oak, a sweet winding river, and charming lawns that will afford him sufficient materials to exercise his genius on ... at the bottom of the hill, which is covered with wood, runs the river, by the side of which Mr Donnellan can make a walk three miles long, of the finest turf that ever was seen. The river is so well disposed, that he can make cascades, and do what he pleases with it.[97]

Today, with the exception of the grounds of the castle and Catholic church, the western half of the park on both sides of Summerhill has become part of the urban landscape of Nenagh (fig. 65). Summerhill itself is fringed by Georgian

history of the diocese of Killaloe, p. 418.   **90** *Civil survey*, 278.   **91** *CIPM*, viii, no. 184.   **92** Gwynn and Gleeson, *A history of the diocese of Killaloe*, p. 288.   **93** Sheehan, *Nenagh and its neighbourhood* (1950), passim.   **94** Bradley, 'The medieval towns of Tipperary' (1985), p. 50.   **95** Sheehan, *Nenagh and its neighbourhood*, pp 24–7.   **96** Sheehan, *Nenagh and its neighbourhood*, pp 26–8.   **97** Delany, *The autobiography and correspondence of Mary Granville, Mrs Delany* (1861), pp 386–8.

65 Nenagh from above. Map Data © Google, DigitalGlobe; Google and the Google logo are registered trademarks of Google Inc., used with permission.

and Victorian buildings, while Dublin Road/Thomas MacDonagh Street has nineteenth-century buildings close to the core of the town, but further along are twentieth-century constructions. Birr Road/Bulfin Road, the side roads and the high point of the park survived for longer in a rural state, having been developed for residential use in the later twentieth century. In this pattern, the roads clearly show the growth of the town to encompass an ever-larger area over time. By contrast, the eastern half of the park still remains a pleasant, leafy, demesne landscape, with Summerville owned by the Christian Brothers, although the house no longer exists, and Riverston and the Riverston Mill remaining as private houses surrounded by trees, gardens, horse paddocks and grazed fields. The river itself, although the banks have been modified by drainage systems, is still a very pleasant place, with small, possibly artificial, stone weirs along its length, suggestive of the cascades that Mrs Delany proposed in the eighteenth century (fig. 66).

This provides a window on the layout of the manor of Nenagh in later-medieval and post-medieval times. The lack of development in much of the park area demonstrates that this was not considered to be a part of the urban fabric of Nenagh, and instead was held in demesne and reserved for the Butlers throughout the later-medieval and post-medieval periods. At some point, however, the layout of the streets was altered and Summerhill was constructed,

66 A 'cascade' at Nenagh as described by Mrs Delany in the eighteenth century.

running through the western part of the park, and separating the castle from the high point and the eastern portion of the former park. Despite development in the west, the land to the east was still undeveloped and the association of the park with the landowner continued in the eighteenth century, when the Donnellans and later the Holmes family both selected the still-sylvan retreat of Derrynenagh as the site for their suburban dwellings. Ironically, the proximity of the park to the town and its suitability for a demesne residence is why the wood-pasture ambience has been retained in the eastern portion, and of all the surveyed parks this is the one that has the most park-like landscape today.

GLENCREE, CO. WICKLOW: AN INVISIBLE PARK

The last known record of the park at Glencree is from 1279/80;[98] however, the latest known Anglo-Norman mention of land rights at Glencree is in 1308, when Nigel le Brun was given land by the king that was valued at one mark per year for each carucate.[99] In the first half of the fourteenth century the area around Glencree passed out of Anglo-Norman control and into the hands of the

98 *CDI*, ii, no. 1633. **99** *IEMI*, no. 160. **100** Price, 'Powerscourt and the territory of Fercullen', 117–19;

O'Tooles. They held it for much of the next two hundred years, although in the early sixteenth century they were briefly dispossessed by the FitzGeralds. Nevertheless, in 1537 they held the territory of Fercullen, which included Glencree and Powerscourt, and, despite these lands being granted to the Talbots, the Talbots surrendered them in exchange for other lands and Fercullen was formally granted to the O'Tooles in 1541.[100] After the rebellion of Brian-an-Chogaidh and Felim mac Tirlagh O'Toole, the lands were forfeited, and were subsequently granted to Sir Richard Wingfield in 1603,[101] after which time Powerscourt remained in the hands of the Wingfields until the twentieth century. The park, however, does not seem to have survived the turbulence of the fourteenth century. In 1540 the lord deputy and the council of Ireland wrote to the king noting that the lands of the O'Tooles were 'nothing but woddes, rockes, greete bogges and barren ground, being unmanured or tilled'.[102] Nevertheless, if it was sparsely occupied in the sixteenth century, the valley soon developed. By the 1660s, the Hearth money rolls record twenty-two houses in Glencree, three in Barnamire and seven in Curtlestown, most of which were sufficiently substantial to have chimneys. By the time of the Powerscourt estate map and the first-edition OS map in the first half of the nineteenth century, the enclosure had been divided into fields and a number of clusters of buildings are found both within and adjacent to the enclosure.[103] Interestingly, in the area to the north of the Glencree to Enniskerry road, field survey showed the presence of more field boundaries than are shown on these or later maps, suggesting that some of the field systems had already become obsolete by the early nineteenth century.

BALYDONEGAN, CO. CARLOW: A DEMESNE AND INDUSTRIAL LANDSCAPE

The Down Survey parish maps show 'Ducanstown and Newgardens' as an arable area of 271 plantation acres and two roods, with a castle on the banks of the River Barrow. The maps also show 'Duckanswood' as almost entirely shrubwood and pasture totalling 228 plantation acres, with both properties owned by James Butler. To the east of this area, the 589 plantation acres of Painestown were owned by James Barry and contained a castle and the parish church of Painestown.[104] While it is likely that this area included the park at Balydonegan, no obvious medieval park boundary features could be identified during fieldwork.

By the late eighteenth century, Painestown had been laid out as the Oakpark demesne and by the time of the first-edition OS map both 'Ducanstown and

Fitzgerald, 'The manor and castle of Powerscourt', 127–39.   **101** Fitzgerald, 'The manor and castle of Powerscourt, County Wicklow', 138.   **102** *State papers*, Hen. VIII, iii, p. 266.   **103** Armstrong, 'Maps of the estates of the Right Honourable Richard, lord viscount Powerscourt'.   **104** Petty, 'Down Survey parish maps'.

Newgardens' and Duckanswood had been split into a number of townlands, while the eastern portion of Oakpark was used as a racetrack and deer park. The modern land-use in the area is very varied since, in addition to suburban housing, there is industrial land alongside the River Barrow, including the now-defunct Irish Sugar plant at Strawhall and a landfill site to the north of this in 'Bestfield or Dunganstown'. Today, the core of Oakpark and the Palladian mansion house are used as a Teagasc crop research centre, while part of the racetrack and deer park have been developed into a golf course and an industrial estate. Although varied, these modern uses of the land have all resulted in significant ground disturbance for both agricultural and industrial uses and very little of Duckanswood remains.

FIELDS, PARKS, GARDENS AND TOWNS

There are forty-six high-medieval parks for which documentary evidence has been found, and of these at least the general location of forty-two is clear. Many of the smaller parks may never be cartographically or physically found, but it has proved possible to identify several of the larger examples in the modern landscape. High-medieval parks could have three possible long-term fates: they could continue in some form, held in demesne and managed separately from the ordinary renanted lands; they could become ordinary agricultural land or they could be lost under urban sprawl.

Survey work in Ireland has shown that cartographic and place-name evidence can be crucial, and many parks in England are also known only from these types of analyses.[105] This potentially low visibility, even in England, where there was cultural continuity through the later-medieval and post-medieval period, is an important point, and explains the even lower visibility of the Irish parks, which have often been subject to much more changeable political and cultural circumstances. Nevertheless, place-names have been surprisingly resilient to the changes of the last seven hundred years, with 'park' elements in the modern townland names at Earlspark, Carrick and Dunamase, while in Maynooth the name survived until early in the nineteenth century. Only at Nenagh is the place-name evidence less clear cut, but even here there is a preponderance of woodland-related names, including the name 'Derrynenagh', which was in use until the eighteenth century.

None of the surveyed parks have had continuity of use throughout the medieval period and into modern times. Despite this, the longevity of some has

---

105 Cantor and Wilson, 'The medieval deer-parks of Dorset: I–XVII', passim; Hoppitt, 'Hunting Suffolk's parks: towards a reliable chronology of Imparkment' (2007), p. 157; Watts, 'Wiltshire deer parks: an introductory survey', 92; Winchester, 'Baronial and manorial parks in medieval Cumbria' (2007), pp 157–9.

been surprising, although it must be borne in mind that the parks examined here are among the largest, best-documented and highest-status parks in the medieval records. Earlspark and Maynooth were both used into the seventeenth century, with Maynooth retaining deer to that time. These were both extant until they were superseded by parks at the new caputs of Portumna House and Carton House respectively. In the cases of Nenagh, Dunamase and Glencree, the parks fell out of use in the fourteenth century. The Butlers may have retained nominal control over Nenagh; however, the evidence suggests that the Mac Uí Brian sept may have had physical possession of the town and castle until the mid-sixteenth century, and certainly the Butlers had only minimal input to the town in the intervening period. At Dunamase there was a complete loss of Anglo-Norman control, with the O'Mores holding the castle and manor until the late sixteenth century, and similarly Glencree was held by the O'Tooles for much of the late-medieval period. Despite these changes in local power structures, both Dunamase and Nenagh seem to have survived intact and in the post-medieval period were retained in demesne. This suggests that although the Gaelic lords had not constructed parks in the high-medieval period, when they obtained them in the fourteenth century they could see a value in keeping them whole. There is no evidence that at this stage they used them to keep deer, but instead, as for the majority of the Anglo-Normans, they were a valuable source of timber and grazing and, if the palings and hedges were maintained, they could be used as securely bounded areas in which to keep cattle. Interestingly, having survived the late-medieval Gaelic resurgence, both Dunamase and Nenagh were given a new lease of life as naturalistic landscape parks of the eighteenth century. At Carrick, which was plagued by absenteeism, the park was very short-lived, becoming tenanted at an early stage and being used as agricultural land throughout the late-medieval and post-medieval periods. At Balydonegan, Co. Carlow, by contrast, Duckanswood, although not described as a park, survived as woodland into the seventeenth century and some of it remains within the Oakpark demesne today.

For those parks that have retained some semblance of their former use, this can be reflected in parkland features surviving, or being recreated within the modern field systems. This association of place with function found expression at Dunamase in the late eighteenth century, when Sir John Parnell sought to revive the past glories of the castle and its demesne by rebuilding part of the castle, planting trees and re-enclosing the high-medieval park. In doing so, as an Anglo-Irish landlord, he sought a return to a perceived Golden Age in which his role as lord of the manor would be unquestioned and his power would be undimmed by new ideas of democracy and equality. The eighteenth and nineteenth centuries were important periods of emparkment in Ireland and Britain, when 'naturalistic' landscape parks became an essential backdrop for large country houses, which in Ireland were built mainly by the Anglo-Irish.[106] As in England, these could contain deer, and if so then the venison was consumed, but their role was not aristocratic hunting.[107] By the eighteenth century the elite had turned their attention to fox-hunting, which was more suited to the enclosed field systems that had come into vogue.[108] There is evidence that some other medieval parks were reinvigorated in the post-medieval period, or that their original location was reused in developing a post-medieval parkland demesne. For example, some of Balydonegan, Co. Carlow, became part of the eighteenth-century Oakpark demesne and similarly at Ferns, Co. Wexford, St Edan's and Ferns Demesne are likely to cover the site of the original park held by the bishop of Ferns.

At Kilkenny the park and garden lay opposite the gate of the castle,[109] which originally faced south-east. The area to the south-east is now all parkland, although there is cartographic and geophysical evidence to show that orchards and gardens previously existed immediately adjacent to the castle.[110] Nevertheless, the land beyond this, which had become a 'Dancing meadow & other small cells', Archerstown, Archersgrove and Sence by the time of the Down Survey, is likely to have been the original high-medieval park.[111]

Unfortunately, where post-medieval demesne landscapes have been developed it is difficult to identify the position of any medieval park within the newer park since more recent features such as lodges and kennels are likely to have obscured the previous phases. Landscaping could be extensive in the post-medieval period, with lakes constructed, ground levelled and new boundaries created. More recently again, many eighteenth- and nineteenth-century demesnes, such as at Oakpark, Co. Carlow, and Carton, Co. Kildare, have been redeveloped into hotels and golf courses, with even greater levels of landscaping taking place as a result, and further obscuring earlier features.

Many parks, especially the smaller ones and those at minor manors, are likely to have become agricultural land at an early date. A square park of fifty statute acres would measure approximately 450m in each direction and the first-edition OS map shows that in the good agricultural soils of eastern Ireland there were many individual fields of that size. Also, many smaller fields currently sit within blocks of land of this size, possibly having their origin in the open field systems of the later-medieval period. As a result, identifying these smaller parks without other evidence such as place-names or landscape features such as recorded or extant woodland can be extremely difficult. The surveyed parks were all large,

106 Reeves-Smyth, 'Demesnes', pp 201–3; Watts, 'Wiltshire deer parks: an introductory survey', 88. **107** Watts, 'Wiltshire deer parks: an introductory survey', 93. **108** Sleeman, 'Mammals and mammalogy' (1997), pp 245–6. **109** *COD*, ii, no. 201. **110** Rocque, 'Survey of the city of Kilkenny' (1758); Tietzsch-Tyler, 'Kilkenny Castle' (2011), 4–5. **111** Petty, 'Down Survey parish maps'.

high-status examples and in general these have at least some areas within them with large, regular fields that appear to be relatively late features. At Dunamase and at Nenagh the lands were retained in demesne until the nineteenth or twentieth century and so were not divided into multiple small tenancies. At Maynooth, although rented out since at least 1652, this was as a portion of an even larger lease to a single tenant, and at the time of Griffith's Valuation there were only two main tenants, as well as a small number of suburban dwelling houses within the 495 acres of the park.[112] At Carrick, there seems to have been a single tenant in 1635, and cartographic evidence from Vallancey's map suggests that the fields are relatively late, although these are small and there were certainly a large number of small tenancies by the time of Griffith's Valuation.[113] At Earlspark, there is also evidence for the late division of fields in the north-eastern quadrant of the park, the field systems in the north-western portion post-date both of the relict roads within the townland and land in the southern portion was divided and sold to families from outside the immediate area in the early twentieth century. In all of these cases, therefore, the land within the former parks has been treated differently to ordinary agricultural land in terms of the way that it has been managed and utilised after becoming obsolete as a park.

The final potential fate of the high-medieval parks was to be partly or wholly swallowed by urban development. Dublin and its surroundings have seen much development in the last century or so, and therefore the Dublin parks are the most likely to have disappeared through urban and suburban expansion. The archiepiscopal manors of Finglas, Shankill, St Sepulchre's (Colonia) and Welshtown all had recorded parks and these manors have subsequently been developed into residential and industrial areas. Similarly, Shanballymore in Baggotrath and Ballykene in Swords are also now in urban areas. At Nenagh, only the eastern half of the park has survived as rural land, while the entire western half has been swallowed up by the town. Fortunately in this case, the streetscape has preserved the outline of the park and much of the development has occurred since the first-edition OS mapping took place; indeed, it may be possible to apply a similar methodology to that used at Nenagh in order to find the outlines of parks in other urban locations.

CONCLUSION

In the 750 years since the peak of Irish high-medieval park-making, the parks have succumbed to a variety of fates. Some have been absorbed into post-

---

112 Griffith's Valuation maps.   **113** Vallancey, 'Military itinerary to the south of Ireland'.

medieval demesne landscapes and hence have retained elements of their former functions and character. Many others have become ordinary agricultural land, with several of the surveyed parks under tillage, while others provide good-quality pasture. For these two categories it is sometimes still possible to locate the park using boundaries and landscape features in conjunction with historical, cartographic and place-name evidence. For parks swallowed up by suburban and urban development, however, we are completely reliant on these indirect indicators. We are therefore fortunate that the first-edition OS maps were created before the nineteenth-century expansion of many of our towns and cities, so holding out the prospect that some of these parks may yet be identified.

CHAPTER EIGHT

Conclusions

FINDINGS

The aim of this book was to investigate Anglo-Norman parks in high-medieval Ireland, specifically in the period from the arrival of the Anglo-Normans in 1169 to c.1350. This has included the evidence for park ownership, distribution and chronology, the function and form of parks, the symbolism of parks in an Irish context and finally an examination of how they initially became obsolete and of what happened to them in the later landscapes. Later-medieval studies have become more popular in Ireland in the past two decades, but only limited work has been carried out to investigate the wider landscape of Anglo-Norman manors and castles.[1] As a result, parks, which were an important aspect of later-medieval culture, have been largely ignored, or have been investigated with a narrow focus that utilised only one type of information or concentrated on a single site or county.

In England, medieval parks have been seen primarily in their role as deer parks. Hunting was also central to aristocratic society in high-medieval Ireland, having practical purposes in developing military skills and in forging social bonds between the elite, as well as important symbolic roles in creating elite identity. For both Anglo-Norman and Gaelic lords, cross-country hunting was a noble pursuit and excellent military training. Parkland hunting was much less strenuous and, for the Gaelic lord, this sedate activity seems to have been meaningless, providing no worthwhile exercise and no expression of power or status. For the Anglo-Normans, however, parkland hunting was perceived as a 'civilised' activity that helped to tame the landscape, while still providing some exercise. It was imbued with connotations of status, the 'divine order' and abundance. Thus, while the Anglo-Normans did introduce hunting parks and fallow deer from England, they perhaps did so in a somewhat half-hearted way in the relatively uncrowded Irish countryside, where lordships were often held as liberties and where there were relatively small areas of royal forest. As with the rest of Europe, deer parks never reached the large-scale penetration that they had reached in the much more crowded countryside of England. In Ireland, as a result, even the great magnates

---

1 For example, Lyttleton and O'Keeffe (eds), *The manor in medieval and early modern Ireland*, passim; O'Conor, 'Medieval rural settlement in Munster', passim.

had only a few parks, compared to the dozens held by English lords. Nevertheless, they could be used as a symbol of Anglo-Norman identity. One possible example of this is at Nenagh, where the park was not enclosed until eighty years after the castle was constructed. The area was already demesne woodland, but in 1299, at a time when political tensions were rising and the crown was concerned with the increasing gaelicisation of the Anglo-Irish lords, Theobald Walter (Butler) suddenly decided to very publicly create a park in his manor. His aim in doing so may well have been to mark himself as a loyal subject of the crown. In fact, the lack of parks and the emphasis on cross-country hunting could, with hindsight, be seen as an early step on the road towards the gaelicisation of the Anglo-Norman nobility in Ireland.

Despite the relative scarcity of parks, the role of deer in them should not be underplayed as both park hunting and venison consumption were indicators of elite status. Venison could not be sold, but could be given as a gift, so that the ability to procure this meat was a mark of high social status and this is reflected in the zooarchaeological record. Some of the elite parks were evidently carefully managed to optimise the venison obtained from them; for example, at Maynooth and Trim the proportion of fallow deer to red deer bones shows that the parks supplied the majority of the venison consumed in the castles.[2]

Since venison could not be sold, deer and venison were not an economically viable reason to have a park; yet it was possible to manage the parks to be a source of some revenue. Timber and underwood were important resources, providing a potentially lucrative source of income. If deer stocks were low or there were no deer, then the pasturage of the park could yield a profit, and although it does not seem to have been common in Ireland for pannage rights to be sold, pigs belonging to the landholder would undoubtedly be set loose within the bounds to avail of the crop of acorns in the autumn. As a secure location within the manor, the parks could also serve to protect cattle, horses and other stock from theft and to impound domestic animals, thereby compelling tenants to pay their fines to the lord's court. While some parks were designed as deer parks, in the majority of examples from Ireland timber, underwood and grazing were much more important than deer, and it is significant that in Ireland it was the ownership of a park, not of deer, that was important as a marker of Anglo-Norman identity.

At least forty-six documented high-medieval parks have been identified, and detailed case studies have been conducted for a number of these. The majority of the parks were east of the Shannon, with outliers in more westerly Anglo-Norman strongholds, and no high-medieval enclosed deer parks were identified

2 Beglane, 'The social significance of game in the diet of later-medieval Ireland'.

in Gaelic Ireland. Several of the parks were owned by senior ecclesiastics such as the archbishop of Dublin and the bishops of Cloyne and Ferns. A number of the parks were associated with the lands of the lordship of Leinster, held by the Marshals, and were subsequently divided by inheritance, while other major magnates holding parks included the de Burghs, FitzGeralds, de Clares and Butlers. There are also a number of references to less significant landowners holding single parks, used for pasture and woodland, and it is notable that some of these were very small.

One finding is that in three of the detailed case studies the likely location of the park lodge was occupied by a monument that would conventionally be described as a ringfort. In two of the others the likely lodge location has been built upon in modern times and so could not be examined for earlier structures. The most likely explanation for these is that early medieval ringforts were taken over as suitable lodge sites due to their locations and their essential similarity to the moated sites that were commonly used for lodges in England.

A decade ago, O'Keeffe raised the question of whether there were designed landscapes in later-medieval Ireland.[3] This book shows that the answer is emphatically 'yes', though they were clearly not as common as in England. Parks were created to demonstrate the power and status of the lord and to do this their sites were carefully selected.

One factor appears to be the incorporation of socially significant earlier landscapes within the park. At Earlspark, the Northern Complex of apparently prehistoric and early medieval monuments is accessed by a road that runs from the town of Loughrea into the park, and the likely site of the park lodge is a large circular enclosure that may be of early medieval or even prehistoric origin. In the late-medieval period the park seems to have continued to be symbolically important, becoming associated with assembly and possibly inauguration. Similarly, at Maynooth, place-name evidence suggests that the park incorporates the site of a *bile* tree, significant as a symbol of kingship to the pre-existing population.

In creating parks, the boundaries were also considered in relation to the views to and from the park. In some cases, such as at Nenagh and Dunamase, the parks abutted the castles, providing an attractive vista from the windows and wall walks, while in other cases the parks were at a distance, but were still visible from the castles. These views showcased the attributes of the manor; they were conceived as part of the structured, ordered layout and formed, for example, part of an arc of seigniorial landscape features at Maynooth. These were not haphazard constructions as they would have been costly to build and to maintain and this

---

3 O'Keeffe, 'Were there designed landscapes in medieval Ireland?', 52–68.

expense would not have been undertaken without careful thought and planning. The high cost may be one reason why there are fewer parks and designed landscapes in Ireland than in England. The evidence suggests that the early promise of the Anglo-Norman colony was not fulfilled, and that castles constructed after 1220 were more modest than earlier examples.[4] It is likely that this is also the case with park construction, with thirteenth-century lords at all levels of elite society being much more cautious about committing money to unnecessary display in less profitable manors. By the fourteenth century, the Anglo-Norman colony in Ireland was in retreat and was under severe military, cultural and financial pressure, so that few parks seem to have been created in Ireland at this time, although this is the period during which emparkment was at its height in England.

Today, many of the Irish parks are ephemeral features that are not imprinted in local memory, but survive only as cartographic features on old manuscript maps, estate maps and Ordnance Survey maps. Two exceptions are at Loughrea and at Dunamase. The park boundary wall at Earlspark, Loughrea, is a dramatic landscape feature that locals have continued to explain by a folktale describing a semi-miraculous event. The park at Dunamase is still surrounded by a low bank. In the late eighteenth century the past glories of Dunamase were recreated and re-envisioned by a conservative landlord who built a demesne wall overlying the medieval boundary. The original role of the parks has been obscured by time and later landscape concepts. When they were created, these were 'parks', which were valuable for timber, pasture and pannage and a source of priceless venison and prestige, and importantly they were multi-functional. To describe them as 'deer-parks' in the sense of the landscaped amenity parks of the eighteenth and nineteenth centuries is to do them a disservice.

Parks were part of the manorial system of demarcating and structuring landholding and as such they were seen as markers of Anglo-Norman 'civilisation' and identity. They were part of the process of creating a sense of place and familiarity in a foreign land. However, unlike in England where they became ubiquitous, in Ireland parks never became an essential feature of a manor. A lord aspired to stock his park with fallow deer, but these were much less accessible in Ireland than in England, and only the highest echelons of society received this ultimate royal gift. The deer did not become common and hence did not filter down the social ladder to the more humble parks of the minor nobility and gentry. While this was their original intention, the Anglo-Normans in Ireland did not live in a transplanted version of an English manor and, as O'Keeffe noted, by leaving England or Wales, they may already have been aware that they had taken the first step in the process of gaelicisation that was to cause such political

---

4 McNeill, *Castles in Ireland*, pp 230–1.

problems in the fourteenth century.[5] There are three periods in which parks were created in significant numbers in Ireland: the Anglo-Norman period, the plantation periods of the later sixteenth to seventeenth century, and the period of Anglo-Irish ascendancy of the eighteenth and nineteenth centuries. The timing of these phases is no coincidence. In each case the parks were mainly created by incoming or resident elites of Anglo-Norman or English origin, and these can be seen as serving two symbolic functions. Firstly, as a form of symbolic violence, they provided a pedagogic statement of power and lordship, controlling access to resources and closing off previously accessible land. Secondly, they sought to impose an English landscape in Ireland, to create a sense of place for the incoming elite and to disassociate the land with its past.

FUTURE RESEARCH DIRECTIONS

In order to undertake a study of this nature, it seemed appropriate to adopt a multidisciplinary approach, incorporating aspects of landscape analysis, zooarchaeology, history, art history and literary studies. This posed a number of practical difficulties, since any one individual is unlikely to be equally knowledgeable and skilled in all these disciplines; however, by examining all aspects of Anglo-Norman parks the aim was to give a more rounded interpretation of a previously neglected subject. This field of research is certainly not complete, and further references to parks are likely to be found in documents not consulted for this study, including estate records and untranslated and uncalendared sources. Furthermore, a review of the extant documents would be of value in identifying mistranslations and ambiguities in the terms used for the males and females of the fallow deer and red deer species and in the terms for woodland and forest. Literary materials and art-historical sources from both the Anglo-Norman and the Gaelic world would also be worth investigating further, as very few have been examined for this study. In relation to the parks themselves, this work has involved fieldwork and detailed desktop research of a relatively small number of examples among the documented sites. Many more of the others may be archaeologically or cartographically visible if they were subjected to equally detailed scrutiny, and thus there is great scope for continued study of the parks, their features and their landscapes.

This book has examined the developments that took place at documented Anglo-Norman high-medieval parks through the later-medieval period, the

---

5 O'Keeffe, 'Concepts of "castle" and the construction of identity in medieval and post-medieval Ireland', 80.

plantation period and into the modern era, but there is also considerable scope to examine those parks created during the plantation and modern periods as studies in their own right. The post-medieval period has arguably been even more poorly served in Irish scholarship than the later-medieval period,[6] and detailed analysis of the reintroduction of the park concept at that time would be a valuable addition to our understanding of the remodelling of the landscape that took place at that point in history. There is also considerable scope for further study into Gaelic society during the high and late-medieval periods. This includes investigating developments in Gaelic hunting practices as well as domestic animal husbandry and timber/wood management. This study has shown that at Dunamase and at Nenagh the high-medieval parks survived essentially intact through the late-medieval period and became post-medieval demesne landscapes. In both cases these were in areas controlled by Gaelic lords, who seem to have retained them for grazing and timber throughout. This study did not identify any parks for fallow deer created by Gaelic lords in the high-medieval period. Nevertheless, examples such as Dunamase and Nenagh demonstrate that certainly by the late-medieval period Gaelic lords saw a value in retaining existing parks and by the seventeenth century there is evidence for them creating new parks and stocking them with deer.

While the era of the Celtic Tiger was instrumental in identifying many previously unknown archaeological sites and in highlighting the palimpsest that is the Irish countryside, it has also brought problems in its wake. Many of the park sites surveyed here have been subject to development within the last few decades, some with no archaeological assessment, and all with absolutely no cognisance of the presence of a high-medieval park in the area. As a result, it is likely that some park-related features such as boundary ditches and banks, relict roads, lodges and gate features may have been inadvertently destroyed during land clearance. Notable possibilities in this regard include the siting of water reservoirs at the highest points at both Earlspark and Nenagh, as well as a telecommunications aerial on the highest point at Earlspark, the construction of housing estates within the parks at Maynooth and Nenagh, and at Carrick there has been recent land clearance of the boundary stream at the eastern end of the park as well as now-abandoned partial construction of housing estates at the western end.

Understanding Anglo-Norman high-medieval parks and the manorial landscapes in which they were placed is important in refining our knowledge of the development of the Irish landscape. They were part of a complex manorial system that included mills, fishponds, roads, fields and the settlements of

---

6 Horning et al., 'Foreword: post-medieval archaeology in and of Ireland' (2007), p. xviii; Rynne, *Industrial Ireland, 1750–1930: an archaeology* (2006), pp 1–14.

ordinary people. The recording of monuments and the processes of awarding planning permission have concentrated on the preservation and excavation of stone monuments and discrete earthwork monuments such as ringforts. Manorial landscapes, including parks, are much more ephemeral, and, as demonstrated here, a single monument can measure over 2km across, making them almost too large to see without the benefit of large-scale cartography. It is therefore imperative that lessons are learnt from the developments in the late 1990s and 2000s and that future planning constraints take into account the possible presence of these ephemeral archaeological monuments, particularly where place-name evidence or the presence of a nearby Anglo-Norman castle suggest that a later-medieval manorial landscape is present.

APPENDIX 1

Parks as a legal concept

Year	Contents of document
1200	Freedom of Knights Hospitaller from works in parks, forests and vivaries.[1]
1216	Duty of guardian to maintain possessions of an heir, including houses, parks, vivaries, ponds, mills, lands and ploughs.[2]
1216	Henry III disafforests all forest that was afforested in the time of his father King John; mentions forests and foresters, warrens and warreners.[3]
1229	Disafforestation of various lands listed in south Dublin; right to make parks in these areas.[4]
1234	Maurice fitzGerald to look after lands of Richard Marshal, late earl of Pembroke, allowing no waste etc. in lands including parks.[5]
1236	Law regarding trespassers in parks and viviaries.[6]
1284–5	Law regarding coursing in another's parks, fishing in another's ponds or lodging in another's manor or house.[7]
1285	Law regarding trespassers in parks and viviaries.[8]
1285	Parks, woods, forests, chases, warrens etc. with regard to writs of novel disseisin.[9]
1287–93	Grant of lands in Munster and Leinster by Juliana de Cogan to John son of Thomas including various rights and types of land including parks.[10]
1290	Charter of Henry III to the Knights Templar that they are free of various duties and costs including works of castles, parks and bridges. They can use their woods as they see fit and have various rights in forests.[11]
1308	Royal decree that roads should be widened through woods and forests, including where parks are present.[12]
1335	William la Zousche Mortymer and Eleanor his wife. Licence to quit claim Kilkenny Castle and lands to John bishop of Ely. Various land types mentioned including parks, warrens, forests etc.[13]
1350	Manors of archbishop of Dublin. Evil-doers broke parks and entered his free warrens, hunted, felled his trees and underwood, took deer, hares, rabbits, pheasants and partridges.[14]

1 *CDI*, i, no. 123.   2 *SIJH*, 9.   3 *Magna Charta* for Ireland, no. XIII; *HMDI*, 65, 67, 71, 72.   4 *CDI*, i, no. 1757; *CAAR*, p. 62.   5 *CDI*, i, no. 2111.   6 *SIJH*, 29.   7 Statutes of Westminster the first (enacted in England 3 Edw. I): *SIJH*, 49.   8 *SIJH*, 65–7.   9 The statutes of Westminster (the second): *SIJH*, 144–5.   10 *RBK*, no. 30.   11 *CDI*, iii, no. 666.   12 Statute of Winchester (enacted in England 13 Edw. I, AD1285): *SIJH*, 256.   13 *CPR*, Edw. III, iii, 106.   14 Ibid., viii, 590.

Year	Contents of document
1361	Grant of lands of Humphrey de Bohun to William, abbot of Walden. Various land types mentioned including parks, warrens, forests etc.[15]
1369	Thomas de la Dale appointed surveyor of lands of Philippa, daughter of duke of Clarence, 'and of the keepers and other ministers and officers of the chaces, parks, woods, hunts and warrens pertaining thereto'.[16]
1369–70	Grant to William de Wyndesore of the castle or manor of Dungarvan 'Le Blackcastle'. Including 'fisheries, chases, parks, woods, warrens, rents and all other appurtenances'.[17]
1373–4	Manors of archbishop of Dublin. Evil-doers broke parks and entered his free warrens, hunted, felled his trees and underwood, took deer, hares, conies, pheasants and partridges.[18]

15 *CFR*, vii, 187.   **16** Ibid., viii, 9–10.   **17** *CPR*, Edw. III, xiv, 222.   **18** Ibid., xv, 309.

Documented parks

Park	Year	Associated names	Summary of documented information
Adare, Co. Limerick	1331	Richard, son of Thomas FitzGerald	Land in the park for which Tathogh Othe renders 13s. 10d. a year.[1]
Ardraghin (Ardrahan), Co. Galway	1321	Thomas fitz Richard de Clare	100 acre brush and thicket that had previously been emparked.[2]
Arscol (Ardscull), Co. Kildare	1282	William de Mohun	Park extended at 13s. 4d.[3]
Baliduwil, Co. Kerry	1286–8	Thomas de Clare	Park of 4 acres good for oxen and for osiers for carts, extended at 12d.[4]
Ballykene, Swords, Co. Dublin	1306	Geoffrey Savage (Sauuage)	Animals impounded in park.[5]
Balydonegan (Dunganstown /Oakpark), Co. Carlow	1305, 1306, 1333	Richard de Burgh, earl of Ulster vs William Waspayl	In 1305, court case about poaching of deer, digging of pit-traps and and trespass.[6]
		William de Burgh (The Brown Earl)	In 1333, park with deer, surrounded by palings. Profits of the park are 8s. a year. Dovecote beneath park, formerly worth 3s. 4d., now ruined. Warren worth 12d. a year in 1333.
Bray, Co. Wicklow	1284, 1311	Christina de Mariscis,	In 1284, Walter de Belinges paid 6s. 8d. for the park.
		Richard le Botiller	In 1311, park surrounded by a ditch that contained 60 acres and was valued at 20s. a year.[7]

---

1 *RBK*, 135.   2 *IEMI*, no. 204.   3 Ibid., no. 46.   4 *CDI*, iii, no. 459.   5 *CJRI*, ii, p. 326.   6 Ibid., 136, 314; *CIPM*, vii, Edw. III, no. 537; *IEMI*, no. 251.   7 *CDI*, ii, no. 2430; *RBO*, no. 10.

Park	Year	Associated names	Summary of documented information
Callan, Co. Kilkenny (2 parks)	1300, 1307, 1350	Joan, countess of Gloucester and Hertford	Acres of land in a park in 1300, park with oak trees, wood worth 6s. 8d. per year in 1307. In 1350, 2s. 6d. rent of 5 acres in the New Park and Cogedanesgrene at 6d. an acre. Further area of c.14 acres did not have tenants. Herbage in the park worth 2s. and wood 27s. 2d.[8]
Carrick, Co. Wexford	1231x4	Richard, earl Marshal	Park separated from Carrick Castle by a river that flows into the Slaney.[9]
Cloyne, Co. Cork	1364	Bishop of Cloyne	Tenants have a duty to make the lord's meadow and park.[10]
Location unknown, Co. Cork	1311	Thomas Cod	Cattle stolen from park.[11]
Curtun, Kinelahun (Courtown), Co. Wexford	1280–1	Christina de Mariscis	Lands include a 'coveria' or preserve, worth 5s.[12]
Donkeryn (Dunkerrin), Co. Offaly	1305	Earls of Ormond	Newly afforested (planted) park.[13]
Donmowe (Dunmoe), Co. Meath	1415	Margaret Darcy, widow of John Darcy	Assignment of dower includes a park held by a tenant.[14]
Dunamase, Co. Laois	1282–3	Roger de Mortimer	A mountain pasture and emparked pasture, together worth 33s. 4d. a year.[15]
Ferns, Co. Wexford	1253	Bishop of Ferns, but land in the king's hand	Wild cattle kept in the park.[16]
Fynglas (Finglas), Co. Dublin (2 parks)	1326	Archbishop of Dublin	24-acre park worth nothing and 71-acre park with grazing worth 2s.[17]

8 *CDI*, v, no. 659; *Handbook*, pp 302–3; *IEMI*, no. 154; *RBO*, no. 25.   9 *CERM*, p. 56.   10 *PRC*, 13.
11 *CJRI*, iii, p. 200.   12 *CDI*, ii, no. 1801.   13 *RBO*, no. 91.   14 *IEMI*, nos 347, 348.   15 *CDI*, ii, no. 2028; *IEMI*, no. 54.   16 *CDI*, ii, no. 297.   17 *CAAR*, 173.

Park	Year	Associated names	Summary of documented information
Garnenan (at Kilkea), Co. Kildare	1228	Walter de Ridelisford	Walter asks to divert road that currently runs through his park of Garnenan[18]
Glencree, Co. Wicklow	1242, 1244, 1251, 1279/80	Royal park	In 1242, fallow deer sent to stock an unnamed royal park in Ireland. In 1244, 60 does and 20 bucks from king's parks in England sent to Dalkey and then to stock king's park at Glencry. In 1251, deer gifted from park to Luke, archbishop of Dublin. In 1279/80, timber trees gifted from park to John de Walhope.[19]
Gowran, Co. Kilkenny	1306	Earls of Ormond	Various lands listed that lie outside, next to and under the park.[20]
Inchiquin, Co. Cork (3 parks)	1321, 1348	Thomas fitzRichard de Clare, Isabella, widow of Gilbert de Clare, Giles de Badelesmere	In 1321, 3 parks: 18 acres at Garranglas and le Haggard and a wood called le Park. 1321 assignment of dower, of which 9 acres in the park, in 1348 60 acre oak wood called 'le Park' worth 5s. in its pasture and not in underwood or in any other profits.[21]
Kicopsentan (Kilmasantan), Co. Dublin	1206–7	John, archbishop of Dublin	Grants a right to make a park and erect a deerleap. Also no requirement to feed foresters.[22]
Kildare, Co. Kildare	1298	Earl of Kildare	Park broken and affers (draught-horses) removed that had previously been impounded for the lord by the sergeant.[23]
Kilkenny, Co. Kilkenny	1375	Alice, widow of Hugh le Despenser, William Ilger, William Lumbard	William Ilger sold on the constableship and associated rights of Kilkenny Castle to William Lumbard, including all rights to the park. The great park was described as being opposite the gate of the castle and containing a dovecote. There were also fishing rights, land, an orchard and a garden associated with the constableship.[24]

18 *CDI*, i, no. 1641.   **19** Ibid., nos 2580, 2671, 3123; ii, no. 1633.   **20** *RBO*, no. 14.   **21** *IEMI*, nos 205, 207, 291; *CIPM*, ix, Edw. III, no. 119.   **22** *CDI*, i, no. 316.   **23** *CJRI*, i, p. 200.   **24** *COD*, ii, no. 201.

Park	Year	Associated names	Summary of documented information
Kilmaynan (Kilmainham), Co. Dublin	1326 1335	Knights Hospitaller of St John of Jerusalem	In 1326, Roberto Gutters had custody of the park and waters. 1335: Hamundo de Lee had custody of the park.[25]
Kylkarban / Kylwarban (Kilcorban), Co. Galway	1334	William de Burgh, earl of Ulster	A carucate of parkland formerly worth 13s. 4d.[26]
Kylka (Kilkea), Co. Kildare	1284	Christina de Mariscis	Pannage of the park 3s. Herbage and pasture in the park 40s.[27]
Le Roche (Castleroche), Co. Louth	1378	Theobald de Verdun	A small plot called park and a garden lying around the castle.[28]
Loughrea, Co. Galway	1333	William de Burgh, earl of Ulster	Park of 7 carucates worth nothing apart from its deer.[29]
Lucan, Co. Dublin	1299	Roesia dePeche and her husband John Hanstede	Rights of reasonable estovers for housebote and hayebote in the park of Lucan.[30]
Maynooth, Co. Kildare	1328	Earl of Kildare, Johanna de Burgh	Extent of manor and assignment of dower. Both mention the park and features within and adjacent.[31]
Nenagh, Co. Tipperary	1299	Theobald Walter (Butler)	In 1299, king's permission sought to divert road to construct park. In 1338–9 lands called Le Dirre are described.[32]
Platyn (Platin), Co. Meath	1305	William de la Ryuere	Animals seized and emparked.[33]
Pouloc, Ulster (possibly north Co. Antrim)	1282	William FitzWarin	Park containing tenants' beasts broken and beasts released.[34]

25 *Registrum de Kilmainham*, 8, 69, 74. **26** *IEMI*, no. 262. **27** *CDI*, ii, no. 2340. **28** *CIRCLE*, PR 2 Rich. II, no. 38. **29** *IEMI*, no. 262; *CIPM*, vii, Edw. III, no. 537. **30** *CJRI*, i, p. 222. **31** *RBK*, nos 119, 120; *RPH, Antiquissime dorso*, no. 41.3. **32** *CJRI*, i, p. 234. **33** Ibid., ii, p. 18. **34** *CDI*, ii, no. 1918.

Park	Year	Associated names	Summary of documented information
Senekyll (Shankill), Co. Dublin (2 parks)	1326	Archbishop of Dublin	A park of oaks and thorns, 30 acres, no value in herbage or sale of under-wood on account of war and another small park, 4 acres no value for want of beasts and on account of war.[35]
Shanballymore (Baggotrath), Co. Dublin	c.1274	Robert Baggot, knight.	'Small park'.[36]
St Sepulchre's Colonia, Co. Dublin ('divers parks')	1326	Archbishop of Dublin	66-acre woodland worth 20s. a year with 'divers parks'.[37]
Trim, Co. Meath	1388, 1400, 1401, 1425, 1425/6, 1427–9, 1430–1 and beyond	de Mortimer family and in the king's hand	Appointment and payment of parkers.[38]
Villa de Hacket (Ballyhackett, Carncastle, Co. Antrim)	1279	John, son and heir of John Bisset	100 acres with a park.[39]
Welshtown, Co. Dublin	1276	Archbishop of Dublin	Wife of Elias le Waleys holds 55 acres with a park, extended at 9d. an acre.[40]
Wexford, Co. Wexford	1275, 1324, 1324–5, 1331, 1335, 1336 (several), 1375/6, 1377, 1378, 1383, 1384, 1389, 1399, 1420	Earl marshal and various heirs	Park of 60 acres containing oak trees and associated with Wexford Castle, in 1324 it is worth nothing save for the pasturing of animals. Part assigned in dower in 1324–5. In 1375–6, pasture in the park worth 13s. 4d. In 1335–6, two separate individuals were assigned the custody of the castle and park of Wexford. Location of the park is detailed in 1378.[41]

35 *CAAR*, 195. **36** Ibid., 146. **37** Ibid., 170–2. **38** *RPH*, pat. 12 Rich. II, no. 38; pat 1 Hen. IV, no. 22; pat 3 Hen. VI, no. 83; close 3 & 4, Hen. VI, no. 46; close 6 Hen. VI, no. 28; *CPR*, Hen. IV, i, 468; *IEP*, 562, 568. **39** *IEMI*, no. 36. **40** *CDI*, ii, no. 1283. **41** *IEMI*, no. 339; *CDI*, ii, no. 1109; *CIPM*, vi, Edw. II, nos 339–40; xiv, Edw. III, nos 152–3; *IEMI*, nos 228, 237; *CPR*, iii, Edw. III, nos 123, 225–6, 257, 272, 320; *CFR*, iv, no. 470; *CIRCLE*, PR I Rich. II, no. 11; Hore, *History of the town and county of Wexford*, v, pp 33, 106, 121, 123–4, 130.

Abbreviations

1297 parliament	*Enactments of the 1297 parliament*, ed. Philomena Connolly. *Law and disorder in thirteenth-century Ireland* (Dublin, 1997)
Acallam na Senórach	*Tales of the elders of Ireland: a new translation* of Acallam na Senórach, ed. Ann Dooley and Harry Roe (Oxford, 1999)
AFM	*Annals of the kingdom of Ireland by the Four Masters* (7 vols), ed. J. O'Donovan (Dublin, 1848–51)
BSA	*The Boke of Saint Albans, 1486*, ed. Berners Juliana and William Blades (London, 1881)
BSD	*The books of survey and distribution*, ed. R.C. Simmington (Dublin, 1949–67)
CAAR	*Calendar of Archbishop Alen's Register, c.1172–1534*, ed. Charles McNeill (Dublin, 1950)
CBC	*The Compossicion book of Conought*, ed. A. Martin Freeman (Dublin, 1936)
CCR	*Calendar of the close rolls perserved in the Public Record Office. Edward I to Richard II*, 28 vols (London)
CDI	*Calendar of documents relating to Ireland, 1171–1307* (5 vols), ed. H.S. Sweetman (London, 1875–86)
Census 1659	*A census of Ireland, c.1659*, ed. Seamus Pender and William J. Smyth (Dublin, 1939)
CERM	*Charters of Earl Richard Marshal of the forests of Ross and Taghmon*, ed. G. Orpen. *JRSAI* IV(1): 54–63 (1934)
CFR	*Calendar of the fine rolls, 1372–1509* (22 vols), ed. H.C. Maxwell Lyte (London)
Chronicles	*Chronicles of England, Scotland and Ireland, 1577* (2008–10)
CICB	*Calendar of the Irish Council Book, 1581–1586*, ed. John P. Prendergaset and David B. Quinn. *Analecta Hibernica, no. 24*, pp 91–180 (1967)
CIPM	*Calendar of inquisitions post mortem and other analagous documents. Henry III to Richard II* (18 vols), various editors (London, 1904–87)
CIRCLE	*A calendar of Irish chancery letters* (chancery.tcd.ie)
Civil Survey	*The Civil Survey, AD1654–56*, ed. R.C Simington (Dublin, 1931–61)
CJRI	*Calendar of the justiciary rolls or proceedings in the court of the justiciar of Ireland preserved in the public record office of Ireland* (3 vols), ed. James Mills and M.C. Griffiths (Dublin, 1905–14)
COD	*Calendar of the Ormond deeds* (6 vols), ed. Edmund Curtis (Dublin, 1932–43)
CPR	*Calendar of the patent rolls Edward I to Richard III*, 18 vols (London)
CPRI Jas I	*Irish patent rolls of James I: Facsimile of the Irish record commissioners' calendar prepared prior to 1830*, ed. M.C. Griffith (Dublin, 1966)

CPRI	*Calendar of the patent and close rolls of chancery in Ireland of the reigns of Henry VIII, Edward VI, Mary and Elizabeth*, ed. James Morrin (1861, Dublin)
CSL	*Crown surveys of lands, 1540–1 with the Kildare rental begun in 1518*, ed, Gearoid Mac Niocaill (Dublin, 1992)
CSMA	*Chartularies of St Mary's Abbey, Dublin, with the register of its house at Dunbrody, and annals of Ireland*, ed. John Thomas Gilbert (Dublin, 1884)
CSPI	*Calendar of state papers relating to Ireland in the reigns of Henry VIII, Edward VI, Mary and Elizabeth, 1509–73* (24 vols), ed. H.C. Hamilton, E.G. Atkinson and R.P. Mahaffy (London, 1860–1912)
DAIKC	*Documents on the affairs of Ireland before the king's council*, ed. G.O. Sayles (Dublin, 1979)
DEP	*Dublin Evening Post*
Discovery	*A discovery of the true causes why Ireland was never entirely subdued and brought under obedience of the crown of England, until the beginning of His Majesty's happy reign. 1612*, ed. John Davies. *Historical tracts* (London, 1786)
Duanaire Finn	*Duanaire Finn: The book of the lays of Fionn* (3 vols), ed. Eoin MacNeill (London, 1908–53)
FJC	*The Annals of Ireland by Friar John Clyn*, ed. Bernadette Williams (Dublin, 2007)
Handbook	*Handbook and select calendar of sources for medieval Ireland in the National Archives of the United Kingdom*, ed. Paul Dryburgh and Brendan Smith (Dublin, 2005)
Histoire du roy	*Histoire du roy d'Angleterre Richard II by Jean de Creton*
HMDI	*Historical and municipal documents of Ireland, 1172–1320*, ed. J.T. Gilbert (London, 1870)
IEMI	*Inquisitions and extents of medieval Ireland*, ed. Paul Dryburgh and Brendan Smith (n.p., 2007)
IEP	*Irish exchequer payments, 1270–1446*, ed. Philomena Connolly (Dublin, 1998)
IRCH	*Inquisitionum in officio rotulorum cancellariae Hiberniae asservatarum, repertorium. vol 1*, ed. James Hardiman (Dublin, 1826)
Itinerary through Wales	*The itinerary through Wales: description of Wales by Giraldus Cambrensis*, ed. E. Rhys and W. Llewelyn Williams (London, 1912)
Itinerary	*An itinerary, by Fynes Moryson, 1617* (Glasgow, 1908)
IZWG	Irish Zooarchaeological Working Group
JCKAS	*Journal of the County of Kildare Archaeological Society*
JOWHS	*Journal of the [Old] Wexford Historical Society*
JRSAI	*Journal of the Royal Society of Antiquaries of Ireland*
Judicial rents	*Return according to provinces and counties of judicial rents. April 1898* (Dublin, 1898)

Kildare estates	*Thomas Emerson's Kildare estates surveys, 1674–97*, ed. Arnold Horner, *JCKAS*, 18:3 (1996–7), 399–429
Leges	*Leges Henrici primi*, ed. L.J. Downer (Oxford, 1972)
Leinster deeds	*Deeds, leases and grants for Maynooth, 1553–1889*. Leinster papers, PRONI D.3078/1/5/1–53
Livre de chasse	*The book of the hunt by Gaston Phoebus*, ed. François Avril; trans. Société de Traduction Integram (Paris)
Livre du Roy Modus	*Le livre du Roy Modus et de la Royne Racio*, ed. Elzéar Blaze (Paris, 1839)
Master of game	*The master of game by Edward second duke of York*, ed. W.A. Baillie-Grohman and F. Baillie-Grohman (London, 1909)
Metrical Dindsenchas	*The Metrical Dindsenchas, pt iv*, ed. Edward Gwynn (Dublin, 1924)
n.d.	no date (given)
NGR	National Grid Reference
NMS	National Monuments Service
n.p.	no place (given)
NRA	National Roads Authority
NUI	National University of Ireland
NUIG	National University of Ireland Galway
OS name books	*Ordnance Survey name books*
OS/OSI	Ordnance Survey Ireland
PDNHAS	*Proceedings of the Dorset Natural History and Archaeological Society*
PRC	*The pipe roll of Cloyne* (Rotulus pipae Clonensis), ed. Paul MacCotter and K.W. Nicholls (Midleton, 1996)
PRONI	Public Record Office of Northern Ireland
RBK	*The red book of the earls of Kildare*, ed. Gearoid Mac Niocaill (Dublin, 1964)
RBO	*The red book of Ormond*, ed. N.B. White (Dublin, 1932)
RDKPRI	*Report of the deputy keeper of the public records of Ireland*, 59 vols (Dublin, 1869–1921)
Registrum de Kilmainham	*Register of chapter acts of the Hospital of Saint John of Jerusalem in Ireland, 1326–39*, ed. Charles McNeill (Dublin)
Rent roll 1684	'Rent roll of the earl of Kildare, 1684'. BL, MS Harley 7200. NLI Microfilm P.1431
RMP	Record of Monuments and Places
RPH	*Rotulorum patentium et clausorum cancellariae Hiberniae calendarium, Hen. II–Hen. VII*, ed. Edward Tresham (Dublin, 1928)
SIJH	*Statutes and ordinances, and acts of the parliament of Ireland, King John to Henry V*, ed. H.F. Berry (Dublin, 1907)
SPH8	*State papers published under the authority of His Majesty's commission* (11 vols) (London, 1834)
State papers	*State papers published under the authority of His Majesty's commission* (London, 1834)

Statute of   *A statute of the fortieth year of King Edward III, enacted in a parliament*
   Kilkenny   *held in Kilkenny, AD1367, before Lionel duke of Clarence, lord lieutenant*
                of Ireland, ed. James Hardiman (Dublin, 1843)
Topographia   *Topographia Hiberniae: The history and topography of Ireland by Gerald*
                of Wales, ed. John J. O'Meara (London, 1982)
UBA   Queen's University, Belfast: radiocarbon sample code

Bibliography

Ainmean-Àite na h-Alba, 'Gaelic place-names of Scotland' [online]. www.gaelicplace names.org, accessed 25 Mar. 2014.

Alexander, Magnus, *Introductions to heritage assets: animal management* (n.p., 2011).

Allsen, Thomas T., *The royal hunt in Eurasia history* (Philadelphia, 2006).

Almond, Richard, *Medieval hunting* (Stroud, 2003).

Andrén, Anders, 'Paradise lost: looking for deer parks in medieval Denmark and Sweden' in Hans Andersson, Peter Carelli and Lars Ersgård (eds), *Visions of the past: trends and traditions in Swedish medieval archaeology* (Lund, 1997), pp 469–90.

Ashcroft, Bill, Gareth Griffiths and Helen Tiffin, *Post-colonial studies: the key concepts* (London, 1998).

Ashe, Geoffrey, *Mythology of the British Isles* (London, 1990).

Bailey, Mark, *The English manor, c.1200–1500* (Manchester, 2002).

Barry, Terry B., *The archaeology of medieval Ireland* (London, 1987).

— 'Rural settlement in medieval Ireland' in Terry B. Barry (ed.), *A history of settlement in Ireland* (London, 2000), pp 110–23.

Beglane, Fiona, 'Deer and identity in medieval Ireland' in Aleksander Pluskowski, Gunther Karl Kunst, Matthias Kucera, Manfred Bietak and Irmgard Hein (eds), *Viavias 3. Animals as material culture in the Middle Ages 3: bestial mirrors: using animals to construct human identities in medieval Europe* (Vienna, 2010), pp 77–84.

— 'Deer in medieval Ireland: preliminary evidence from Kilteasheen, Co. Roscommon' in Thomas Finan (ed.), *Medieval Lough Cé* (Dublin, 2010), pp 145–58.

— 'Parks and deer-hunting: evidence from medieval Ireland' (PhD, NUI Galway, 2012).

— 'The social significance of game in the diet of later-medieval Ireland', *Proceedings of the Royal Irish Academy* (2015), 1–30.

— 'Theatre of power: the Anglo-Norman park at Earlspark, Co. Galway, Ireland', *Medieval Archaeology*, 58 (2014), 321–32.

Bennett, Isabel, 'Preliminary archaeological excavations at Ferrycarrig Ringwork, Newtown Td., Co. Wexford', *JOWHS*, 10 (1984–5), 25–43.

Birrell, Jean, 'Deer and deer farming in medieval England', *Agricultural History Review*, 40:II (1992), 112–26.

Blair, John and Nigel Ramsey, *English medieval industries* (London, 2001).

Bond, James, 'Forests, chases, warrens and parks in medieval Wessex' in Michael Aston and Carenza Lewis (eds), *The medieval landscape of Wessex: Oxbow monograph 46* (Oxford, 1994), pp 134–44.

— and Kate Tiller, *Blenheim: landscape for a palace* (2nd ed. Stroud, 1997).

Bouchard, Constance Brittain, *Strong of body, brave and noble: chivalry and society in medieval France* (Ithaca, NY, 1998).

Bourdieu, Pierre, *Distinction: a social critique of the judgement of taste* (Cambridge, MA, 1984).

— 'The forms of capital' in N.W. Biggart (ed.), *Readings in economic sociology* (Oxford, 2008), pp 46–58.

Bourke, Angela, 'Irish stories of weather, time and gender: Saint Brigid' in Marilyn Cohen and Nancy J. Curtin (eds), *Reclaiming gender: transgressive identities in modern Ireland* (New York, 1999), pp 13–32.

Bradley, John, 'The medieval towns of Tipperary' in William Nolan and Thomas G. McGrath (eds), *Tipperary: history and society* (Dublin, 1985), pp 34–59.

— 'Urban archaeological survey, pt vi: County Laois' (unpublished report, 1986).

— 'Early urban development in County Laois' in Pádraig G. Lane and William Nolan (eds), *Laois: history and society: interdisciplinary essays on the history of an Irish county* (Dublin, 1999), pp 257–82.

Brady, Niall and Kieran O'Conor, 'The later-medieval use of crannogs in Ireland', *Ruralia*, 5 (2005), 127–36.

Broderick, John, 'The IreAtlas townland database' [online]. www.seanruad.com/, accessed 18 Sept. 2009.

Brown, Gordon S., *The Norman conquest of southern Italy and Sicily* (Jefferson, NC, 2003).

Brown, R.A., *English castles* (3rd ed. London, 1976).

Bunachar loghinmneacha na hÉireann, 'Place-names database of Ireland' [online]. www.logaimn.ie accessed 16 Nov. 2011.

Butler, Vincent, 'Preliminary report on the animal bones from Dunamase, Co. Laois, 93E150, 1994 season' (unpublished report, 1995).

Campbell, Bruce M.S., *English seigniorial agriculture, 1250–1450* (Cambridge, 2000).

Cantor, Leonard M., 'The medieval parks of Leicestershire', *Leicestershire Archaeological and Historical Society*, 66 (1970–1), 9–24.

— 'Forests, chases, parks and warrens' in Leonard M. Cantor (ed.), *The English medieval landscape* (London, 1982), pp 56–85.

— and J. Hatherly, 'The medieval parks of England', *Geography*, 64 part 1:282 (1979), 71–85.

— and J.D. Wilson, 'The medieval deer-parks of Dorset: I', *PDHNAS*, 83 (1962), 109–16.

— 'The medieval deer-parks of Dorset: I–XVII', *PDNHAS*, 83–99 (1962–80).

— 'The medieval deer-parks of Dorset: II', *PDNHAS*, 84 (1963), 145–53.

— 'The medieval deer-parks of Dorset: III', *PDNHAS*, 85 (1964), 141–52.

— 'The medieval deer-parks of Dorset: VIII', *PDNHAS*, 90 (1968), 241–8.

Carden, Ruth F., Allan D. McDevitt, Frank E. Zachos, Peter C. Woodman, Peter O'Toole, Hugh Rose, Nigel T. Monaghan, Michael G. Campana, Daniel G. Bradley and Ceiridwen J. Edwards, 'Phylogeographic, ancient DNA, fossil and morphometric analyses reveal ancient and modern introductions of a large mammal: the complex case of red deer (Cervus elaphus) in Ireland', *Quaternary Science Review*, 42 (2012), 74–84.

Carey, Vincent P., 'The end of the Gaelic political order: the O'More lordship of Laois, 1536–1603' in Pádraig G. Lane and William Nolan (eds), *Laois: history and society: interdisciplinary essays on the history of an Irish county* (Dublin, 1999), pp 213–56.

Chapman, Donald and Norma Chapman, *Fallow deer* (Machynlleth, Powys, 1997).

Clancy, Thomas Owen, 'Kingmaking and images of kingship in medieval Gaelic literature' in Richard Welander, David J. Breeze and Thomas Owen Clancy (eds), *The Stone of Destiny: artefact and icon* (Edinburgh, 2003), pp 85–106.

Clinton, Mark, *The souterrains of Ireland* (Dublin, 2001).

Colfer, Billy, 'Medieval Wexford', *JOWHS*, 13 (1990–1), 5–29.

Collins Dictionary, *Collins pocket English dictionary* (London, 1981).

Comerford, M., *Collections relating to the dioceses of Kildare and Leighlin*, 3 (Dublin, 1886).

Cooney, Gabriel, 'Building the future on the past: archaeology and the construction of national identity in Ireland' in M. Diaz-Andreu and T. Champion (eds), *Nationalism and archaeology in Europe* (San Francisco, 1996), pp 146–63.

Cooper, Alan, 'The king's four highways: legal fiction meets fictional law', *Journal of Medieval History*, 26:4 (2000), 351–70.

Coote, Charles, *Statistical survey of the Queen's County* (Dublin, 1801).

Cosgrove, A. (ed.), *A new history of Ireland, II: medieval Ireland, 1169–1534* (Oxford, 1987).

Crawford, H.S., 'Mural paintings in Holy Cross Abbey', *JRSAI*, 5:2 (1915), 149–50, pl. xiv.

Creighton, Oliver, *Castles and landscapes* (London, 2002).

— 'Castle studies and archaeology in England: towards a research framework for the future', *Château Gaillard*, 23 (2008), 79–90.

— *Designs upon the land: elite landscapes of the Middle Ages* (Woodbridge, 2009).

— 'Room with a view: framing castle landscapes', *Château Gaillard*, 24 (2010), 37–49.

Crouch, David, *The image of aristocracy in Britain, 1000–1300* (London, 1992).

Cummins, John, *The hound and the hawk: the art of medieval hunting* (London, 1988).

— 'Veneurs s'en vont en Paradis: medieval hunting and the "natural" landscape' in John Howe and Michael Wolfe (eds), *Inventing medieval landscapes: senses of place in western Europe* (Gainesville, FL, 2002), pp 33–56.

Cunningham, Bernadette, 'From warlords to landlords: political and social change in Galway, 1540–1640' in Gerard Moran (ed.), *Galway: history and society* (Dublin, 1996), pp 97–130.

— 'Richard Burke (c.1572–1635) and the lordship of Clanricard' in Jane Fenlon (ed.), *Clanricard's Castle: Portumna House, Co. Galway* (Dublin, 2012), pp 32–48.

Currie, Christopher K., 'Fishponds as garden features, c.1550–1750', *Garden History*, 18:1 (1990), 22–46.

DAD-IS, 2014. Domestic animal diversity information system (DAD-IS), food and agriculture organization of the United Nations [online]: dad.fao.org, accessed 2 Feb. 2015.

Danagher, Ed, *Monumental beginnings: the archaeology of the N4 Sligo Inner Relief Road* (Dublin, 2007).

De Paor, Liam, *Landscapes with figures: people, culture and art in Ireland and the modern world* (Dublin, 1998).

Delaney, Dominic, *The Rock of Dunamase* (Vicarstown, 1996).

Delany, Mary, *The autobiography and correspondence of Mary Granville, Mrs Delany* (London, 1861).

Denham, Sean, 'Animal exploitation in medieval Ireland' (PhD, Queen's University, Belfast, 2008).

Díaz Vera, Javier E., *A changing world of words: studies in English historical lexicography, lexicology and semantics*, 141 (Amsterdam, 2002).

Doherty, Charles, 'Kingship in early Ireland' in Edel Bhreathnach (ed.), *The kingship and landscape of Tara* (Dublin, 2005), pp 3–31.

Doran, Linda and James Lyttleton (eds), *Lordship in medieval Ireland* (Dublin, 2007).

Down, Kevin, 'Colonial society and economy' in A. Cosgrove (ed.), *A new history of Ireland, II: medieval Ireland, 1169–1534* (Oxford, 1987), pp 439–91.

Duffy, Patrick J., David Edwards and Elizabeth FitzPatrick (eds), *Gaelic Ireland, c.1250–c.1650: land, lordship and settlement* (Dublin, 2001).

—, 'The territorial identity of Kildare's landscapes' in William Nolan and Thomas McGrath (eds), *Kildare: history and society* (Dublin, 2006), pp 1–33.

Durham Hedgerow Partnership, *Hedge laying and coppicing: field boundaries technical advice shee*t, 1 (Durham, n.d.).

Edwards, Nancy, 'The archaeology of early medieval Ireland, *c.*400–1169: settlement and economy' in Dáibhí O'Cróinín (ed.), *Early medieval Ireland* (London, 2005), pp 235–300.

Einhorn, Eric, *Old French: a concise handbook* (Cambridge, 1974).

Elrington Ball, Francis, *A history of the county of Dublin*, 4 (1906).

Empey, C.A., 'The Norman period, 1185–1500' in William Nolan and Thomas G. McGrath (eds), *Tipperary: history and society* (Dublin, 1985), pp 71–91.

English Heritage, 'List entry: Littywood moated site, 1017856' [online]. http://list. english-heritage.org.uk/resultsingle.aspx?uid=1017856, accessed 16 Nov. 2011.

Enright, Michael J., *Lady with a mead cup: ritual prophesy and lordship in the European warband from La Tène to the Viking Age* (Dublin, 1996).

Eppinger, Michael, *Field guide to trees and shrubs of Britain and Europe* (London, 2006).

Everson, Paul, 'Bodiam Castle, East Sussex: a fourteenth-century designed landscape' in David Morgan Evans, Peter Salway and David Thackray (eds), *The remains of distant times* (Woodbridge, 1996), pp 66–72.

Fenlon, Jane, 'Portumna: a great, many windowed and gabled house' in Jane Fenlon (ed.), *Clanricard's Castle: Portumna House, Co. Galway* (Dublin, 2012), pp 49–82.

Finan, T., 'Introduction: Moylurg and Lough Cé in the later Middle Ages' in T. Finan (ed.), *Medieval Lough Cé* (Dublin, 2010), pp 11–14.

Finan, T. and K. O'Conor, 'The moated site at Cloonfree, Co. Roscommon', *Journal of the Galway Historical and Archaeological Society*, 54 (2002), 72–87.

Finch, Jonathan and Kate Giles (eds), *Estate landscapes* (Woodbridge, 2007).

Fitzgerald, Walter, 'Maynooth Castle', *JCKAS*, 1 (1895), 223–39.

— 'Historical notes on the O'Mores and their territory of Leix, to the end of the sixteenth century', *JCKAS*, 6:1 (1909), 1–88.

— 'The manor and castle of Powerscourt, County Wicklow, in the sixteenth century, formerly a possession of the earls of Kildare', *Journal of the County Kilkenny Archaeological Society*, 6 (1909–11), 127–39.

FitzPatrick, Elizabeth, 'Assembly and inauguration places of the Burkes in late-medieval Connacht' in Patrick J. Duffy, David Edwards and Elizabeth FitzPatrick (eds), *Gaelic Ireland, c.1250–c.1650* (Dublin, 2001), pp 357–74.

— 'An Tulach Tinóil', *History Ireland* (spring 2001), 22–6.

— '*Leaca* and Gaelic inauguration ritual in medieval Ireland' in Richard Welander, David J. Breeze and Thomas Owen Clancy (eds), *The Stone of Destiny: artefact and icon* (Edinburgh, 2003), pp 107–21.

— *Royal inauguration in Gaelic Ireland* (Woodbridge, 2004).

— 'Native enclosed settlement and the problem of the Irish "ring-fort"', *Medieval Archaeology*, 53 (2009), 271–307.

— '*Formaoil na Fiann*: hunting preserves and assembly places in Gaelic Ireland', *Proceedings of Harvard Celtic Colloquium*, 32 (2013), 95–118.

— and Raymond Gillespie (eds), *The parish in medieval and early modern Ireland: community, territory and building* (Dublin, 2006).

Flanagan, Deirdre and Laurence Flanagan, *Irish place-names* (Dublin, 2002).

Fletcher, John, 'The rise of British deer parks: their raison d'être in a global and historical perspective', *Landscape Archaeology and Ecology*, 6 (2007), 31–44.

— *Gardens of earthly delight* (Oxford, 2011).

Frame, Robin, 'English officials and Irish chiefs in the fourteenth century', *English Historical Review*, 90:357 (1975), 748–77.

Franklin, Peter, 'Thornbury woodlands and deer parks, pt 1: the earl of Gloucester's deer parks', *Transactions of Bristol and Gloucestershire Archaeological Society*, 107 (1989), 149–69.

Frazer, James George, *The golden bough: a study in magic and religion* (London, 1922).

Frost, James, *The history and topography of the county of Clare* (Dublin, 1843).

Gardiner, Mark, 'The quantification of assarted land in mid- and late twelfth-century England', *Haskins Society Journal*, 21 (2009), 165–86.

Gibbons, Michael and Tommy Clarke, 'Deer parks', *Carloviana* (1990/1), 4–5.

Gilbert, John M., *Hunting and hunting reserves in medieval Scotland* (Edinburgh, 1979).

Glasscock, R.E., 'Land and people, c.1300' in A. Cosgrove (ed.), *A new history of Ireland, II: medieval Ireland, 1169–1534* (Oxford, 1987), pp 205–39.

Gleeson, Dermot F., 'The castle and manor of Nenagh', *JRSAI*, 6:2 (1936), 247–69.

— 'Drawing of a hunting scene, Urlan Castle, Co. Clare', *JRSAI*, 6:1 (1936), 193.

— 'The priory of St John at Nenagh', *JRSAI*, 68 (1938), 201–16.

Grant, Raymond, *The royal forests of England* (Stroud, 1991).

Grogan, Eoin and Annaba Kilfeather, *Archaeological inventory of County Wicklow* (Dublin, 1997).

Grose, Francis, *The antiquities of Ireland: the first volume* (London, 1791).

— *The antiquities of Ireland: the second volume* (London, 1795).

Gwynn, Aubrey and Dermot F. Gleeson, *A history of the diocese of Killaloe* (Dublin, 1962).

Hadden, George, 'The origin and development of Wexford town, pt 3: the Norman period', *JOWHS*, 2 (1969), 3–12.

— 'The origin and development of Wexford town: pt 4', *JOWHS*, 3 (1970–1), 5–10.

Hall, V. and L. Bunting, 'Tephra-dated pollen studies of medieval landscapes in the north of Ireland' in P.J. Duffy, D. Edwards and E. FitzPatrick (eds), *Gaelic Ireland, c.1250–c.1650* (Dublin, 2001), pp 207–22.

Hansson, Martin, *Aristocratic landscape: the spatial ideology of the medieval aristocracy* (Stockholm, 2006).

Harris, S. and Derek W. Yalden, *Mammals of the British Isles: handbook* (4th ed., Southampton, 2008).

Hartland, Beth, 'The liberties of Ireland in the reign of Edward I' in Michael Prestwich (ed.), *Liberties and identities in the medieval British Isles* (Woodbridge, 2008), pp 200–16.

Hawkins, Laurence, 'Killeenadeema' in Pat O'Looney (ed.), *Killeenadeema aille: history and heritage* (Loughrea, 2009), pp 45–7.

Henning, Jessica, '"Bos Primigenius" in Britain: or, why do fairy cows have red ears?', *Folklore*, 113:1 (2002), 71–82.

Herbert, Máire, 'Goddess and king: the sacred marriage in early Ireland' in Louise Olga Fradenburg (ed.), *Women and sovereignty* (Edinburgh, 1992), pp 264–75.

Hodkinson, Brian J., 'Excavations in the gatehouse of Nenagh Castle, 1996 and 1997', *Tipperary Historical Journal* (1999), 162–82.

— , 'A summary of recent work at the Rock of Dunamase, Co. Laois' in J.R. Kenyon and K. O'Conor (eds), *The medieval castle in Ireland and Wales* (Dublin, 2003), pp 32–49.

Hooke, Della, 'Medieval forests and parks in southern and central England' in C. Watkins (ed.), *European woods and forests: studies in cultural history* (1998), pp 19–32.

Hoppitt, Rosemary, 'Hunting Suffolk's parks: towards a reliable chronology of imparkment' in Robert Liddiard (ed.), *The medieval park: new perspectives* (Macclesfield, 2007), pp 146–64.

Hore, Herbert Francis, *History of the town and county of Wexford*, 6 vols (London, 1900–11).

Horner, Arnold, *Irish historic towns atlas, 7: Maynooth* (Dublin, 1995).

Horning, Audrey, Ruari O'Baoill, Colm Donnelly and Paul Logue, 'Foreword: post-medieval archaeology in and of Ireland' in Audrey Horning, Ruari O'Baoill, Colm Donnelly and Paul Logue (eds), *The post-medieval archaeology of Ireland, 1550–1850* (Dublin, 2007), pp xviii–xx.

James, Noel David Glaves, *A history of English forestry* (Oxford, 1981).

— *An historical dictionary of forestry and woodland terms* (Oxford, 1991).

Jaski, Bart, *Early Irish kingship and succession* (Dublin, 2000).

Jennison, George, *Animals for show and pleasure in ancient Rome* (Philadelphia, 2005).

Johnson, Matthew, *Behind the castle gate: from medieval to Renaissance* (London, 2002).

Johnston-Luik, E.M., 'Parnell, Sir John' in James McGuire and James Quinn (eds), *Dictionary of Irish biography* (Cambridge, 2009), online at http://dib.cambridge. org/viewReadPage.do?articleId=a7202.

Kealhofer, Lisa, 'Creating social identity in the landscape: Tidewater, Virginia, 1600– 1750' in Wendy Ashmore and A. Bernard Knapp (eds), *Archaeologies of landscape* (Oxford, 1999), pp 58–82.

Kelly, Fergus, *Early Irish farming: a study based mainly on the law-texts of the 7th and 8th centuries AD* (Dublin, 2000).

Kelly, James, 'The parliamentary reform movement of the 1780s and the Catholic Question', *Archivium Hibernicum*, 43 (1988), 95–117.

King, D.C., *The castle in England and Wales* (Beckenham, 1988).

Kinsella, Thomas *The Tain* (Oxford, 1969).

Knapp, A. Bernard and Wendy Ashmore, 'Archaeological landscapes: constructed, conceptualized, ideational' in Wendy Ashmore and A. Bernard Knapp (eds), *Archaeologies of landscape* (Oxford, 1999), pp 1–32.

Knox, Hubert Thomas, 'Occupation of the county of Galway by the Anglo-Normans after AD1237', *JRSAI*, 31 (1901), 365–70.

— 'Occupation of Connaught by the Anglo-Normans after AD1237', *JRSAI*, 32 (1902), 132–8.

Kohn, Margaret, 2011. 'Colonialism' in Edward N. Zalta (ed.), *The Stanford encyclopedia of philosophy* (fall 2011).

Le Fanu, Thomas Philip, 'The royal forest of Glencree', *JRSAI*, 23 (1893), 268–80.

Leask, H.G., 'Irish castles, 1180–1310', *Archaeological Journal*, 93 (1936), 143–99.

— *Irish castles and castellated houses* (Dundalk, 1941; repr. 1977).

Ledwich, Edward, *Antiquities of Ireland* (Dublin, 1804).

Lee, Sidney, *Dictionary of national biography*, l (London, 1897).

Leerssen, Joep, 'Wildness, wilderness and Ireland: medieval and early modern patterns in the demarcation of civility', *Journal of the History of Ideas*, 56:1 (1995), 25–39.

Leslie, Stephen, *Dictionary of national biography*, 66 (London, 1885).

Lewis, Samuel, *A topographical dictionary of Ireland*, 2 vols (London, 1837).

Liddiard, Robert, *Landscapes of lordship* (Oxford, 2000).

— 'The deer parks of Domesday book', *Landscapes*, 1 (2003), 4–23.

— *Castles in context: power symbolism and landscape* (Cheshire, 2005).

Linnard, W., *Welsh woods and forests* (Llandysul, 2000).

Lister, Adrian M., 'The morphological distinction between bones and teeth of fallow deer (*Dama dama*) and red deer (*Cervus elaphus*)', *International Journal of Osteoarchaeology*, 6:2 (1996), 119–43.

Lodge, Edmund, *The genealogy of the existing British peerage* (London, 1838).

Long, Patricia, 'Ancient hunting in County Kildare', *Seanda*, 3 (2008), 38–9.

Lucas, Anthony T., 'The sacred trees of Ireland', *Journal of the Cork Historical and Archaeological Society*, 68 (1963), 16–54.

Luscombe, David and Jonathon Riley-Smith, *The new Cambridge medieval history, c.1024–c.1198: pt 1* (Cambridge, 2004).

Lydon, James, 'The impact of the Bruce invasion, 1315–27' in A. Cosgrove (ed.), *A new history of Ireland, II: medieval Ireland, 1169–1534* (Oxford, 1987), pp 275–302.

— 'A land at war' in A. Cosgrove (ed.), *A new history of Ireland, II: medieval Ireland, 1169–1534* (Oxford, 1987), pp 240–74.

— *The lordship of Ireland in the Middle Ages* (Dublin, 2003).

Lyttleton, James and Tadhg O'Keeffe (eds), *The manor in medieval and early modern Ireland* (Dublin, 2005).

Mac Coitir, Niall, *Irish trees: myths, legends and folklore* (Cork, 2003).

MacBain, Alexander, *An etymological dictionary of the Gaelic language* (Stirling, 1911).

MacCotter, Paul, *Medieval Ireland: territorial, political and economic divisions* (Dublin, 2008).

MacDonald, Philip and David McIlreavy, 'Data structure report: site evaluation and excavation at Crew Hill (Cráeb Telcha), near Glenavy, County Antrim, 2007' (unpublished report on behalf of NI Environment and Heritage Service, 2007).

MacWeeney, Alen and Richard Conniff, *Ireland: stone walls and fabled landscapes* (London, 1998).

McCarthy, Martina, 'Earlspark and Moanmore East townlands, Loughrea, Co. Galway: report on an archaeological geophysical survey' (2010).

McCormick, Finbar, 'The effect of the Anglo-Norman settlement on Ireland's wild and domesticated fauna' in Pam J. Crabtree and Kathleen Ryan (eds), *MASCA research papers in science and archaeology: supplement to vol. 8* (Philadelphia, 1991), pp 40–52.

— 'Early evidence for wild animals in Ireland' in Norbert Benecke (ed.), *The Holocene history of the European vertebrate fauna* (Berlin, 1998), pp 355–71.

— 'Archaeology: the horse in early Ireland' in Mary McGrath and Joan C. Griffith (eds), *The Irish draught horse: a history* (Cork, 2005), pp 17–29.

— 'Appendix IV: the faunal remains' in Ann Lynch (ed.), *Tintern Abbey, Co. Wexford: Cistercians and Colcloughs: excavations, 1982–2007* (Dublin, 2010), pp 227–32.

— 'The animal bones from Carrickfin, Co. Donegal' (unpublished report, n.d.).

— 'The mammal bones from Ferrycarrig, Co. Wexford' (unpublished report, n.d.).

McDowell, R.B., 'The age of the United Irishmen: reform and reaction, 1789–94' in T.W. Moody and W.E. Vaughan (eds), *A new history of Ireland, IV: eighteenth-century Ireland, 1691–1800* (Oxford, 1986), pp 289–373.

McErlean, Thomas, 'The archaeology of parks and gardens, 1600–1900: an introduction to Irish garden archaeology' in Audrey Horning, Ruairí Ó Baoill, Colm Donnelly and Paul Logue (eds), *The post-medieval archaeology of Ireland, 1550–1850* (Dublin, 2007), pp 275–88.

McKeon, James, 'Anglo-Norman frontier urban settlement in the Plantaganet realm' (PhD, NUI Galway, 2008).

McNeill, Tom, *Anglo-Norman Ulster: the history and archaeology of an Irish barony, 1177–1400* (Edinburgh, 1980).

— *Castles in Ireland: feudal power in a Gaelic world* (London, 1997).

— 'Lost infancy: medieval archaeology in Ireland', *Antiquity*, 76 (2002), 552–6.

— 'The view from the top', *Les Cahiers de l'Urbanisme* (Sept. 2006), 122–7.

Mileson, Stephen A., 'The importance of parks in fifteenth-century society' in Linda Clark (ed.), *Of mice and men: image, belief and regulation in late-medieval England* (2005), pp 19–38.

— 'The sociology of park creation in medieval England' in Robert Liddiard (ed.), *The medieval park: new perspectives* (Macclesfield, 2007), pp 11–26.

— *Parks in medieval England* (Oxford, 2009).

Mills, James and M.J. McEnery (eds), *Calendar of the Gormanston register* (Dublin, 1916).

Mitchell, F. and M. Ryan, *Reading the Irish landscape* (Dublin, 1998).

Moorhouse, Stephen, 'The medieval parks of Yorkshire: function, contents and chronology' in Robert Liddiard (ed.), *The medieval park: new perspectives* (Macclesfield, 2007), pp 99–127.

Moreland, John, *Archaeology and text* (London, 2001).

Morton, Karena, 'Iconography and dating of the wall paintings' in Conleth Manning, Paul Gosling and John Waddell (eds), *New survey of Clare Island, 4: the abbey* (Dublin, 2005), pp 97–121.

— and Christoph Oldenbourg, 'Catalogue of the wall paintings' in Conleth Manning, Paul Gosling and John Waddell (eds), *New survey of Clare Island, 4: the abbey* (Dublin, 2005), pp 61–95.

Moss, Rachel, 'Romanesque sculpture in north Roscommon' in Thomas Finan (ed.), *Medieval Lough Cé* (Dublin, 2010), pp 119–44.

Muir, Richard, *The new reading the landscape* (Exeter, 2000).

Munby, Julian, 'Wood' in John Blair and Nigel Ramsey (eds), *English medieval industries* (London), pp 379–406.

Murphy, Margaret, 'Henry of London (d. 1228)' in Seán Duffy, Ailbhe MacShamhráin and James Moynes (eds), *Medieval Ireland: an encyclopedia* (2004), pp 212–13.

— and Kieran O'Conor, 'Castles and deer parks in Anglo-Norman Ireland', *Eolas: Journal of the American Society of Irish Medieval Studies*, 1 (2006), 51–70.

— and Kieran O'Conor, *Roscommon Castle: a visitor's guide* (Boyle, 2008).

— and Michael Potterton, *The Dublin region in the Middle Ages* (Dublin, 2010).

Murray, Emily, 'Faunal remains from Maynooth Castle' (unpublished report, n.d.).

Newman, Conor, *Tara: an archaeological survey* (Dublin, 1997).

Ní Dhonnchadha, Máirín, 'Caillech and other terms for veiled women in medieval Irish texts', *Éigse: a Journal of Irish Studies*, 28 (1994–5), 71–96.

Nicholls, K.W., 'Gaelic society and economy in the high Middle Ages' in A. Cosgrove (ed.), *A new history of Ireland, II: medieval Ireland, 1169–1534* (Oxford, 1987), pp 397–438.

— 'Woodland cover in pre-modern Ireland' in Patrick J. Duffy, David Edwards and Elizabeth FitzPatrick (eds), *Gaelic Ireland, c.1250–c.1650* (Dublin, 2001), pp 181–206.

— *Gaelic and gaelicized Ireland in the Middle Ages* (Dublin, 2003).

NMS, 'Excavations database' [online]. www.excavations.ie, accessed 14 June 2011.

NMS, 'National Monuments Service' [online]. www.archaeology.ie, accessed 16 Nov. 2011.

NRA, 'NRA archaeological database' [online]. http://archaeology.nra.ie/Home/Search/, accessed 8 Jan. 2012.

Nugent, Louise, 'Pilgrimage in medieval Ireland' (PhD, UCD, 2009).

Nugent, Patrick, 'The dynamics of parish formation in high-medieval and late-medieval Clare' in Elizabeth FitzPatrick and Raymond Gillespie (eds), *The parish in medieval and early modern Ireland* (Dublin, 2006), pp 186–208.

O'Conor, Kieran, 'The Anglo-Norman period in Co. Laois' (MA, UCD, 1986).

— 'The origins of Carlow Castle', *Archaeology Ireland*, 11:3 (1997), 13–16.

— *The archaeology of medieval rural settlement in Ireland* (Dublin, 1998).

— 'The ethnicity of Irish moated sites', *Ruralia*, 3 (1999), 92–102.

— 'Motte castles in Ireland: permanent fortresses, residences and manorial centres', *Château Gaillard*, 20 (2002), 173–82.

— 'Medieval rural settlement in Munster' in John Ludlow and Noel Jameson (eds), *Medieval Ireland: the Barryscourt lectures, i–x* (Cork, 2004), pp 225–56.

— 'Gaelic lordly settlement in 13th- and 14th-century Ireland' in I. Holm, S. Innselet and I. Øye (eds), *Utmark: the outfield as industry and ideology in the Iron Age and the Middle Ages* (Bergen, 2005), pp 209–21.

— 'Castle studies in Ireland: the way forward', *Château Gaillard*, 23 (2008), 329–39.

—, Niall Brady, Anne Connon and Carlos Fidalgo-Romo, 'The Rock of Lough Cé, Co. Roscommon' in Thomas Finan (ed.), *Medieval Lough Cé: history, archaeology and landscape* (Dublin, 2010), pp 15–40.

— and Ciaran Parker, 'Anglo-Norman settlement in Co. Longford' in Martin Morris and Fergus O'Ferrall (eds), *Longford: history and society* (Dublin, 2010), pp 75–99.

O'Donovan, John, 'Ordnance Survey letters: Co. Galway' (1838).

O'Keeffe, Tadhg, 'Concepts of "castle" and the construction of identity in medieval and post-medieval Ireland', *Irish Geography*, 34:1 (2001), 69–88.

— 'Were there designed landscapes in medieval Ireland?', *Landscapes*, 5:2 (2004), 52–68.

— 'Trim's first cousin: the twelfth century donjon of Maynooth Castle', *Archaeology Ireland*, 27:2 (2013), 26–31.

O'Leary, Edward, 'The Rock of Dunamase', *JCKAS*, 6:2 (1909–11), 161–71.

O'Sullivan, Catherine Marie, *Hospitality in medieval Ireland, 900–1500* (Dublin, 2004).

O'Sullivan, Jerry, 'Nationalists, archaeologists and the myth of the golden age' in Michael A. Monk and John Sheehan (eds), *Early medieval Munster: archaeology, history and society* (Cork, 1998), pp 179–89.

Ó Cléirigh, Cormac, 'The impact of the Anglo-Normans in Laois' in Pádraig G. Lane and William Nolan (eds), *Laois: history and society: interdisciplinary essays on the history of an Irish county* (Dublin, 1999), pp 161–82.

Ó Corráin, Donnchadh, 'Ireland, *c.*800: aspects of society' in Dáibhí O'Crónin (ed.), *Early medieval Ireland* (London, 2005), pp 549–608.

Ó hÓgáin, Dáithi, *Myth, legend and romance: an encyclopedia of the Irish folk tradition* (London, 1991).

— *The lore of Ireland: an encyclopedia of myth, legend and romance* (Woodbridge, 2006).

Oram, Richard, 'Castles, concepts and contexts: castle studies in Scotland in retrospect and prospect', *Château Gaillard*, 23 (2008), 349–59.

Orpen, Goddard H., *Ireland under the Normans, 1169–1333*, 4 vols (Oxford, 1911–20).

Orser, Charles, 'Symbolic violence, resistance and the vectors of improvement in early nineteeth-century Ireland', *World Archaeology*, 37:3 (2005), 392–407.

— 'Symbolic violence and landscape pedagogy: an illustration from the Irish countryside', *Historical Archaeology*, 40:2 (2006), 28–44.

— 'Estate landscapes and the Cult of the Ruin: a lesson in spatial transformation in rural Ireland' in Jonathan Finch and Kate Giles (eds), *Estate landscapes: design, improvement and power in the post-medieval landscape* (Woodbridge, 2007), pp 77–94.

Otway-Ruthven, A.J., *A history of medieval Ireland* (New York, 1968).

Pluskowski, Aleksander, 'The social construction of medieval park ecosystems: an interdisciplinary perspective' in Robert Liddiard (ed.), *The medieval park: new perspectives* (Macclesfield, 2007), pp 63–78.

Potterton, Michael, *Medieval Trim: history and archaeology* (Dublin, 2005).

Price, Liam, 'Powerscourt and the territory of Fercullen', *JRSAI*, 83:2 (1953), 117–32.

— *The place-names of Co. Wicklow* (Dublin, 1980).

Prunty, Jacinta, *Maps and mapmaking in local history* (Dublin, 2004).

Rackham, Oliver, *Trees and woodland in the British landscape* (London, 1976).

— *The history of the countryside* (London, 1987).

Rahtz, P.A., *Excavations at King John's hunting lodge, Writtle, Essex, 1955–7* (London, 1969).

Reetz, Elizabeth C., 'The elite landscape of Leamaneh Castle, County Clare' (MA, NUIG, 2003).

Reeves-Smyth, Terence, 'Demesnes' in F.H.A. Aalen, Kevin Whelan and Matthew Stout (eds), *Atlas of the Irish rural landscape* (Cork, 1997), pp 197–205.

— 'Natural history of demesnes' in John Wilson Foster and Helena C.G. Chesney (eds), *Nature in Ireland: a scientific and cultural history* (Dublin, 1997), pp 549–72.

Richardson, Amanda, *The forest, park and palace of Clarendon, c.1200–1650* (Oxford, 2005).

Rollin, *The ancient history of the Egyptians, Carthaginians, Assyrians, Babylonians, Medes and Persians, Macedonians and Grecians* (Baltimore, 1832).

Roy, James Charles, 'Caher na Earle (the earl's chair)', *Journal of the Galway Archaeological and Historical Society*, 52 (2000), 144–54.

Rynne, Colin, *Industrial Ireland, 1750–1930: an archaeology* (Cork, 2006).

Schmid, E., *Atlas of animal bones* (Amsterdam, 1972).

Serovayskaya, Yu J., 'Royal forests in England and their income in the budget of the feudal monarchy from the mid-twelfth to the early thirteenth centuries' in C. Watkins (ed.), *European woods and forests: studies in cultural history* (1998), pp 33–8.

Sheehan, M.B., *Nenagh and its neighbourhood* (Bray, 1950).

Sherlock, Rory, 'An introduction to the history and architecture of Bunratty Castle' in Roger Stalley (ed.), *Limerick and south-west Ireland: medieval art and architecture* (Oakville, 2011), pp 202–18.

Shirley, Evelyn Philip, *Some account of English deer parks: with notes on the management of deer* (London, 1867).

Simms, Katharine, 'Warfare in the medieval Gaelic lordships', *Irish Sword*, 12 (1975), 98–108.

— *From kings to warlords: the changing political structure of Gaelic Ireland in the later Middle Ages* (Woodbridge, 1987).

— 'Native sources for Gaelic settlement: the house poems' in Patrick J. Duffy, David Edwards and Elizabeth FitzPatrick (eds), *Gaelic Ireland, c.1250–c.1650* (Dublin, 2001), pp 246–67.

Sleeman, Patrick, 'Mammals and mammalogy' in John Wilson Foster and Helena C.G. Chesney (eds), *Nature in Ireland: a scientific and cultural history* (1997), pp 241–61.

Smith, Spencer, 'Medieval parks, gardens and designed landscapes of north Wales and the Shropshire Marches', *Welsh Historic Gardens Trust Bulletin*, 63 (2012), 4–6.

Smyth, Alfred P., *Celtic Leinster* (Dublin, 1982).

Soderberg, John, 'Wild cattle: red deer in the religious texts, iconography and archaeology of early medieval Ireland', *International Journal of Historical Archaeology*, 8:3 (2004), 167–83.

Spellissy, Sean, *The history of Galway* (Limerick, 1999).

St John Brooks, Eric, 'The family of Marisco', *JRSAI*, 7th ser., 1:1 (1932), 22–38.

— 'The de Ridelesfords', *JRSAI*, 81 (1951), 115–38.

Stout, Geraldine and Matthew Stout, 'Early landscapes: from prehistory to plantation' in F.H.A. Aalen, Kevin Whelan and Matthew Stout (eds), *Atlas of the Irish rural landscape* (Cork, 1997), pp 31–63.

Stout, Matthew, *The Irish ringfort* (Dublin, 2000).

Stringer, Keith, 'States, liberties and communities in medieval Britain and Ireland, c.1100–1400' in M. Prestwich (ed.), *Liberties and identities in the medieval British Isles* (Woodbridge, 2008), pp 5–36.

Stuhmiller, Jacqueline A., 'The hunt in romance and the hunt as romance' (PhD, Cornell, 2005).

Sweetman, David, *Medieval castles of Ireland* (Woodbridge, 1999).

Sykes, Naomi, *The Norman conquest: a zooarchaeological perspective* (Oxford, 2007).

— and Ruth F. Carden, 'Were fallow deer spotted (OE *pohha/*pocca*) in Anglo-Saxon England? Reviewing the evidence for *Dama dama dama in early medieval Europe*', *Medieval Archaeology*, 55 (2011), 139–62.

—, Judith White, Tina E. Hayes and Martin R. Palmer, 'Tracking animals using strontium isotopes in teeth: the role of fallow deer (*Dama dama*) in Roman Britain', *Antiquity*, 80 (2006), 948–59.

Taylor, Christopher, Paul Everson and R. Wilson-North, 'Bodiam Castle, Sussex', *Medieval Archaeology*, 34 (1990), 155–7.

Taylor, Patrick, *The Oxford companion to the garden* (Oxford, 2006).

Thiebaux, Marcelle, 'The mediaeval chase', *Speculum*, 42:2 (1967), 260–74.

Tietzsch-Tyler, Dan, 'Kilkenny Castle', *Castle Studies Group Bulletin*, 13 (summer 2011), 4–5.

Tilley, Christopher, *A phenomenology of landscape: places, paths and monuments (explorations in anthropology)* (Oxford, 1994).

Tomlinson, Roy, 'Forests and woodlands' in F.H.A. Aalen, Kevin Whelan and Matthew Stout (eds), *Atlas of the Irish rural landscape* (Cork, 1997), pp 122–33.

Toynbee, Jocelyn M.C., *Animals in Roman life and art* (London, 1973).

Tuan, Yi-Fu, *Space and place: the perspective of experience* (Minneapolis, 1977).

Vaux, William Sandys Wright, *Nineveh and Persepolis: an historical sketch of ancient Assyria and Persia, with an account of the recent researches in those countries* (London, 1850).

Vera, Franz, *Grazing ecology and forest history* (2000).

— 'The wood-pasture theory and the deer park: the grove – the origin of the deer park', *Landscape Archaeology and Ecology*, 6 (2007), 107–12.

Verdon, Jean, *Travel in the Middle Ages* (Notre Dame, IN, 2003).

Visscher, P.M., D. Smith, S.J.G. Hall and J.L. Williams, 'A viable herd of genetically uniform cattle', *Nature*, 409 (2001), 303.

Waddell, John, *Foundation myths* (Bray, 2005).

Wallace, Angela, 'Excavation of an early medieval cemetary at Ratoath, Co. Meath' in Michael Potterton and Chris Corlett (eds), *Death and burial in early medieval Ireland in the light of recent archaeological excavations* (Dublin, 2010), pp 297–317.

Watt, J.A., 'The Anglo-Irish colony under strain, 1327–99' in A. Cosgrove (ed.), *A new history of Ireland, II: medieval Ireland, 1169–1534* (Oxford, 1987), pp 352–96.

— 'Gaelic polity and cultural identity' in A. Cosgrove (ed.), *A new history of Ireland, II: medieval Ireland, 1169–1534* (Oxford, 1987), pp 314–51.

Watts, Kenneth, 'Wiltshire deer parks: an introductory survey', *Wiltshire Archaeological and Natural History Magazine*, 89 (1996), 88–98.

— 'Some Wiltshire deer parks', *Wiltshire Archaeological and Natural History Magazine*, 91 (1998), 90–102.

Webb, Alfred John, *A compendium of Irish biography: comprising sketches of distinguished Irishmen, and of eminent persons connected with Ireland by office or by their writings* (Dublin, 1878).

Weir, Hugh W.L., 'Deer parks of Clare', *The Other Clare*, 10 (1986), 54–5.

Westropp, T.J., 'Earthwork near Curtlestown, Co. Wicklow', *JRSAI*, 43:2 (1913), 185–6.

Wickham, Chris, *Land and power: studies in Italian and European social history, 400–1200* (London, 1994).

Williamson, Tom, *Rabbits, warrens and archaeology* (Stroud, 2007).

Winchester, Angus J.L., 'Baronial and manorial parks in medieval Cumbria' in Robert Liddiard (ed.), *The medieval park: new perspectives* (Macclesfield, 2007), pp 165–84.

Woodman, P., M. McCarthy and N. Monaghan, 'The Irish quaternary fauna project', *Quaternary Science Reviews*, 16 (1997), 129–59.

Young, Charles, R., *The royal forests of medieval England* (Philadelphia, PA, 1979).

MAPS

Armstrong, William, 'Maps of the estates of the Right Honourable Richard, lord viscount Powerscourt, in the county of Wicklow and Dublin' (1816).

First-edition OS map, 'First edition, 6-inch-to-the-mile maps' (1837–42).

Griffith's Valuation, 'Griffith's valuation maps' (1847–64).

Larkin, W., 'A map of the county of Galway' (1819).

Petty, William, 'Down survey parish maps' (*c.*1656).

Petty, William, '*Hiberniae delineatio* atlas of Ireland' (1685).

Rocque, John, 'Survey of the city of Kilkenny' (1758).

Rocque, John, 'The manor of Maynooth' (1757).

Sherrard, Brassington and Green, 'Survey of the manor of Maynooth, Co. Kildare' (1821).

Taylor, Alexander, 'A map of the county of Kildare' (1783).

Taylor, George and Andrew Skinner, 'Maps of the roads of Ireland' (1778).

Vallancey, Charles, 'Military itinerary to the south of Ireland' (1776).

Glossary

There are numerous specialist terms associated with later-medieval parks, hunting, woodland, forestry and agriculture. The reader is referred particularly to James for an extensive list and more detailed descriptions than are given here, while other sources used here are noted individually.[1]

Affer	Draught horse.[2]
Agistment	Pasture of cattle and pigs in a forest.
Assart	Area of land within a later-medieval forest from which trees and shrubs had been cleared for cultivation. Could also be used as a verb, 'to assart'.
Browse	Foliage, brushwood and small branches that were cut and fed to deer.
Buck	Male fallow deer.[3]
Calf	Young red deer.[4]
Caput	Chief place of an estate, whether a barony or an individual manor.[5]
Carucate	Area of land that could be ploughed by a single plough team in a season. This could vary between 60 and 180 acres, although 120 acres was usually used by both the English and the Irish exchequer.[6]
Chase, Chace	Similar to a **forest**, but with rights held by a nobleman, not by the king.
Coneygarth	Artificial rabbit warren.[7]
Demesne	Lands retained in the lord's hand, rather than let to tenants.[8]
Disafforest	To free a forest or portion of forest from forest law and return it to civil law.
Dispark	To throw open a park or to convert it to agricultural land.
Doe	Female fallow deer.[9]
Empale	To erect a fence around an area; for example, in order to establish a park.
Empark/ impark	To convert an area into a park by enclosing it with a fence or wall.
Estovers	Right of a tenant to take certain necessary materials from the land. Some of the more common included **firebote, haybote, housebote** and **ploughbote**.

1 James, *An historical dictionary of forestry and woodland terms*, passim. **2** Javier E. Díaz Vera, *A changing world of words: studies in English historical lexicography, lexicology and semantics*, 141 (2002), pp 233–4. **3** Harris and Yalden, *Mammals of the British Isles: handbook* (4th ed., 2008), p. 595. **4** Ibid., p. 573. **5** McNeill, *Castles in Ireland*, p. 245. **6** MacCotter, *Medieval Ireland*, p. 25. **7** Williamson, *Rabbits, warrens and archaeology*, pp 12, 17. **8** Gilbert, *Hunting and hunting reserves in medieval Scotland*, p. 408. **9** Harris and Yalden, *Mammals of the British Isles*, p. 595. **10** Ibid.

Fawn	Young fallow deer.[10]
Firebote	Right of a tenant to take necessary firewood from woodland.
Forest	Area of land in which hunting and timber rights belonged to the king or a nobleman, regardless of the ownership of the land.
Hart	In later-medieval times, a male red deer of six years or over.[11]
Haybote or Hedgebote	Right of a tenant to take wood for fencing from woodland.
Hind	Female red deer.[12]
Housebote	The right of a tenant to take wood for housebuilding and maintenance from woodland.
Justiciar	Chief governor in place of the king.[13]
Liberty	Lordship where the lord, as opposed to a royal official, was responsible for administering justice.[14]
Lymer	Hound that worked individually to find a deer suitable for hunting.
Osier	Coppiced willow used for basketry or wickerwork[15]
Pale	Vertical fence timber.
Pannage	Form of **agistment** in which pigs were allowed to root in woods for acorns.
Park	Enclosed area of land.
Ploughbote	Right of a tenant to take wood needed to construct or maintain ploughs from woodland.
Rut	Mating season for deer.
Stag	Male red deer, in later-medieval times only those aged five years, but now commonly referring to all adult males.[16]
Timber	Oak, ash and elm trees over twenty years old, although other economically useful species could be included.
Underwood	Young trees, coppice and bushes growing beneath larger trees.
Venison	Meat of deer and of wild pig. In modern usage only deer meat is included.
Vert	Trees and bushes.
Vivary	Pond in which fish were bred.[17]
Warren	Right to hunt beasts of the warren, but also an artificial construction to rear rabbits.[18]
Waste	Any action that destroyed **vert**, but particularly unauthorised tree felling.
Wood pasture	Land used both for trees and for grazing animals.[19]

11 *Master of game*, p. 29.   **12** Harris and Yalden, *Mammals of the British Isles*, p. 573.   **13** McNeill, *Castles in Ireland*, p. 246.   **14** Ibid.   **15** Collins Dictionary, *Collins pocket English dictionary* (1981). **16** Harris and Yalden, *Mammals of the British Isles*, p. 573; *Master of game*, p. 29.   **17** Currie, 'Fishponds as garden features, c.1550–1750' (1990), 22.   **18** Williamson, *Rabbits, warrens and archaeology*, p. 17. **19** Rackham, *The history of the countryside*, p. 119.

Index